MAGICAL USE OF THOUGHT FORMS

A PROVEN SYSTEM OF MENTAL & SPIRITUAL EMPOWERMENT

Dolores Ashcroft-Nowicki and J.H. Brennan

Llewellyn Publications
Woodbury, Minnesota

FIRST EDITION
Eighth Printing, 2012

Cover design by Gavin Dayton Duffy

The Magician tarot card used in this book is from the Rider-Waite Tarot Deck ®, known also as the Rider Tarot and the Waite Tarot, reproduced by permission of U.S. Games Systems, Inc., Stamford, CT 06902 U.S.A. Copyright 1971 by U.S. Games Systems, Inc. Further reproduction prohibited. The Rider-Waite Tarot Deck™ is a registered trademark of U.S. Games Systems, Inc.

Library of Congress Cataloging-in-Publication Data
Ashcroft-Nowicki, Dolores.
    Magical use of thought forms : a proven system of mental & spiritual empowerment / by Dolores Ashcroft-Nowicki and J. H. Brennan.
        p. cm.
    Includes bibliographical references (p.).
    ISBN 13: 978-1-56718-084-8
    ISBN 10: 1-56718-084-1
    1. Magic. 2. Parapsychology. I. Brennan, J. H. II. Title.

BF1611 .A78 2001
133–dc21

2001046294

Llewellyn Worldwide does not participate in, endorse, or have any authority or responsibility concerning private business transactions between our authors and the public.
    All mail addressed to the author is forwarded but the publisher cannot, unless specifically instructed by the author, give out an address or phone number.
    Any Internet references contained in this work are current at publication time, but the publisher cannot guarantee that a specific location will continue to be maintained. Please refer to the publisher's website for links to authors' websites and other sources.

Llewellyn Publications
A Division of Llewellyn Worldwide Ltd.
2143 Wooddale Drive
Woodbury, MN 55125-2989
www.llewellyn.com
Llewellyn is a registered trademark of Llewellyn Worldwide Ltd.
Printed in the United States of America

MASTER A PROVEN SYSTEM OF MENTAL AND SPIRITUAL EMPOWERMENT

Magical Use of Thought Forms is a extraordinary exposition of a fundamental esoteric technique. While background theory is well covered, the heart of this book lies in practical techniques, the vast majority of which have never appeared in print before. These are advanced magical methods that have all been tested in the field.

Detailed and accurate visualization is the basis of 99 percent of magical training. But if visualization remains no more than simple imagery, it will not give the results required by the serious occultist. Mental constructs need to be linked to the actual manipulation of astral matter.

In *Magical Use of Thought Forms,* you will learn the art of observation and new visualization techniques that both train the inner eye to build correct images and improve manipulation skills when dealing with astral matter. Finally, you will be shown how to build up a specific collection of imaginal "patterns" that can be used as an astral construction set, allowing complex structures to be created.

J. H. BRENNAN AND DOLORES ASHCROFT-NOWICKI

ABOUT THE AUTHORS

Dolores Ashcroft-Nowicki is one of the most respected and experienced esoteric practitioners currently at work in the British Isles. She teaches seminars on the topic worldwide.

J. H. Brennan is a writer whose work has appeared in more than fifty countries. He is the author of over seventy books, including: *The Magical I Ching, Magick for Beginners,* and *Time Travel.*

TO WRITE TO THE AUTHOR

If you wish to contact the authors or would like more information about this book, please write to the authors in care of Llewellyn Worldwide and we will forward your request. The authors and publisher appreciate hearing from you and learning of your enjoyment of this book and how it has helped you. Llewellyn Worldwide cannot guarantee that every letter written to the authors can be answered, but all will be forwarded. Please write to:

Dolores Ashcroft-Nowicki and J. H. Brennan
℅ Llewellyn Worldwide
2143 Wooddale Drive
Woodbury, MN 55125-2989

Please enclose a self-addressed stamped envelope for reply, or $1.00 to cover costs. If outside U.S.A., enclose international postal reply coupon.

Many of Llewellyn's authors have websites with additional information and resources (visit www.servantsofthelight.org).
For more information, please visit our website at
http://www.llewellyn.com

For Jacks—
from both of us.

CONTENTS

CONTENTS

ACKNOWLEDGMENTS

Writers have a hard life, which is why families are important to us, so the first acknowledgments must go to those closest to us: Michael and Jackie and those amazing kids that somehow grew up while we weren't looking and are now paying mortgages of their own. Heaven knows they don't see much of us once we have a literary bee buzzing in our minds and a deadline sitting on the shoulder like Long John's parrot.

Then there are the friends who understand when we don't write or phone, agents like Sophie who are worth their weight in platinum, and publishers who have perfected the art of waiting for their writers to produce that last page.

And then, of course, there are the readers. Herbie and I have decided to acknowledge you, the reader—and not only those who read *this* book, but all those who have read the books we have written in the past, because you are the root cause of our need to write. We write so you can read, enjoy, learn, practice, and, hopefully, ask for more.

To all of you: family, friends, agents, publishers, and readers, we raise a glass of poteen and say *Slainté!*

Introduction

A WORD ABOUT BONA FIDES

THIS IS SUCH AN ODD book that a word of explanation is required.

It's written, in collaboration, by two authors who, between them, have managed (much to their own amazement) to collect more than a century of experience in the occult arts. Since it's no harm to know your mentors, here's who they are and how they got together:

Dolores Ashcroft-Nowicki was born on Jersey, one of the Channel Islands that lie between the southwest coast of Britain and the coast of France. She was ten years old when World War II broke out and the Nazis invaded, necessitating her evacuation onto mainland Britain. There she endured the Blitz on Liverpool night after night, cooped up in air raid shelters listening to the drone of German warplanes overhead, the ack-ack fire and the terrifying explosions as sticks of bombs reduced the city to rubble.

Even as a child, Dolores showed signs of what was then called "being fey," an expression that has no real modern counterpart but carries the feel of someone who is a little otherworldly, a little psychic, a little imaginative, a little eccentric. It was no surprise. She came from a fey family. Both her parents were Third Degree Initiates of the Western Mysteries. Household conversation tended to center on spiritualism, ghosts, Theosophy, and other esoteric matters. But the emotional pressures of war were to change the feyness into something else, something much more rich and strange.

One night, listening to the crump-crump of the approaching bombs, Dolores found herself . . . elsewhere.

Behind the house where the family had been billeted by the War Office, stood a hastily built and totally inadequate bomb shelter. It consisted of a concrete base and a square structure, two bricks in thickness, with another layer of concrete for a roof. Inside were wooden benches and nothing else.

In this flimsy building the family passed night after night as the raids continued. The noise, fear, and daily death of school friends had taken its toll on the young mind, and brought it close to breaking point. During one particularly bad raid, Dolores was sitting with her head in her mother's lap, fingers in her ears, when something happened that was to change her life.

The noise died away, the fear began to lessen, and she could no longer feel the pressure of her mother's arms around her. Lifting her head, she found herself in an entirely different place. She stood on a plateau set amid high snow-covered mountains. Sparse, stunted bushes grew here and there and although she did not feel it, she knew it was normally extremely cold here. Before her was a fire that offered her a sense of warmth and welcome. Seated around it in a silent circle was a group of orange-robed figures. One raised his head. It was a young face, but with eyes that were centuries old. He smiled and indicated that she should take her place in the circle, which she did.

It seemed to the child that she stayed for many hours soaking in the silence, the peace, and, above all, the companionship of those around her. Nothing was said during that visit, or the subsequent visits that occurred as the Battle of Britain continued. She learned that she was taken only when the danger was greatest, when it seemed that her mind must give way under the weight of fear.

The bombing finally eased as Hitler realized that it accomplished nothing and drained his resources. On the final visit to her snowbound plateau, Dolores was silently directed to observe the mountainous background, as if to fix it in her mind. She knew then it would be her last time here, and it was at this time that information was put into her mind that all this had been for a purpose. She was also informed that these people had once been part of her life and she was among friends who could be called upon when the need was great.

Over thirty years later, she recounted this story to her teacher, the late W. E. Butler, describing the strange outline of the mountains. Without a word he got up and fetched a book from his library. He opened it at a picture of high, snow-covered mountains. They were instantly recognizable. Butler explained that in this area there had been for centuries a lamasery of a special kind, and that it still existed. She had, he told her, been given protection to safeguard her immature mind from excessive trauma and that she was by no means the only one under such protection.

She hadn't understood it at the time, of course, but clearly something had wanted to make contact. It was a presage of things to come.

While all this was going on, across the water in Ireland Herbie Brennan was also beginning to chart his earliest esoteric experience—albeit of a very different sort. He was a precocious child, addicted to reading from an early age. But his choice of reading was bizarre. In place of Enid Blyton and Rupert Bear, he began to devour books on yoga, oriental mysticism, and, above all, hypnosis. He hypnotized his first subject, a school friend, when he was only nine.

In his teens he began a study of mesmerism, which many believe to be an early form of hypnosis, but isn't. Mesmerism involves the manipulation of subtle energies, with results quite different from hypnotic trance. The interest in subtle energies drew him toward magic, but books on the subject were at a premium in Ireland at the time.

Then one day while searching on a market stall, he came across a little work titled *Magic, Its Ritual Power and Purpose,* which purported to contain information about the mysterious "Kings of Edom" briefly mentioned in the Bible. The author was somebody called W. E. Butler. Herbie bought the book. Days later, he began hunting for the author's other works and eventually obtained a copy of *The Magician, His Training and Work,* which described training techniques used in the Western Esoteric Tradition.

There was a London contact address at the back of Butler's books, recommended by Butler for those who wished to go further in their esoteric studies—it was the address of the Society of the Inner Light.

The Society of the Inner Light was founded by the psychic and occultist Dion Fortune (Violet Penry-Evans, née Violet Firth), who was herself trained by the Hermetic Students of the Golden Dawn, a magical Order that initiated the Irish poet William Butler Yeats and his nemesis, Aleister Crowley. It offered training based on the Qabalah, a potent system of ancient mysticism and magic that forms the foundation of the Western Esoteric Tradition.

Dolores survived the war and trained as an actress at R.A.D.A. (the Royal Academy for the Dramatic Art), but alongside her career ambitions was a growing interest in magic. One day while on a visit to London, she went to the old Aquarian Press store to pick up a tarot deck for her mother. There were some secondhand books on the shelves, and among them she discovered a medieval grimoire, one of the notorious "black books" of magical practice. She was leafing through it avidly when a hand fell on her shoulder.

"You don't need that," said an ominous voice. "You need this."

She turned, and the shop's proprietor handed her a copy of a little book titled *Magic, It's Ritual Power and Purpose.*

Herbie Brennan took nearly two weeks to apply for training with the Society of the Inner Light. Dolores—and her husband, Michael—had their applications in the post within three days.

Their training involved four years of daily meditations and visualizations along with theoretical study of the ancient tradition. Detailed records were kept and submitted, with membership of the Society open only to those who completed the course. Few did. Magical training was (and still is) very hard work.

Herbie was initiated into the Society of the Inner Light on his twenty-fourth birthday, the absolute minimum age the Society would accept a full member at the time. Dolores and her husband were initiated in 1968. Herbie and Dolores managed to miss one another completely.

Herbie's initial training was at the hands of Margaret Lumley-Brown, a psychic of the highest reputation even among that company of magicians. She was the Society's own cosmic mediator and an expert, from first hand experience, on the world of faery. Dolores' official mentor in the Inner Light was C. C. Chichester, its warden, but her most abiding influence was the man whose little book had set her on the path four years before—W. Ernest Butler.

Both Dolores and Herbie eventually left the Inner Light in good standing, still without meeting one another. Herbie began to cast around for ways to extend his esoteric experience and stumbled on a five-year training program called the Helios Course, written by Gareth Knight and run by W. Ernest Butler. He promptly signed up. Dolores, meanwhile, was training personally as a Cosmic Mediator with Ernest Butler. (Butler himself had been trained directly by Bishop Robert King and Dion Fortune, who founded the Inner Light.)

It's almost a relief to learn that while it took several more years, Dolores and Herbie got together eventually. By then Dolores had become Director of Studies for the Servants of the Light, the international Mystery School that developed out of Ernest Butler's Helios Course. Herbie, a loner by inclination, had a lengthy period of esoteric practice under his belt, including reincarnation research and a specialization in the Astral Plane. There wasn't much stopping them before they met, but there was no stopping them afterward.

Over a period of years, Dolores Ashcroft-Nowicki and Herbie Brennan embarked on a program of magical experimentation designed to advance the frontiers of esoteric knowledge, a program that included work on:

- evocation to visible appearance;

- the creation of ghosts by ceremonial means;

- contact with spirit entities;

- revival of ancient oracular systems;

- gross psychokinetic effects;

- astral projection;

- deep trance phenomena;

- past life investigation, and much, much more.

A great deal of their work involved the direct or indirect use of thought forms. Much of it was concerned with the Astral Plane. The personal experience they obtained forms the foundation of the book you are reading now.

It's a book that contains information published nowhere else, the fruits of many years of investigation. Some of it results from research, some from experimentation, and some from data supplied by Inner Plane sources in contact with the authors. You will learn about:

- the Triangle of Causation: desire, emotion, and imagination;

- the three-point location of occult power in the physical brain;

- the triune persona of a human being;

- the Occult Art of Observation.

Within the book are detailed instructions on collecting mental and physical images, information about dealing with perspective on the Astral Plane, instructions on storing and recalling nonvisual memories of emotions, and building up desire as fuel for a potent astral engine.

The use of advanced astral structures is dealt with in key segments covering:

- the creation of an astral homunculus;

- Egyptian tomb guardians;

- astral landscapes;
- controlling what you create.

But before you begin the practical work, you have a treat in store. For the book opens with some of the most fascinating and instructive case studies you will ever read. Studies that will literally change the way you think about reality and lay the theoretical foundation for the work ahead.

Enjoy.

"The real voyage of discovery consists not in seeing new landscapes,
but in having new eyes."

MARCEL PROUST

Part One

THE NATURE OF REALITY

1 WOLF MAN

MANUELA GARCIA HAD A bad marriage. Nobody got divorced in northern Spain in 1849, but Manuela managed a separation, taking her daughter Petronila with her. She was living without her husband in the remote village of Rebordechao when a handsome young peddler came calling at her door.

The peddler was thirty-year-old Manuel Blanco Romasanta, a native of Riguiero, another village some distance away. He traveled the area selling various items from his pack, and captured Manuela's attention with one of his specialties, a lace veil from Portugal. It was a delightful, delicately worked article, and while she couldn't afford it, her beauty captivated the peddler as much as the veil captivated her. Romasanta soon became a regular caller at Manuela's home.

Although this story is true, it has distinct fairy-tale elements—the beautiful and innocent girl, the isolated village, the handsome peddler. Anyone familiar with fairy tales will spot the danger signs at once. Handsome peddlers tend to be trouble for innocent girls. But perhaps Manuela Garcia hadn't read enough fairy tales, or perhaps she was just flattered by the attention. Whatever the reason, she allowed the relationship to flourish. Romasanta seemed like such a nice man. He was attentive to her, attentive to her daughter, and very concerned about their financial difficulties.

One day Romasanta presented them with a solution to the money problems. He had, he said, arranged jobs for both of them as house servants to a kindly priest in the port city of Santander, the capital of Cantabria province, situated on a southern inlet of the Bay of Biscay. The priest was a good man, he said. They would be treated like family. A delighted Manuela and her daughter set off with Romasanta for Santander. It was the last anyone ever saw of them.

Manuela had relatives in Rebordechao, including a sister named Benita. Weeks after their departure, Romasanta returned to the village carrying letters from Manuela saying how happy she was in her new post. Benita was so impressed that she too agreed to go to Santander, where Romasanta promised to find her a position with a wealthy family. She took her young son with her.

Once again Romasanta returned to Rebordechao with letters, this time from Benita and her son. A woman named Antonia Rua read them and, like the others, departed with Romasanta for a new life in the great city. With them went her daughter, Peregrina. When Romasanta returned to the village, he took it upon himself to look after Antonia's older daughter, Maruja. Nearly a year and a half later, Antonia wrote to Maruja asking that she join her in Santander. When Maruja accepted, Romasanta offered to accompany her on the trip, as a chaperone.

This was the beginning of a flourishing business for Romasanta. On his village sales route he told of the money to be made in the big city, where loyal, hard-working servants were at a premium. He was, he claimed, very well connected and could arrange work for virtually anybody who wanted it. And lots of people did. Romasanta escorted them from their homes and took them away. He accepted no money for his services. He did it all from the goodness of his heart.

But the country folk of Northern Spain were far from stupid. Many of them thought Romasanta was too sweet to be wholesome. Rumors started that he wasn't taking people to Santander at all, but killing them in the mountains for their body fat. (In a superstitious age, it was widely believed that Portuguese witches used human fat in their potions and were prepared to pay large sums of money for it.)

Romasanta denied it all, but eventually the rumors grew so persistent that he left Rebordechao for good and took up residence in Castile. There he changed his name to Antonio Gomez, ceased peddling, and took up a trade as a nail-maker. Later he moved to the village of Verin, where he worked as a farm hand.

One day in 1852, three Rebordechao villagers happened to visit Verin. They recognized Romasanta and reported his real identity to the mayor. This worthy promptly had him arrested and jailed in the nearby town of Allariz.

At this point, Romasanta surprised them all—he announced he was a werewolf.

The werewolf legend, based on the idea that some people have the ability to turn themselves into wolves, is one of humanity's oldest and most widespread myths. Danish, Gothic, Old Norman, Serbian, Slovakian, Russian, Greek, Romanian, French, German, Slavic, indeed every Indo-European language without exception had its own word for, and myth of, the werewolf. As long ago as the fifth century B.C., the Greek historian Heroditus recorded that an entire Scythian tribe called the Neuri changed into wolves once a year, stayed that way for several days, then changed back again. (Heroditus no more believed this story than you do, but the point is that the myth of the werewolf was a living tradition more than two thousand years ago.)

France has had more than its fair share of werewolf lore, possibly because natural wolves were once abundant in that country. In 1574, for example, a hermit named Gilles Garnier was burned alive after he confessed to killing and eating two children while in the form of a wolf. Jacques Roulet, a French beggar, was a little more lucky. When he admitted to being a werewolf at Angers in 1598, the court simply ordered him to be committed to an insane asylum. All the same, Roulet was discovered when hunters tracked two wolves that had torn a young boy apart.

In the same year at St. Claud, a woman named Gandillon was arrested after attacking two children in an orchard. One of them, who later died, described his assailant as a wolf equipped with human hands. Gandillon's entire family was arrested and all members were subsequently observed to spend a great deal of time on all fours in their cells. Her brother Pierre eventually confessed to the practice of witchcraft and to being a werewolf, with the result that they all went to the stake.

In neighboring Germany, another country that once harbored a large wolf population, Peter Stumf admitted to a twenty-five-year reign of terror as a werewolf, during which he killed and ate numerous woman and children, including his own son. He made the change with the aid of a magical wolfskin belt (an item that frequently features in werewolf lore). A Cologne court sentenced him in 1589. He was broken on the wheel, beheaded, and his body burned.

There is a strong suspicion that the confessions in some of these early cases—and many others like them—were obtained by torture, but the Romasanta affair was different. Although no one put pressure on him and any hard evidence gathered at that point was slim, he voluntarily confessed to many murders, including four of which nobody had accused him. He explained to the jury at his trial that when the urge gripped him, he would strip himself naked and roll on the ground, arising minutes later as a wolf.

In wolf form, he felt energized and invulnerable. He could run for miles without tiring, felt fear of nothing, and was intoxicated by a sense of freedom. Typically, he would rip out the throat and lungs of his victims, then eat the bodies, leaving only their gnawed bones. It was only when he returned to human form that he felt the slightest guilt.

According to his own testimony, Romasanta had been a werewolf for a long time—since the age of thirteen, in fact. He believed that a relative, possibly one of his own parents, had placed a curse on him, causing him to feel the blood urges. He fought them for a time, but after six months or so, gave in. He went up into the mountains at Couso, where, accidentally or otherwise, he happened on two men from Valencia who were also werewolves. They all changed together and ran as a pack for several days before changing back into human form. From then on, Romasanta's fate was sealed.

While still in custody, Romasanta suddenly announced he had lost his blood lust (on a saint's day) and the curse had been lifted. He became cooperative and took the judge to remote locations where he dug up the bones of his victims.

Despite the convenient lifting of the "curse," Romasanta was condemned to death in April 1853. In Spanish law, a death sentence had to be confirmed by a special court. A new defense lawyer denounced the "medieval superstition" of werewolves and argued strongly that Romasanta was insane—a man so mad he would admit to anything. A medical expert from Britain forwarded testimony suggesting Romasanta might have been hypnotized into believing he was a werewolf. In any case, it was obvious he did not really change into a wolf but was suffering from a specific form of lunacy known as "lycanthropy" that made him believe he became a wolf. Clearly he was not responsible for his actions.

The court accepted these arguments and commuted the death sentence to life imprisonment. In a bizarre development, this was changed back to a death sentence (by strangulation) following newspaper pressure, then commuted again to perpetual imprisonment by a special order of the queen. Romasanta died in jail some years later.

It is tempting to accept the defense arguments in this case, especially as the theory that certain people can imagine themselves as wolves is borne out by the experience of the American travel writer W. B. Seabrook.

Some time in the 1930s, Seabrook was in a flat overlooking New York's Times Square with a small group of friends that included a career diplomat and a Russian émigré he called Magda. They were consulting an oracle known as the I Ching.

The I Ching, as the name implies, is of Chinese origin and is sometimes claimed to be the oldest book in the world.[1] It is consulted by means of six-lined figures known as hexagrams. There are sixty-four in all, each with a different meaning. Because the lines themselves have different meanings, too, the oracle is capable of delivering more than four thousand answers and is generally used as a system of divination. Seabrook's party was, however, using it as an aid to a special meditative state.

The technique they used was to create a hexagram, then visualize it on a closed wooden door. This picture was held in the mind until the door opened of its own accord, at which point the practitioner "stepped through" by an act of imagination, into a visionary scene beyond.

In the flat above Times Square, it was the Russian émigré Magda who got into trouble using the I Ching this way. The hexagram she drew has the Chinese name Ko, which is usually translated as "Revolution." In its original sense, however, it means an animal's pelt, which changes over the course of a year by molting.

After concentrating on the mental picture for some time, Magda claimed she was lying naked "except for a fur coat" in the snow, then it was moonlight and she was running through the woods at great speed. Her face took on a feral appearance and she became aggressive. Suddenly she howled like a wolf. When the men attempted to wake her, she snarled, snapped, and bit them fiercely. It was quite a time before they could overpower her and get her out of trance.

Magda, fortunately, was no worse for her experience (although her companions went searching for the Band-Aids). But it is a short step to suppose someone like Romasanta might, through madness (or even hypnosis as the expert witness suggested), periodically imagine himself to be a wolf and carry his delusion as far as murder.

---

1. For a full exposition of this fascinating work, see *The Magical I Ching,* by Herbie Brennan (St. Paul, Minn.: Llewellyn Publications, 2000).

All the same, there are problems with this explanation.

The first is that it occurred to the original jury that Romasanta might be mad, and the court ordered a medical examination. He was found to be suffering from no physical illness, was of sound mind, and highly intelligent. The most the doctors could discover was that he sometimes lost his temper under stress.

His actions were not those of a periodic madman, either. Again and again he lured women and children away from their villages, sometimes patiently taking a year or more to gain their confidence. He did not simply run amok when seized by some violent lunacy.

But the most curious factor of all was the distances Romasanta had to travel. From Rebordechao, where he found his first victim, to Santander, where he took her before she was killed, is a distance of four hundred miles. Another victim came from Viana, on the Portuguese border, which is even farther. It was rugged, desolate terrain and the most common way to cross it was on foot. Romasanta owned neither horse, donkey, nor any other form of transport, yet he crossed and recrossed this vast area with ease and in far less time than he should have. Furthermore, he seemed wholly immune from attack by an indigenous wolf population so ferocious that the animals often besieged whole villages, particularly in winter, in search of food.

The belief in werewolves did not die with Romasanta. As late as 1930, a French farmer was accused of changing into a wolf at night. Even more recently, in 1946, a Navajo Indian reservation in America was attacked by a vicious creature widely believed to be a werewolf.

Today, of course, the legend of the werewolf is more widespread than ever thanks to books and movies like *The Howling* and *An American Werewolf in London*. Audiences are well accustomed to the realistic metamorphosis of man into wolf through the magic of special effects.

But is it even remotely possible for people to actually change into wolves?

2 ANOMALIES

WEREWOLVES ARE NOT the only unlikely creatures with a widespread provenance. From the werefoxes and werehares of China to the werecats of tropical Africa, there is a whole menagerie of animals into which certain humans are reputed to change.

In *The Way of the Shaman,*[1] Professor Michael Harner writes:

> The connectedness between humans and the animal world is very basic in shamanism, with the shaman utilizing his knowledge and methods to participate in the power of that world. Through his guardian spirit or power animal, the shaman connects with the power of the animal world, the mammals, birds, fish, and other beings. The shaman has to have a particular guardian in order to do his work, and his guardian helps him in certain special ways.

The choice of spirit was never arbitrary, for it was believed that a link with a particular animal was already there,

---

1. Michael Harner. *The Way of the Shaman* (New York: Bantam Books, 1986).

forged by the nature of the shaman, even though the shaman might not be aware of it. Thus the spirit would often make itself known, in visions or dreams, before the shaman practiced those techniques that called it to him. This calling had many benefits. Says Harner:

> A power animal or guardian spirit, as I first learned among the Jivaro, not only increases one's physical energy and ability to resist contagious disease, but also increases one's mental alertness and self-confidence.[2]

When the shaman entered nonordinary reality in search of the animal, she would often become temporarily possessed by it. This naturally led to the concept of were animals, the belief—which to many tribes was a matter of simple experience—that certain individuals could literally shapeshift and become the animal concerned.

But were animals are only one example of a whole range of curious phenomena that we all know to be impossible, yet have for centuries been supported by countless legends, myths, and even eyewitness accounts.

When Irish author Bram Stoker crafted his legendary vampire Dracula, the character was based on a fifteenth-century Balkan noble named Vlad the Impaler and named after *dracul*, the Rumanian word for devil. But Stoker did not create the vampire legend, although he added immeasurably to it. There is a mention of blood-drinking ghosts in Homer's *Odyssey*. In Hebrew mythology, Adam's first wife Lilith is described as a vampiric character, preying on babies. The same theme is taken up in Arab, Celtic, and Roman mythology, all of which contain references to blood-drinking demons of one sort or another. But the vampire legend familiar today derives directly from an outbreak of vrykolka activity throughout the Balkans and Greece in the seventeenth century. According to popular belief and what purported to be widespread eyewitness reports, vrykolkas were resurrected corpses that fed on the blood of the living. In Hungary, the Magyar term for them was *vampir*, a word that, with only a slight change, carried the legend into the English-speaking world. By 1746, the first scholarly work on the creatures had appeared, written by Dom Augustine Calmet, a French monk.

---

2. *The Way of the Shaman.*

Bilocation—the appearance of the same person in two different places at once—is another impossibility, but one apparently achieved by several Christian monks and saints. The list of bilocators includes St. Anthony of Padua, St. Ambrose of Milan, St. Severus of Ravenna, and, in modern times, Padre Pio, an Italian monk. Some of the appearances have been well attested. When Pope Clement XIV was on his deathbed, he had a visit from St. Alphonsus Maria de Ligouri, who was seen by several members of the Papal Court at the pope's bedside. But Alphonsus was confined to his cell at the time—four-days' journey away.

Another ability frequently attributed to saints is levitation. St. Joseph of Cupertino and St. Theresa of Avila were both reputed to do it frequently. One eyewitness swore Theresa remained airborne, eighteen inches off the ground, for about half an hour. The great Tibetan yogi Milarepa went one better: according to contemporary accounts, he was able to walk and even sleep while levitating. In the nineteenth century, the spiritualist medium Daniel Dunglas Home surprised several witnesses by floating out of a third story window and into another. The Italian medium Amedee Zuccarini was photographed levitating with his feet some twenty inches above the nearest support.

In a somewhat similar category is the experience of a British psychologist named Kenneth Batcheldor, who became interested in the widespread reports of table-turning during the Victorian craze for spiritualism. Batcheldor set up groups to investigate, and, after several months of experimentation, developed a system that allowed tables to move by themselves under tightly controlled test conditions. His work culminated with infrared video of a table levitated several inches off the floor with no one touching it.

Levitating tables also featured in an experiment carried out by Dr. George Owens and his wife, Iris, two members of the Canadian Society for Psychical Research, who decided they would try to make an artificial ghost. To this end, they and fellow members of their group created a fictional character named Philip who lived during Cromwellian times (mid-seventeenth century) at a place called Diddington Manor in England. Philip had an affair with a gypsy girl named Magda; his wife found out and denounced Magda as a witch. When she was burned at the stake, Philip committed suicide by throwing himself from the battlements of his ancestral home.

The romantic tale was entirely fictional, except for the detail of Diddington Manor, which actually does exist. The Owens group pinned photos of the manor around the walls of their room and sat regularly in a classical spiritualist séance to make contact with the character they had created. After several months, they were rewarded by a paranormal rapping. A code was soon established to allow them to communicate with the entity behind the rapping . . . the entity turned out to be Philip, and gave its history in the terms of the fictional life story already agreed.

But Philip added so many accurate historical details to the account that the sitters began to wonder if they might have accidentally hit on a real person. Research showed they had not, yet Philip exhibited a far greater familiarity with the Cromwellian period than any member of the group. Furthermore, he proved able to levitate tables and once "walked" one up a short flight of steps.

A variation on the Philip experiment was conducted by Dolores and myself in Britain using techniques of ritual evocation to speed up the process. As a result, a member of our group was temporarily possessed by the "spirit" of an entirely fictitious Saxon priestess.

Astral projection is another well-attested impossibility. My first experience of the phenomenon occurred when I rose in the middle of the night to visit the bathroom and discovered I could not open the bedroom door. After a puzzling moment, I discovered my hand had passed through the doorknob and my (physical) body was still lying in bed beside my wife. It took me six attempts to persuade the body to get up. During one of them I strolled through a solid wall.

This (strictly temporary) ability seems almost humdrum when set beside what happened to Benedetto Supino in 1982. A schoolboy at the time, he was reading a comic in a dentist's waiting room when the paper went on fire. Since that time, anything he touches scorches and he has proved capable of setting things alight just by looking at them. Examined by doctors at the Tivoli Medical Center, he was pronounced "entirely normal"—a diagnosis both he and his family might question.

In 1967, another teenager, Anne-Marie Schaberl, exhibited even stranger powers—although at first no one realized they were emanating from her. The trouble started in a lawyer's office in Rosenheim, Germany, when the lighting system became faulty. The lawyer, Sigmund Adam, had a special meter installed that showed unusual electrical surges. In an attempt to solve the problem, he exchanged his strip lighting for ordinary bulbs and had a direct cable installed. When neither worked, he put in his own generator . . . which made no difference either.

Then, while still grappling with the electrical problem, Adam received a gigantic phone bill—far in excess of what was normal. When outgoing calls were monitored, it was discovered that somebody in the building was calling the speaking clock several times a minute, and managing to do so faster than the normal connection time would allow.

In desperation, one of Europe's leading parapsychologists, Professor Hans Bender of Freiburg, was called in. He discovered widespread poltergeist activity associated with Schaberl, who could cause overhead lights to start swinging just by walking down a corridor.

The generation of poltergeist effects is just one of a number of "wild talents," like telepathy and distant viewing, that have been put to the test in recent years and found to be genuine, if sometimes erratic. Nor are these talents confined to humans. The British scientist Rupert Sheldrake decided to investigate the common belief among dog and cat owners that their pets could read their minds. In a televised version of one of his experiments, an owner was taken from her house and driven around for some hours before being told she could return. At the precise second she turned back for home, a synchronized camera showed her dog moving to his spot at the window where he normally waited for her. (If dogs can read minds, cats seem capable of seeing the future. Mrs. B. N. Harris of Harrowgate, England, reported that while living in Tiverton Road, Exeter, during World War II, she watched a steady stream of felines padding out of the city toward Tiverton . . . just ahead of a devastating air raid.)

Sheldrake is the scientist who developed the theory of "morphic resonance"— the idea that once a critical number of people have learned something, it becomes easier for the population as a whole to learn it. Through experiments, he showed that this was true of schoolchildren learning poetry, and noted that simple skills can sometimes become available to an entire animal or bird population without having to be learned at all.

Most of the oddities so far mentioned might be categorized as unusual abilities, but there is a whole other category of phenomena that seem to be of a completely different type.

What, for example, are we to make of the fact that worldwide reports of black helicopter sightings were filed in 1938? The first helicopter flight was made by a Frenchman in 1907, but the machine was capable only of a brief vertical ascent. In 1930, a prototype chopper managed forward as well as vertical movement, but it was not until 1939—a year after the worldwide sightings—that Igor Sikorsky built the first practical machine.

In 1887 and 1888, a manlike creature with wings was reported performing aerial maneuvers over New York and New Jersey. The reports were never taken seriously, yet the creature—or something like it—reappeared in the Ohio River Valley during 1966 and 1967. It was described as winged, gray, man-sized, man-shaped, with red eyes—and was seen by more than a hundred witnesses.

A rain of pink frogs fell on Stroud, in Gloucestershire, England, on October 24, 1987. Naturalist Ian Darling confirmed that the frogs were albinos (the pink color came from the blood flowing beneath their pale skin), but could give no explanation about where they came from. Presumably it was the same place that caused a similar rain of pink frogs on nearby Cirencester two weeks earlier.

Strange rains are far from unusual. Downpours of frogs have been reported from Pennsylvania, Minnesota, Indiana, and Massachusetts—to name just a few locations in the United States. There was a rainfall of herring at Argylshire in Scotland in 1817.

The conventional explanation of this phenomenon is that whirlwinds have scooped up the unfortunate creatures, carried them a distance, then deposited them as rain. If so, the whirlwinds are curiously selective, managing to scoop only frogs from their ponds and carefully segregating herring from the myriad of fish available in the sea. Besides which, the rainfalls have never been confined to amphibians and fish.

There was a fall of large yellow mice on Bergen, Norway, in 1578. A year later it rained lemmings. Burning sulphur fell on Magdenburg, Germany, in 1642. Black eggs pelted down on Port-au-Prince, Haiti, in 1786. Animal feed fell in Iran in 1828. San Francisco had a rain of beef—yes, beef—in 1851. Cinders have fallen in Illinois; lizards on Sacramento; snakes on Memphis, Tennessee; worms in West Virginia; silver coins in Russia; banknotes in France and Germany; peaches in Louisiana; mud, wood, glass, and pottery in Cuba. Black "snowflakes" as large as table tops fell on the east coast of the Baltic Sea in 1687. They were found to be rafts of black algae and infusoria.

In 117 A.D., four thousand men of Roman Army's Ninth Legion marched northward out of Dunblane, Scotland, and disappeared. There were no dispatches, no reports of any battle, no bodies, or any other sign of a disaster. The men simply vanished.

The British consul in Vienna, Benjamin Bathurst, was examining a team of horses on November 25, 1809, in the German town of Perleberg, when he vanished. His valet and secretary saw him walk around to the other side of the horses, at which point he disappeared. People have been disappearing just as mysteriously ever since, including the Toronto businessman who walked into his office and never came out and several individuals who vanished while people were actually looking at them.

The few case studies quoted represent the barest skimming on the surface of a vast literature of anomalies. Such reports have profound implications. If people can be in two places at once or disappear into thin air, if dogs can read minds and cats can tell the future, if a girl can generate a poltergeist and Romasanta really could change into a wolf, then we need to revise our ideas about the nature of reality.

3 EVOCATION

PEMA TENSE WAS nine years old in 1939 when he became a monk at the Drepung Monastery, near Lhasa in Tibet. Neither his vocation nor his age was unusual. At that time one (male) Tibetan in four took to the religious life, and most of them began training when they were only children.

Pema learned to read the Buddhist scriptures, memorizing long passages by heart. His teachers discovered a musical talent, so he was trained in the curious deep-throated overtone chanting that can ruin the vocal cords if indulged in for too long. He ate a frugal, satisfying diet, vegetarian more by necessity than choice—most monks would eat meat when they could get it. He drank copious quantities of cool, oily, salted tea: cool because water boils at low temperatures in the high altitudes of Tibet, oily because Tibetans add butter, creating a high energy concoction that helps them withstand the weather, salted because they like the taste.

The outbreak of World War II did not impinge on Pema Tense. Since the Anglo-Tibetan Convention imposed by force of arms in 1904, Tibet had been an isolated country. The number of resident foreigners could be counted on the fingers of one hand and even transient visitors were few and far between. Only Nazi Germany sent small parties into the country at regular intervals between 1937 and 1945, and even they had no military agenda—they were in search of occult knowledge that could aid the Third Reich.

Pema, too, was in search of occult knowledge. A great many Tibetans entered the monasteries because it was the accepted thing to do. The life, while hard, was often less hard than the life outside. Monks—called lamas in Tibet— were respected and enjoyed unprecedented security. (At least until the Chinese invasion of 1950.) But Pema had other motivations. From earliest childhood he had shown a profound interest in spiritual and religious matters. His family privately considered him the reincarnation of a high lama. Pema himself made no such claims, perhaps wisely, but he certainly aspired toward esoteric wisdom.

He found little enough of it in Drepung. The great monastery was a sprawling structure very similar to a medieval town with a population running into tens of thousands. There was much ceremonial and religious observance, but as Pema grew older he began to suspect that observance was all there was—actual understanding seemed to be lacking. He consulted his superiors, who were in no way dismayed by his questions. One of them suggested he needed a personal guru.

The guru-chela relationship is a very ancient convention in the Orient. The *chela* (pupil) binds himself utterly to the guru (teacher), often acting as an unpaid servant in return for teaching. Pema was quite prepared to do anything needed of him, but where to find the guru?

There is a belief in the Western Esoteric Tradition that when the pupil is ready, the teacher will appear. This belief is shared in the East. Pema, by then a teenager, curbed his natural impatience and set to wait. While he did, he continued the monastic disciplines of Drepung. The repetitive practice was something that was to stand him in good stead.

The most elevated and revered spiritual teachers in Tibet are known as Rinpoche, a title that means "Precious One." Usually the title is appended to the individual's given name, as in Lungdep Rinpoche or Chanden Rinpoche. But when word reached Pema of a particularly holy guru, his name was given as Kang Rinpoche, perhaps best rendered as "Jewel of the Snows," and not so much a name and a title as a title in its own right. The Kang Rinpoche, sometimes known as Kailas ("The Crystal"), is the sacred mountain, navel of the earth. In Tibetan, Hindu, and Jain myth, this mountain is believed to be located partly in a metaphysical dimension and partly in the remote fastness of the Himalayas somewhere between China and India. It appeared the guru was named for the mythic mountain.

When Pema sought him out, he quickly discovered why. Kang Rinpoche lived at a distance that would have been a day's walk from the monastery, but higher up in the mountains in such an inaccessible little hut that it took Pema two full days to reach him. When he did, Kang Rinpoche refused to take him as a chela.

This sort of rejection would have been shattering for a Westerner (especially after the hard climb), but for Pema it was more or less expected. Gurus tended to play hard to get; and good gurus hardest of all. Pema settled down to wait. Fortunately he had anticipated the development and brought some rations with him. After a week, Kang Rinpoche relented.

Thus a cold and, by then, very hungry Pema began his training. Prior to the Chinese invasion, Tibet's esoteric tradition was a unique blend of shamanism and Buddhism that greatly encouraged the practice of meditation and the personal examination of psychic contents. With centuries of practice behind it, the tradition was obviously the repository of much spiritual wisdom. But it also embodied a rich store of information about the nature and structure of the human mind, more so perhaps than the scientifically oriented psychology schools of the West. This was something Pema was destined to discover for himself.

Although now prepared to permit his new chela into the hut—and even share a little food—the reluctant guru explained to Pema that the most valuable lessons were learned not from fallible mortals, but from the gods. To that end, he advised Pema to familiarize himself with a mystic creature called a Yidam, one of the country's most powerful tutelary deities. As a start, he suggested that the young man spend several months reading about the Yidam in sacred scriptures and studying its many representations.

So Pema found himself back where he started, among his old friends at Drepung Monastery, engaged on a boring study program that held none of the attraction and glamour of his esoteric ambitions. All the same, he stuck at it.

One of the first things he found was that the Yidam had a fearful, almost demonic, aspect—something not uncommon in Tibetan deities. It also had a fearsome reputation. Evocation of a Yidam was looked on as extraordinarily dangerous. Many scriptures warned against it.

Nonetheless, when Pema returned to the hut of Kang Rinpoche, this was precisely what his guru instructed him to do. As preparation he showed the boy how to construct a *kylkhor.*

In Western esoteric practice, spirit evocation to visible appearance involves the use of a "circle of art," usually protected by divine names, in which the magician stands. The spirit form (hopefully) appears in a triangle, similarly fortified, drawn outside the circle. In Tibet, by contrast, the spirit is evoked inside the circle while the magician stays outside, but the principle is much the same: it's the circle that protects the magician. In the West, the magic circle can be drawn or painted, or sometimes set out using tape or rope. The Tibetan circle, the kylkhor, is a more elaborate affair, made sometimes from colored chalks, but more often from colored sands.

The technique of building a kylkhor is fascinating. The magician is equipped with several pots of multicolored fine, dry sands, a metal funnel open at both ends, and a short stick. When the funnel is filled with sand from a pot, rubbing it rhythmically with the stick produces a controlled trickle of sand from the narrow end, which can be used to draw shapes. With practice, lines no wider than a single grain of sand can be produced. The rubbing motion also produces a sound, the pitch and rhythm of which is trance-inducing.[1] As the magician concentrates on producing the elaborate designs involved in the kylkhor, he sinks into a trance state that enables his intent to fortify the circle.

Although easy enough to describe, the correct construction of a kylkhor is a skilled operation, and it took Pema Tense several months to learn the procedure properly. But eventually his guru was satisfied. Pema was instructed to tramp off into the Tibetan wilderness in search of a high altitude cave "suited to the Yidam's manifestation."

What sort of cave is suited to the manifestation of a deity? First, it had to be large enough for Pema to draw a full-size kylkhor on the floor, with room left over for him to watch the manifestation in comfort. Next, it had to be remote so there was no chance of casual passersby disturbing the operation. Finally, it was required to have an ambiance suited to a deity, which means it had to be dimly-lit, but not gloomy, with pleasing proportions and a high ceiling—a fitting place, in other words, for a god to find himself. The instruction that the cavern should be at a high altitude was particularly interesting. The entire Tibetan plateau has an average elevation of fifteen thousand feet. In the higher, mountainous regions, the oxygen content of the air is so low that Westerners can hardly survive and even native Tibetans find exertion difficult. Such an environment, Western scien-

---

1. Exactly the same technique is used to construct Tibet's famous "sand mandalas," elaborate and complex pictures that are destroyed after completion as an object lesson in impermanence.

tists insist, is conducive to hallucinatory experience. The Tibetans take a different view: They believe it facilitates psychical ability.

Pema got lucky. He found his cavern inside three days—something his guru took as a sign that the Yidam liked him. Kang Rinpoche inspected the cave—making the climb without difficulty, despite his age—and pronounced it suitable. He supplied Pema with minimal rations, and told him to make his home in the cavern and draw a kylkhor on the floor as he had been instructed. He was then to embark on a routine of daily meditation during which he was to visualize the Yidam within the kylkhor.

As a guide to his visualizations, Pema had his memories of the various pictures of the Yidam he had studied at Drepung. Kang Rinpoche instructed him to make his visualization fully detailed, so he could "see" individual items of the Yidam's clothing right down to the individual colors of the symbols it displayed. Then came the bad news: he was to remain in the cave engaging in this routine throughout the daylight hours without a break until he was able to see the Yidam as if it were physically present.

Here was another of those intriguing parallels with Western esoteric training. Magicians following the Qabalistic tradition are often urged to practice their visualization skills until the visualized element appears objectively real to them. They are not normally required to visualize a deity or spirit, however, but rather some small practice object like a rose or a geometrical symbol drawn on a piece of paper. Indeed, most beginners are specifically instructed not to visualize an entity or a living person, since this might lead to unwelcome complications. Besides, as anyone who has tried the technique can attest, even visualizing a simple flower as if it were physically real can take weeks, months, or sometimes even years of hard, mind-numbing practice.

Pema did not find it easy, either. Although a diligent chela with nothing else to do, he discovered his food was running out before he achieved his objective. He began to ration himself to a single, frugal meal a day, a difficult and dangerous practice in the freezing cold of his cavern. Even then, it seemed as if he must soon be torn between the risk of starvation and his vow to obey his guru in all things, including the details of the present operation. But before the situation became completely critical, he awoke one morning to find some food had been left near the mouth of the cave. He assumed it came from Kang Rinpoche. Thereafter, small portions of food were left at irregular intervals. Most of the time Pema was hungry, but he never actually starved.

It took him several months in that lonely, freezing cavern, but the day came when, for just the briefest moment, Pema thought he actually saw the towering figure of the Yidam flicker inside the kylkhor. Days later it happened again. The creature was there for no more than an instant each time, but in the coming week, it happened more and more often. Pema redoubled his efforts and eventually the Yidam came and stayed for several seconds, then half a minute, then a minute. At first it was hazy, like smoke, but gradually more and more details emerged. As they did, Pema became frightened, for, true to the scriptural descriptions, the Yidam was a fearsome-looking creature. But frightened or not, he never once wavered, continuing his visualizations and trusting that the kylkhor would restrain anything that manifested. The day arrived when the Yidam squatted in the kylkhor, glaring out at him with glowing eyes, as real as a monastic statue or a mountain bear. Pema decided his task had been achieved. He ate the last of his food, then started down the mountain to report to Kang Rinpoche.

His guru was delighted. He told Pema very few pupils reached the stage of calling the Yidam to visible appearance. But at the same time, the job was far from finished. Being able to see the Yidam was a great thing, but a teaching deity was useless if you couldn't hear what it wished to say to you. Consequently, Pema was instructed to return to his cave, continue with his visualizations, but now concentrate on the task of hearing the Yidam's voice. Kang Rinpoche told him he should not cease his efforts until the Yidam spoke to him.

This proved even more difficult than calling the deity to visible appearance. After weeks of effort, Pema found he could imagine the Yidam's voice quite vividly and sometimes it "said" things inside his head apparently of its own accord, but Kang Rinpoche had anticipated such a development and warned that it was not enough. The voice of the Yidam had to be heard objectively, just as its form was seen objectively.

Two more months went by before it happened. Pema awoke one morning from a deep exhausted sleep to find the Yidam already present within the kylkhor. As he prepared himself for his early meditations, the creature, quite distinctly, spoke his name.

Although overjoyed by the development, Pema knew instinctively it would not be enough and waited several more weeks before reporting back to his guru. By that stage the Yidam spoke to him regularly and even gave him what seemed like excellent advice on his spiritual development. Once again, Pema started down the mountain.

As before, Kang Rinpoche was pleased with his pupil. But again he warned that the task was not yet over. Pema had to seek the blessing of the Yidam. He had to persuade it to come to the edge of the circle and lay hands upon his head. Most important, he had to feel the Yidam's hands. In other words, he had to work to give the creature solidity.

This proved the most difficult aspect of the entire operation. It took Pema six months of intensive effort before he was successful in solidifying the deity to such an extent that he could feel its touch. But when he reached this stage, something quite extraordinary happened. When the Yidam laid its hands upon his head in blessing, a flow of energy entered Pema's spine and he felt as if his body lit up from within like a lamp. For the moment and for many hours afterward, he felt strong, energized, invulnerable. He knew he was at last making real progress without need of reassurance from his guru.

Nonetheless, he did return to his guru to report the news. Kang Rinpoche must have sensed something of importance had occurred, for he left his hut to meet the boy. When Pema told him what had transpired, Kang smiled delightedly and replied that the boy's task was almost over. He had to do only one more thing, and that was to persuade the Yidam to leave the magic circle of the kylkhor. When it did so, if all went well, it would take its place behind Pema's left shoulder and walk with him all the days of his life.

So Pema climbed back to his cave to complete this astounding operation of esoteric practice. The Yidam appeared on his mental command, solid, vocal, powerful. Although fearsome in appearance, it was now familiar and Pema was no longer afraid of it. His guru had made it clear that the fact the deity had deigned to manifest to the degree it had was an indication that it favored him and would do him no harm. This was the reason he could safely require it to leave the circle.

For once, something went easily—or at least comparatively easily. Although the creature was reluctant at first, it took Pema only three days to persuade it to step outside the circle. Sure enough, it took up a position behind his left shoulder exactly as the guru had predicted. Overjoyed, Pema went back down the mountain at once. The towering figure of the Yidam lumbered after him.

Kang Rinpoche met them both on the rocky apron that fronted his little hut. He did not have to wait for Pema's report—it was obvious the boy had succeeded. "You are released from your vows to me," he said gravely. "Go on your way. You have now equipped yourself with a teacher far more powerful than I could ever be."

So Pema thanked his old master and left, with the Yidam at his shoulder. For the next few weeks, he wandered the Tibetan wilderness, talking with the deity and receiving the wisdom of its words. But then, for no good reason, doubt began to set in. Although the Yidam knew many things Pema did not and could do many things Pema could not do, Pema was still haunted by the idea that he had somehow constructed the entity rather than calling it up. Eventually the doubts became so strong that he returned to Kang Rinpoche.

Kang Rinpoche was furious. He ordered Pema to return to his mountain cavern and embark on a rigorous routine of meditation until he had rooted out the blasphemous doubts. He was appalled that the young man should be so disrespectful of the deity that had consented not only to manifest, but to talk to him and help him.

Pema did as he was ordered, but although he meditated on the problem daily for several weeks, he could not resolve his doubts. If anything, they grew stronger. Eventually he decided his only course was to apologize and throw himself on the mercy of his guru. This he did. Returning down the mountain he actually knelt before Kang to confess that he still could not shake the feeling the Yidam was somehow unreal.

"But can you not see it?" asked Kang.

Pema nodded miserably. "Yes, Master."

"Can you not hear it?"

"Yes, Master."

"Do you not feel its hands upon your head and sense the power of its blessing?"

"Yes, Master."

"Is it not as solid and real and present as the Himalayas themselves?" demanded Kang.

"It is, Master, and yet I am convinced it is no more than the creation of my mind."

Kang Rinpoche smiled unexpectedly. "You have learned your lesson well, Pema," he said.

Pema suddenly knew what Kang Rinpoche was trying to teach him. The whole experience was actually a test of the pupil. If he succeeded in creating a Yidam that would walk and talk with him, his guru would tell him his studies were ended since he now had the wisest and most powerful teacher possible. The pupil who accepted this was deemed a failure—and sent off to spend the rest of his life in an uncomfortable hallucination. The pupil who expressed doubts had learned the lesson that even the most powerful deities were no more than creations of the human mind.

But Pema went further. No sooner had he understood Kang's words than he was struck by the realization that the world around him, the world he had always believed so real, was no more than a thought form, a waking dream manufactured inside his own head and projected outward, exactly as he had done with the Yidam.

In this way, Pema achieved enlightenment.

4 SCIENCE AND MAYA

Herbie on: optics and illusion; the way we "create" reality; Einstein, relativity, and the nature of our world; the disappearance of time; the disappearance of matter; the uncertainty of everything; the world as a dream state; why we live inside a thought form.

AS LONG AGO AS the nineteenth century, Western science began to suspect there might be something to the Buddhist doctrine that the world was *maya* (illusion). The suspicion arose from, of all things, the study of optics.

Most of us assume the external world is something absolute and objective that exists outside ourselves and is the same for everyone. Nineteenth-century scientists held the same opinion. They believed there really was something out there and it was their job to weigh, measure, and dissect it. But optics raised the first small question mark.

You are aware of external reality through the action of your senses. They are your windows to the world. For a majority of people, the most important of these windows is sight. Most of us experience ourselves as living just behind the eyes and "looking out" into our immediate environment. It's like using a literal window.

However it feels, the science of optics was the first of the sciences to teach that this widespread perception is just plain wrong. Our eyes are not windows through which we observe a common reality. They are part of a system that functions in a different way entirely.

What we are pleased to call the objective world is visible only in the presence of light. A study of optics indicates that rays of light (as they were thought of in the nineteenth century) bounce off objects around us and stimulate our eyes to form an upside-down image of the object. That word "image" is important, for it is our first hint that we do not perceive reality directly. What we actually perceive is a semblance of reality created by the interaction of light rays, our eyes, the object itself, and our brain, which turns the image the right way up.

This doesn't sound too far removed from direct perception, but it was enough to create a tiny worm of doubt in the minds of some scientists. And, like Pema Tense after he got his Yidam, that small worm was destined to grow and grow. In the early days, however, the realization had less to do with objective reality than with the fact that we all perceive objective reality somewhat differently.

I experienced this phenomenon personally many years ago when I worked closely with a professional photographer. He was a talkative individual with a habit of commenting, in detail, on the scenery visible through the window when we traveled anywhere by car. It took me only a short time to realize that what he saw through the window was different from what I saw—in some cases very different. He was aware of textures. I was not. Our color vision differed. And there was a considerable variation in emphasis.

I was prepared to accept these differences as subjective, but nineteenth-century scientists were more subtle. They noted that color, for example, was not something that existed "out there," but was a phenomenon arising out of the interaction of specific parts of the light spectrum on the retina of the human eye. This interaction was then interpreted by the human brain as a particular experience. Thus, while you and I might agree to call the experience "red," there is no way of telling whether we are actually undergoing the same experience. All we can say was that the color experience given by certain objects is consistent. We cannot say it is the same.

This is easy enough to understand when we're talking about color—and frankly, not terribly important. But some scientists—and indeed philosophers—went further. Was it, they suggested, not valid to say that all the visual characteristics of an object (and not just its color) were the result of the way individual brains interpreted light striking the retina?

If this was so—and it certainly seemed to be—then visual reality, as we experience it, was not so much something out there as it was an analogue of something out there created by our brains. So we were never perceiving reality directly, but rather examining a mental model of reality.

This was an uncomfortable thought, but one that has proved amenable to experimental verification. It is possible to make eyeglasses that have the effect of turning everything you see upside down. But if you wear them consistently for more than a few days, everything suddenly turns the right way up again. Your brain compensates by "flipping" your perception of reality. Reality itself (presumably) remains as it has always been.

Once the optical scientists realized what was happening with our visual perception, it quickly became clear that the basic insight applied equally to other senses. Although taste and smell involve the transfer of chemicals from "out there," the experience of both is just as much a construction of the brain as sight. The same goes for sound, which is the brain's interpretation of the action of atmospheric vibrations on a membrane in the inner ear. A Zen koan asks if a tree falling in the forest makes a sound when there is nobody there to hear it. Science has long answered that it does not.

All the same, nineteenth-century science was a million miles away from accepting the Buddhist conclusion that neither the tree, the forest, nor the listener actually existed. There was, after all, still the sense of touch, which might give a distorted idea of reality (like the fable of the three blind men examining an elephant), but at least showed there must be something out there. If seeing wasn't always believing, feeling remained God's honest truth.

In the twentieth century, all that was to change.

The first indication of the change came in 1905 when Albert Einstein (then just twenty-six years old) published his *Special Theory of Relativity*. This was extended eleven years later into the much more comprehensive *General Theory of Relativity*. Between them, the theories revolutionized physics. As a side-effect, they began a massive change in the way science understands reality.

The two aspects of relativity theory that triggered the change were Einstein's insights into the nature of time and his prediction of the existence of Black Holes.

Time, like the external world, was something everybody experienced. Philosophers likened it to a river, carrying us inevitably from the past into the future. It was the ultimate one-way trip, and its nature was something of a mystery. Einstein discovered it didn't exist.

Or rather, he discovered it didn't exist in its own right as something distinct and separate. Instead, his mathematics told him that time was just an aspect of what we'd always thought of as space. With this realization he began using the term "spacetime" (or spacetime continuum) to indicate that space and time could no longer be considered different things. They were actually parts of a greater unit.

The implications of this discovery were as disturbing in their own way as the earlier realization that we do not experience reality directly. They meant that one part of our experience—time—was not only indirect but incorrect. Everything we had always believed about time, everything we positively knew about time, was quite wrong.

The business with the Black Holes showed it wasn't the only thing we'd got wrong.

Einstein's *General Theory of Relativity* wasn't called *"The General Theory of Relativity."* It was titled (in translation) something like *Field Equations Pertaining to the Nature of Gravity.* As that title implies, most of the thrust of the paper was concerned with whatever it is that keeps you from floating off the planet into outer space.

Since the days of Isaac Newton, gravity had been associated with matter. Wherever you had a lump of matter anywhere in the universe, you had gravity as well. The bigger the lump, the more the gravity.

What Einstein's investigations showed was that when you had a really big lump of matter—more than three times bigger than our sun, to be exact—the gravity associated with it would be so strong that the matter would begin to collapse in on itself.

It is our familiar experience that when things collapse under their own weight, they end up as smaller things—their constituent parts are pressed closer together. But Einstein's calculations showed that if the original lump of matter was big enough, the collapse was open-ended. The lump didn't end up as a smaller, more compact lump—it disappeared altogether. In its place you had a sort of gravity well, an area of space where gravity was so powerful it sucked everything in from its immediate surroundings . . . even light. This cosmic vacuum cleaner was quickly dubbed a Black Hole.

Einstein's calculations indicated that if you could pass through a Black Hole, you would enter a completely new spacetime continuum—a parallel universe.

Although the discovery totally annihilated our commonsense view of reality—how is it possible to understand a reality "outside" the only reality we can experience?—the impact was a lot less than you might imagine, even within the scientific community. There was a number of reasons for this. One was that Einstein's Black Holes were a mathematical construction. Nobody knew whether they existed in the real world. Another was that if they did exist, there was no way you could move through one.[1]

By the time astronomers confirmed that Black Holes were a physical reality and fresh calculations showed most opened into not just one parallel universe but a multitude, science had become accustomed to dealing with the new realities as a theoretical construct. Since the Black Holes discovered were very, very far away, parallel universes didn't have much to do with the price of beans. We all began slowly to slide back into the old habit of thinking of reality as the objective world (the single "real" objective world) that existed, as the world anybody could see out there.

But more problems were on the way.

In 1926, two fine physicists, Walter Heisenberg and Erwin Schrödinger, managed to come up quite independently with the principles of a whole new theory of physics—quantum mechanics. It turned out to be the best way of looking at reality that humanity has ever devised. It solved problem after problem that had defeated physicists for years. It indicated time after time, with pinpoint accuracy, exactly how things worked.

In the early 1930s, an experiment in quantum physics showed—yet again!—that the world was not what it seemed. There were two ways of interpreting the results of this experiment (which revolved around the paths taken by subatomic particles). One suggested that the parallel realities predicted by relativity theory were not far away beyond a Black Hole in some distant galaxy, but right beside us as we speak. In fact, according to this explanation, we weave in and out of parallel universes all the time, depending on which of a whole series of possibilities we realize.

The other explanation was a lot more far-fetched. It postulated that an act of observation could cause the universe to split in two, allowing for the emergence of two conflicting possibilities. The split universe would reform into a single unit once a "decision" was made about which of the possibilities became actual.

---

1. The frequent jaunts through Black Holes in shows like *Star Trek* are pure fiction. In a Black Hole, even the slight difference in gravitational action between your head and your feet would be enough to tear you into atoms.

The second, more far-fetched theory is accepted by a majority of physicists today, a measure of how far the findings of quantum mechanics differ from common sense.

But if experiments like this have shown that reality works very differently to the way we perceive it, they still do not dismiss reality as illusional. That had to wait for new ways of examining the subatomic world.

Since the days of the ancient Greeks, philosophers and later scientists believed matter to consist of atoms—tiny building-block particles that were as small a lump of reality as it was possible to get. Consequently, by definition, you couldn't split an atom.

But it turned out this wasn't so. Although atoms certainly were the building blocks of matter, they could be—and eventually were—split. What scientists thought they found inside was even smaller bits of matter. These were labeled subatomic particles: little bits of stuff that are smaller than an atom.

Figuring out subatomic particles was a tricky business. Many of them were invisible not just to the naked eye, not just to optical microscopes, but invisible by definition.

Normally you see something because light bounces off it. But it turned out that light is not rays, as the early pioneers believed. We now know light itself is composed of subatomic particles (called photons). And light is just too grainy for some of the things scientists are interested in looking at. A light particle, instead of bouncing off, will knock any particle smaller than itself out of the way.

Technicians eventually developed something called an electron microscope, which didn't use light at all, but recorded the result of bouncing electrons—which are smaller than photons—off the thing they wanted to look at. This worked very well, but only up to a point. Physicists insisted on finding subatomic particles that were even smaller than electrons.

In physics, when you can't see a thing directly, you have to make a model of what you think it looks like, based on the way it interacts with other things. The earliest model of the inside of an atom was a miniature solar system. In the middle was a nucleus, equivalent to the sun, while orbiting it were particles, equivalent to planets. Lots of people—although not lots of scientists—still think the inside of an atom is like that. But quantum mechanics has taught us that it isn't.

The problem, as quantum mechanics discovered, is that particles aren't actually particles. A particle is a tiny, little lump of something, like a miniature cannonball. But subatomic particles don't always behave like little cannonballs.

They sometimes behave like waves. And it seems that subatomic particles aren't either waves or cannonballs—they're both at the same time.

As techniques improved and physicists started finding smaller and smaller particles, the hunt went on for the ultimate particle, the twentieth-century equivalent of the Greek atom, the bit of something (wave-cum-cannonball) that was absolutely as small as you could get. This ultimate particle would, of course, be the building block of all other particles, just as the atom was the building block of matter.

They didn't find it. There was no ultimate particle. If you went down deep enough into an atom, there was nothing at all!

This is so bizarre most people still find it hard to believe, but according to the very best investigations of the very best theory that physicists have ever developed, the world of matter is made out of absolutely nothing.

That's not another way of saying it's made out of energy (which it is), because energy is made out of absolutely nothing, too. In their most fundamental form, energy (the wave) and matter (the particle) arise out of a void. They appear as mysteriously as the rabbit from a conjurer's hat—more mysteriously, in fact, since we at least know there's some trick involved with the rabbit.

It's bad enough to be told that if you look deeply enough into the world there's nothing there. It's even worse to learn that its apparent stability is purely statistical. Assuming you exist right now, there's a very good chance you will continue to exist in a second from now. But it's only a chance. There are small, but very real, odds that you will stop existing altogether. If it's any consolation, this doesn't just apply to you—it applies to your house, your town, your country, your world . . . even the entire universe.

At any given moment, it's odds-on that the universe will exist, but it is not a certainty.

While scientists were still reeling from those discoveries, quantum mechanics produced another surprise from up its sleeve. This was the Heisenberg uncertainty principle, based on the discovery that you could measure the speed of a particle or you could measure its position, but you couldn't measure both. The reason turned out to be as bizarre as anything Lewis Carroll ever wrote. It was the act of observation that screwed things up. Just looking at the particle influenced its behavior. Therefore, a mental interaction can, at bedrock level, change the nature of reality. The conclusion is inescapable. Science has demonstrated what Buddhism has always taught: we inhabit a world of maya or illusion.

Specifically, we inhabit a thought form.

What lies underneath the thought form? Over the centuries, mystics and psychics have left intriguing reports of an energy structure beneath the familiar appearance of matter; and while this is no more the ultimate reality than our illusion of matter itself, it does seem to represent a deeper perception of the way things actually are. With a little effort and a lot of practice, you can experience this depth perception for yourself.

Find yourself a quiet space and a lighted candle. Sit comfortably and stare into the candle flame. Now slowly close your eyes until they are little more than slits. At some point in the process, you will find you are looking at narrow rays of light radiating outward from the candle flame. If you open your eyes a little, they will disappear. Close them to a slit and the rays are back again.

There is nothing psychic or mystic about the perception so far. What you are experiencing is an optical reflex that will always arise if you stare at a light source through slitted eyes. Play with the rays for a few minutes, opening and closing your eyes to watch them appear and disappear. Then, when you are thoroughly familiar with them, close your eyes completely and take a moment to imagine what you have just seen. Hold the rays in your mind's eye, then slit your eyes again to check your visualization against its source.

Now go outside and find yourself some growing plants—trees, shrubs, bushes, flowers. As you examine them, strongly visualize the strands of light you saw in the candle as emanating from the plants. If you do this correctly, you will find you are imagining a network of light energy linking all the growing structures. You may even become aware that the network extends to animals as well—sheep, cattle, domestic pets, even humans (including yourself).

This is a simple, easy exercise that repays frequent repetition. What it does is begin to retrain your mind. With practice and perseverance, a mental "click-over" will eventually occur so you are no longer imagining the energy structures, but actually seeing them. You have, in other words, permitted yourself a personal experience of a deeper level of reality.

But one of the great disappointments of esoteric practice is that discovering reality is your own creation does not give you the power to change it permanently. However much physics you read, however many mystical writings you study, the world remains stubbornly solid. In theory, you should be able to build your next home by thinking it into existence. In practice, you still have to lay the bricks like anybody else.

What creates such an enduring semblance of solidity? The answer seems to be consensus. The world is what a majority of its inhabitants agree it to be. The consensus view is taught from earliest childhood—babies are literally trained to see their environment in a particular way. It is reinforced throughout the remainder of your life. The mechanics of maintaining the illusion quickly become unconscious. Before you know it, you are trapped in a dream that will last until the day you die.

All the same, the insight that the world is a dream state can be useful. It indicates that, at its most fundamental, the universe doesn't obey the rules of rational physics—as the physicists themselves have now discovered.

It obeys the laws of psychology.

5 MATHEMATICS OF REALITY

FOR CENTURIES, THE MOST consistent and powerful scientific tool for the exploration of reality has been mathematics. Few scientists—and even fewer occultists—realize it was once a closely guarded esoteric art.

Up to the sixth century B.C., mathematics (as far as we know) was used only to count and calculate. Although many of the calculations were quite complex—the Egyptians and Babylonians in particular had sophisticated accounting systems and could perform impressive engineering computations—the whole vast edifice of mathematics as it is understood today simply did not exist.

Pythagoras of Samos changed all that.

The name Pythagoras is known to every schoolchild through his famous geometric theorem stating that the square on the hypotenuse of a right-angled triangle is equal to the sum of the squares on the other two sides. But few are taught that the historical Pythagoras was an occult philosopher whose researches brought him a profound understanding of the nature of reality.

As a young man, Pythagoras spent twenty years traveling the world in search of occult knowledge. Although legend has it he voyaged as far afield as India and

Britain, he was particularly attracted to the mathematical techniques and tools of ancient Egypt, which formed part of an initiate wisdom believed to have originated in antediluvian times. The practical application of this wisdom was both obvious and impressive. The temples and pyramids of Egypt were the envy of the ancient world, but the work was done with the aid of formulae handed down from remote antiquity and not really understood.[1] These old techniques were used like recipes. They were followed. They got results. But nobody knew why. There was no understanding of the relationships between numbers or the patterns they formed.

Pythagoras collected all the information he could, then set sail for home, the Aegean island of Samos, with the intention of founding a Mystery School devoted to researching the formulae he had collected. But he arrived on Samos to discover that the new ruler, Polycrates, had turned its liberal culture into an intolerant tyranny.

Polycrates actually invited Pythagoras, who had already made a name for himself as a philosopher, to join the imperial court, but Pythagoras declined and went off to live in a cave instead. He took on a pupil and eventually established the Semicircle of Pythagoras, the school he had long dreamed of, but was foolish enough to preach social reform. The tyrant Polycrates reacted predictably, and Pythagoras was forced to flee to the city of Croton, in what is now southern Italy but was then part of Greece. There he attracted the patronage of Milo, the city's wealthiest man. With his support, Pythagoras founded the Pythagorean Brotherhood, a six-hundred strong esoteric school that took mathematics so seriously one of its members was sentenced to death for the discovery of irrational numbers.

The Pythagorean Brotherhood believed that the study of numbers was the key to spiritual secrets and would bring them closer to the gods. They were particularly intrigued by perfect numbers, which could be discovered by adding up a number's divisors.[2] The number 6 is perfect because its divisors—1, 2 and 3—add up to itself. The number 28 is perfect for the same reason: here the divisors are 1, 2, 4, 7, and 14.

---

1. The existence of these formulae and the mystery of how they were originally developed is a fascinating study in its own right, but one beyond the scope of the present book. Interested readers are referred to Herbie Brennan's trilogy *Martian Genesis, The Atlantis Enigma,* and *The Secret History of Ancient Egypt* (London: Piatkus Books, and New York: Dell Books).

2. If a number can be divided by a second number without leaving a remainder, the second number is known as a divisor.

Pythagoras himself came to realize there was a relationship between numbers and nature. Natural phenomena is governed by laws that can be described using mathematical formulae. One of the most striking examples is the way in which harmony in numbers is reflected by harmony in music.

Iamblichus records how Pythagoras was walking past a blacksmith's forge when he noticed that while several of the hammers striking the anvil produced harmonious sounds, one did not. He rushed inside and examined the hammers, eventually weighing each one. This led to the discovery that harmonious hammers had simple weight ratios to each other—half, two-thirds, three-quarters, and so on. There was no such weight ratio in the hammer that produced the discord.

Following this insight, Pythagoras went on to examine the relationship between the length of the strings in a Greek lyre and the notes it produced. Once again he found that number governed harmony. It was this discovery that laid the foundation of mathematics as the basis of modern science. Today, its calculations and formulae underpin physics, chemistry, much of biology, and a whole host of other things. Without it, engineering would be impossible, the world we live in a very different place.

Yet, apart from relatively simplistic systems like numerology and Qabalistic gematria, mathematics has largely been abandoned by the occult community. This is a pity, for there are indications that math may be used to underpin certain occult doctrines just as securely as it supports scientific discovery. Ironically, the discovery has been made by a young physicist with an interest in the esoteric. To understand his reasoning requires some basic mathematical knowledge, but hopefully this can be acquired without either the herculean effort or grinding boredom you were forced to endure at school.

We need to begin with the simplest of all mathematical forms—natural numbers. Natural numbers might well be (and often are) called counting numbers, since that is their basic function. They were developed at the dawn of history, almost certainly for the purposes of trade. They enable you to discover the many things you have after your circumstances change.

Imagine you are an impoverished shepherd in Palestine somewhere around 1500 B.C. Your flock contains only ten sheep. Lulled by the drone of insects and the summer heat, you doze off in the noonday sun and four of your sheep wander off. When you awaken, you realize at once that some have gone—but how many? Fortunately, your knowledge of natural numbers can help you. All you need to do is count the sheep you have left (six), and simple subtraction tells you that you need to look for four.

Natural numbers are also extremely useful to you at the market. When things go well and you buy two more sheep for your flock, addition tells you that you now have twelve. Sell five and you are left with seven . . . but now you have five silver coins in your purse as well.

Natural numbers begin at one and march off over the horizon: 1, 2, 3, 4, 5, 6 . . . there is no theoretical end to the natural numbers you might have, since however great the sum they represent, you can always add one more. They stretch to infinity.

But what happens if you sell all your sheep?

Even in the Babylon of the third millennium B.C., it was appreciated that a symbol representing the state of having no sheep could be useful in mathematics. Thus the number zero was born. It showed there was nothing there at all. It displayed an absence of sheep—or anything else for that matter. It represented an empty space.

That empty space comes in very useful in certain mathematical systems (like our own) in which the position of a number changes its value. Take a look at the following brief table:

$$5$$
$$51$$
$$511$$
$$5,111$$

Each number has a 5 in it, but the value of the 5 changes line by line. In the second line it is ten times more valuable than in the first. By the time you reach the last line, it is a thousand times more valuable. But what would happen if the numbers you were counting contained no 1s or any other natural number? How would you tell that the values of the 5s were different then? The answer is to insert zero as a placeholder:

$$5$$
$$50$$
$$500$$
$$5,000$$

In this context, zero isn't a number at all, but rather the absence of a number. Several philosophers in ancient Greece wanted it to stay this way. Aristotle even argued that it should be outlawed altogether. He noted that if you treated zero as a number (rather than the absence of a number), it disrupted the whole natural order. Try dividing something by zero and you get an incomprehensible result.

But zero survived this prestigious assault, and by the sixth century A.D., Hindu mathematicians had accepted it as a number in its own right and hang the consequences. A hundred years later, the sage Brahmagupta remarked that division by zero was rather a neat definition of infinity. Thus, natural numbers no longer started at 1 as in the old days, but at zero. The progression toward infinity began: 0, 1, 2, 3, 4, 5 . . . and so on.

In the ancient world it seemed bizarre and unnatural to try to subtract six apples from four apples—any fool could see it couldn't be done. But the merchants of the Middle Ages had a very healthy respect for debt. They knew what it meant when a customer said, in effect, *Sell me six bolts of fine silk. I will pay you for four of them now and owe you for two.* It was deals like that which developed the concept of negative numbers. You could record the transaction as 4 - 6 = -2. The final figure showed how much you were owed.

Negative numbers might have no physical analogue in the way positive numbers had, but they still had an obvious connection with the real world. Today, most schoolchildren instinctively recognize that if you subtract five from three, the result is two less than zero, or -2. Therefore, they have little trouble with a natural number array that runs:

$$. . . -4, -3, -2, -1, 0, 1, 2, 3, 4 . . .$$

Even the briefest glance is enough to show the matrix extends to infinity both ways.

Negative numbers introduced a degree of abstraction into mathematics, but only a degree. What happened next was the step of such importance both to science and, as we shall shortly see, to the occult.

All natural numbers, negative and positive, can be multiplied in accordance with certain strict mathematical rules. These rules, as you probably learned at school, are as follows:

1. A positive number multiplied by another positive number will always give a positive result.

2. A positive number multiplied by a negative number will always give a negative result.

3. A negative number multiplied by a negative number will always give a positive result.

The rules work, but they also lead you into some weird territory. The first step is straightforward enough. Ask yourself which number, multiplied by itself, will give you the number 4. Even if you are a bigger duffer at mathematics than I am, the answer (2) will probably occur to you at once. Since the question you asked is absolutely equivalent to finding the square root of 4, you can say the square root of 4 is 2.

So far, so good. But if you look at rule 3 above, you will quickly discover the square root of 4 can also be -2. If you multiply -2 by -2, the result again equals 4. Because a minus multiplied by a minus will always result in a positive, the minus signs cancel each other out.

Still, no harm in that. There's nothing to say you can't have two perfectly accurate answers to the same question. Mathematicians take account of the positive and minus aspects of square roots by writing $\sqrt{4} = \pm 2$, another way of saying the square root of 4 equals +2 or -2.

Where things start to go bananas is when you ask yourself what the square root of -4 might be.

Clearly the answer isn't 2. We've already seen that 2 is one of the square roots of +4. But it isn't -2 either, since -2 multiplied by itself will, like any other minus number, give you a positive result. Now you might be tempted to say that -2 multiplied by +2 will give you -4 (which it will), but that still doesn't solve the problem of the square root. To find a square root, you must discover a number that, multiplied by itself, will result in your target number. Minus 2 is not the same number as +2 (otherwise I could pay off all my debts simply by owing them).

So how do you calculate the square root of -4? The answer seems to come straight from Alice in Wonderland. You simply imagine a number that, when multiplied by itself, will give you -4. And so people won't confuse it with a real number, you put the letter "i" (for imaginary) after it.

This sounds so much like something the Red Queen might have told Alice that I need to reassure you it has become a perfectly valid mathematical tool. The most fundamental of all imaginary numbers is the square root of -1, which was first written simply as "i" itself: $\sqrt{-1} = i$, which means the square root of -1 is an imaginary number I am going to represent by the letter "i" for imaginary. But then mathematicians quickly realized that even an imaginary number might be negative or positive, so they rewrote the little equation more accurately as $\sqrt{-1} = \pm i$, which means the square root of -1 is the positive or negative form of the number I am going to imagine is the square root of -1 and represent by the letter "i".

Although put this way, it might not seem mathematicians had gotten very far, but experience was to show they had actually taken a giant step. If the square root of -1 was $\pm i$, then obviously the square root of -4 was $\pm 2i$. From there you could develop a whole series of imaginary numbers that had valid mathematical relationships with one another. In fact, you could exactly match every natural number with its imaginary equivalent. Instead of the familiar linear expression of natural numbers:

$$\ldots -4, -3, -2, -1, 0, 1, 2, 3, 4 \ldots$$

you developed this sort of diagram:

-4i

-3i

-2i

-1i

$$\ldots -4, -3, -2, -1, 0, +1, +2, +3, +4 \ldots$$

+1i

+2i

+3i

+4i

Diagrams notwithstanding, it seems obvious that imaginary numbers have no equivalent in the real world. The number 2i does not represent a pair of sheep, a brace of pheasant, or anything else we would recognize on a woodland walk. Nor does it represent the sheep that are, so to speak, missing if we took four away from the original pair. Even -2i would not represent those missing sheep. Imaginary numbers do not stand for anything recognizable. They simply exist as a construct of the human mind that arose from a manipulation of certain mathematics that did relate to the real world.

And yet—which is where reality once again disappears down a rabbit hole— you can use imaginary numbers to make calculations that predict the outcome of physical events. Worse still, you can combine them with natural numbers almost any way you please and your calculations still give physical results.

Why this should be is a complete mystery within the current scientific paradigm. Mathematicians, scientists, and, more importantly, engineers, know that imaginary numbers really do work, but have no idea how.

Physics student James Bechrakis of Winnipeg, Canada, points out there is an aspect of esoteric theory that neatly bridges the gap. He relates imaginary numbers to astral magic.

Astral magic is a collection of techniques originating in deep prehistory that involve manipulation of the human imagination in an attempt to generate physical plane results. There is a much fuller examination of astral energies later in this book, but for the moment it is enough to say that magicians from primitive shamans to modern practitioners of the Western Esoteric Tradition have noted empirically that imaginal techniques, properly applied, really do seem to work.

In his study of physics, Bechrakis was exposed to imaginary numbers. He first noted that they did not exist in reality—that is, in three dimensions—but, when applied properly, at least in quantum mechanics and other regions of physics, the "imaginary" components reduced to zero and the answer became "real." Imaginary numbers are, for example, used in quantum mechanics to produce the Lorentz Transformations, which translate position, velocity, time, momentum, and energy values between reference frames. Bechrakis' parallel study of esoteric practice led him to ask a novel question: *Does this not resemble how astral magic works?*

The more he thought about it, the more obvious the parallels became. In magic, the wanted outcome is visualized in relevant symbolism to produce observable results. In complex algebra, the mathematician was presented with a problem that defied regular math. In order to solve it he defined an imaginary system of numbers. Armed with this imaginary (astral?) number system, he could now tackle the problem and come up with a result that agreed with experimental values. But if the numbers used technically don't exist except in the back of the human mind somewhere, then was this not a magical process?

Magicians would be hard-pressed to disagree. It seems James Bechrakis has discovered a magical operation hidden in the core system relied upon by all analytical science. His first published paper on the topic is included as appendix B of this book.

6 THOUGHTS DETECTED

FOR MANY OF US, the findings of physics and the insights of the mystics seem very far away. We may accept in theory that the world is a thought form, but the knowledge hardly impinges when we're running for a bus.

Part of the trouble is that we're all too familiar with thought forms—you make them in your head all the time, don't you?—and they share none of the characteristics of the "external" world. Where the world is substantial, our thought forms are nebulous. Where the world is vivid, our thought forms are vague. Where the world is stable, our thought forms are fleeting. It seems almost impossible to believe (in the gut where it counts) that the two are essentially the same thing.

If only there was a way of showing that a thought form—the sort you make in your head—had some sort of actuality outside your head. If only you could show the thought form in your head really did have something in common with what we still believe to be the real world.

Interestingly enough, there is a way to do just that.

In 1556, a treatise on mining—*De re metallica,* by Georgius Agricola—contained the first recorded reference to a *virgula divina,* a device used to find silver ore. It transpires that the virgula was a forked hazel stick. What was being described was a dowsing rod.

Dowsing has an ancient lineage. There are some indications it may have been used in ancient Greece and Rome, but it came into real prominence during the Middle Ages in Europe. From there it seems to have spread into Africa and America through the process of colonization. Today it is a worldwide practice.

In its most fundamental form, dowsing is a technique that employs a forked stick in an attempt to find underground water sources. The dowser holds the fork—usually hazel, rowan, or willow—by its two prongs, pulling them outward so the stick is in a state of delicate equilibrium. As the instrument passes over a water source, something causes it to tremble, dip, or raise distinctly.

What the "something" might be is an open question. In the past, dowsers have claimed they are detecting a specific radiation. Critics meet this with the rational, if somewhat dismissive, idea that the dowser unconsciously seeks natural geological indicators of the presence of water and causes the stick to react accordingly.

Neither explanation is particularly satisfactory. It is, of course, within the bounds of possibility that water gives off a hitherto unsuspected radiation. But dowsing seems perfectly capable of detecting metals, minerals, buried treasures, archaeological remains, and even dead bodies. It is difficult to believe that all these things produce unknown radiations. And what are the "natural geological indicators" for the presence of a corpse?

The problem is compounded by the fact that not all dowsers use a forked stick. Some use L-shaped rods, others use a pendulum, and a few can even manage it by holding out their empty hands. More mysterious still, there is substantial evidence that dowsing may be as successfully carried out over a map as over the terrain itself—a development that suggests dowsing may be a psychic skill.

But however nebulous the theory, the fact remains that dowsing works.

Several years ago, I bought a very old and somewhat isolated Irish cottage—so isolated, in fact, that it had no running water. Because of this, it was necessary to drill a well.

Well drilling in Ireland—and presumably elsewhere—is carried out by a contractor who arrives with boring gear on the back of a monstrously large truck. But before work starts, there's an obvious problem: where do you drill? Machinery this size costs a lot of money and the longer you use it, the higher the bill. Run it too long and you price yourself out of the market. So the trick is to drill at precisely the spot where there's water—and drill there the first time.

This is not an easy trick to pull off. Even highly paid geologists can get it wrong. But my well-drilling contractor didn't show up with a geologist. He arrived with a dowser who cut a forked stick from the hedge, walked around the overgrown garden, and said, "Drill here." He'd stopped at a spot where the stick suddenly dipped in his hands. He seemed absolutely sure of his conclusion. His whole job was done in less than five minutes.

Between the time the rig moved in and the drilling actually started, I had a visit from another water diviner, a young Englishman who had noticed the Well Drilling In Progress sign. He used metal rods rather than a forked stick, but confirmed that water was available at the spot where the first diviner indicated. He added the interesting information that it would be found at about twenty feet, but suggested continuing to drill to seventy feet, where there was "a good source of clean water that will never run dry." Drilling started the next day and the rig struck water at eighteen feet, only two feet short of the depth predicted. The contractor advised continuing, and at seventy feet he felt satisfied he'd located a permanent source. "You've got a lake down there," he told me.

I was so intrigued by the whole experience that I questioned the contractor about his use of dowsers. He was a down-to-earth man with little interest beyond getting the job done. He told me that in his experience in Ireland and abroad, most well-drilling contractors hired dowsers in preference to geologists "although some of them don't admit it."

But dowsing is capable of finding more than water—or even the metals, minerals, archaeological remains, and bodies already mentioned. Some of the things it can detect are weird indeed.

In the days when I was still socially acceptable, I received an invitation to dinner at the home of a Guinness heiress. During the course of the evening, the talk turned to ghosts and our hostess remarked that her castle was reputed to be haunted by a Gray Lady. There were two ghost-hunters in the party, and one of them offered to try to track the apparition with the aid of a pendulum.

A summoned butler appeared with the necessary materials on a silver tray, and a pendulum was made up on the spot. The ghost-hunter strolled off into the castle corridors, the pendulum swinging freely from her hand. The rest of us trailed after her like a line of ducks.

Eventually she halted in a small room. "This is where the ghost was seen," she said with confidence. And a startled hostess confirmed that she was right.

As a longtime member of the Society for Psychical Research, I know the evidence for ghostly apparitions is close to overwhelming. (Although whether ghosts are actually spirits of the dead is a very different matter.) Some of them seem to leave traces after their appearance. A good number of people can sense these traces as cold spots or areas in which they feel "spooky," "creepy," or otherwise uncomfortable. With dowsing rods or a pendulum, even very faint traces, which would otherwise go unnoticed, may be picked up. I was so intrigued by the results of the Guinness ghost-hunt that I began to wonder if it might be possible to detect even more subtle traces.

Around that time, a British television documentary was broadcast, based on an experiment carried out in the English countryside. The experiment itself was in two parts. In the first, an assistant was asked to walk across an open meadow shining an electric torch on the ground behind him. (The experiment was carried out in daylight.) All traces of his passage were then carefully obliterated, and a dowser challenged to discover the route the man had taken. The dowser did so with ease.

The second part of the experiment was a repeat of the first, but with one important difference. The torch, still switched on, was carried inside a lightproof box. Once again the dowser was able to determine the path taken. The commentator assured viewers that the experiment had been repeated several times with the same result. There followed a lengthy discussion about whether light left traces and some comment about the possibility that dowsers reacted to stray photons.

The whole thing struck me as an interesting example of the way unconscious assumptions can sometimes ruin experimental procedure. In this case, the assumption was that since the assistant carried a torch, the dowser had to be picking up traces of light. This assumption survived the second half of the experiment, which (to me at least) showed conclusively that it was not light he was detecting. Yet clearly he was detecting something. The only question was what.

Among several possibilities, it occurred to me that a man who believes himself to be laying down a light track has to be concentrating on what he is doing. If so, could the dowser have picked up not the light track, but the thought form? This idea begged another question: Was it even possible for a dowser to detect a thought form in the first place? I decided to conduct an experiment—one I hope you will take the trouble to repeat. To do so, you may need to know a little more about dowsing equipment.

Figure 6-1: L-shaped Rod

Although the forked stick is traditional, L-shaped rods or a pendulum are far easier to use. If you can't buy rods locally, you can make a pair quite easily from two wire coathangers (the hangers that came back with the last of your dry-cleaning will work well). Untwist them, bend the wire until it forms an L, then use wire-cutters to trim the ends. Hold one rod loosely in each hand so they are parallel to each other, as shown in figure 6-1, then walk slowly over the area you want to dowse. When you pass over water, the rods will move of their own accord to cross. (Or sometimes separate outward.) To dowse for a specific metal, keep a small sample in one hand or in your pocket while you dowse. Using your pendulum takes a little more preparation. While the rods are an all-purpose instrument, the pendulum is more specific. For this reason, it needs to be "tuned in."

It was a British archaeologist named Tom Lethbridge who discovered how to tune a pendulum. At the time he moved to Devon in 1957, most pendulum dowsers used a heavy weight and a short string so their instruments would not blow about in the wind. Lethbridge had the idea that it might be interesting to find out whether pendulums of different lengths would react to different things. To test his theory, he made a long pendulum and wrapped the string around a pencil so the length could easily be varied.

You use a dowsing pendulum by swinging it in a shallow arc, as shown in figure 6-2.

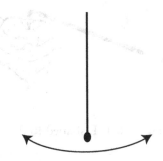

Figure 6-2: Dowsing Pendulum

Once it starts, it will continue to swing to and fro almost indefinitely as you walk from place to place. You know you have gotten a dowsing reaction (like the forked stick bending or the rods crossing) when, at a given spot, the pendulum stops swinging two and fro and starts to describe a circle. (Figure 6-3.)

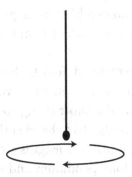

Figure 6-3: Pendulum Swinging in a Circle

Again, like the rods, this is not something you do to the pendulum. As far as the dowser is concerned, the pendulum reacts of its own accord.

Lethbridge put a silver dish on the floor and swung his pendulum over it. Carefully, he varied the length of the string until the pendulum suddenly started to circle. He measured the length of the string (twenty-two inches) and concluded that a twenty-two-inch-long pendulum was "tuned" to the "wavelength" of silver. Over a long series of experiments, he discovered lengths for a wide variety of different things: copper was thirty inches, grass sixteen inches, apples eighteen inches, and so on. He even discovered it was possible to tune the pendulum to abstract emotions (like anger) simply by visualizing them clearly. He and his wife Mina picked up stones and threw them against a wall. The pendulum could be tuned to detect which stone was thrown by the man and which was thrown by the woman.

By the time his experiments were finished, Tom Lethbridge was convinced he had made a fundamental discovery about pendulum dowsing. He wrote a number of books in which he gave the precise pendulum lengths for various substances. But those lengths aren't listed here. Lethbridge's discovery wasn't quite what he thought. It turns out that while certain pendulum lengths help you dowse for different things, these lengths are not the same for everybody. So while a twenty-two-inch pendulum would detect silver for Tom Lethbridge, it would not necessarily detect silver for you. What you have to do is find the particular lengths that work for you.

In other words, you have to tune your own pendulum.

When everything's ready, practice with your rods and/or your pendulum until you're confident that you can detect a particular item like a coin or a bowl of water. Once that's accomplished, you're ready to try the experiment I did. Have a friend or, better still, a small group of friends, visualize the item you wish to detect at a specific location. (Keep the actual item well out of the way.) Then dowse as before.

You will find, as I did, that when you pass over the spot where your friends imagine the item to be, you will get a dowsing reaction . . . to the thought form they have created.

The experiment as I've described it isn't very scientific. It's open to the objection that since you know where your friends are visualizing the object, you may be unconsciously influencing the equipment. You may, of course, tighten up your procedure by having your friends visualize the object without telling you exactly where, but it might be even more interesting to try a different experiment.

This one originates in Sweden and was first carried out—with dramatic success—by a small group of psychical researchers. The results were later duplicated in Ireland by a similar group. The procedure is as follows:

1. Dowse outside until you find a nine-by-nine foot (approximately) open area that generates no reactions at all. The experiment can't be carried out successfully indoors, as electrical wiring—which surrounds most buildings—interferes with results.

2. Mark a spot close to the center of the space you've dowsed.

3. Pick a small object such as an ornament or figurine to act as a target.

4. Select two people to conduct the first part of the experiment. These two go outside alone and out of sight of anyone else. One stands on the marked spot and watches, while the other conceals the target object somewhere in the vicinity.

5. Once this is done, both individuals should alert their colleagues, then leave the scene.

6. A dowser from the group, working alone and without an audience, then goes out and walks in a small circle around the marked spot where the watcher stood.

7. When he gets a dowsing reaction (as he will), the point at which the reaction occurred should also be marked.

8. The dowser should then repeat the process walking in a second, larger circle.

9. A line drawn, joining the three marks, will point to the hidden object.

This is a description of the experiment in its most basic form, but it has several exciting variations. The Swedish group discovered that you don't have to hide an actual object. A single "watcher" standing on the marked spot could select an arbitrary target—like a church spire on the horizon—concentrate on it for a moment, then leave. The dowser could still pick up the "psi track" leading to the target.

Even more peculiar, it transpired that where an object was used, the watcher did not have to know where it was hidden. It was enough for the watcher to form a clear picture of the object in his mind before leaving his marked spot. If two marked spots were used and the watcher visited each of them, then visualized the target object, the actual location of the target could be obtained by triangulation—where the two psi tracks crossed was where the target was hidden.

The group took his process to its ultimate on one occasion when they used it in an attempt to trace a murderer. In Sweden at the time, police were searching for a serial killer and had issued an Identikit picture of a suspect. Using the picture as their target, the group carried out three large-scale triangulations and transferred the psi tracks to a map. They crossed at a village where the suspect was subsequently arrested.

It was quickly discovered that the psi track was not any form of electromagnetic trace. Hiding the object in a metal box made no difference, nor did hiding it under water. The experience with the Identikit picture indicated you did not even have to visualize the actual target—a reasonable representation was enough. Careful examination showed that the "track" was not laid along the ground, but hung in the air a few feet above it.

The conclusion is inescapable. Psi tracks are thought forms, but thought forms you can detect and measure under rigid scientific conditions. They are, in other words, part of what we think of as the objective world.

Just how much a part is underlined by the work of the United States psychiatrist Dr. Morton Schatzman, who carried out extensive psychological tests on a subject he named "Ruth." According to his paper in the *New Scientist*,[1] Ruth had a natural ability to create thought forms of such intensity that they appeared objectively real to her.

When a reversing checkerboard pattern is displayed on, for example, a television set, the flashing image triggers what is known as a visual evoked response, clearly discernable on an electroencephalogram (EEG) taken of the subject's brain waves. Dr. Schatzman had Ruth watch such a pattern and found her brain produced the normal response. He then instructed her to visualize her daughter standing between her and the television set.

Ruth did so, and her EEG returned to normal, exactly as if something was blocking her view of the flashing checkerboard.

---

1. *New Scientist* 87 (1980): 935.

7 THE MYSTERIOUS ASTRAL

Herbie on: magicians and the Astral Plane; why there is no mention of the astral in the grimoires; Astral Plane and the Qabalah; the Big Bang; parallels between physics and the ancient doctrines; imagination as the foundation of the universe.

VIRTUALLY EVERY BOOK on magic published in the last 150 years deals extensively with the Astral Plane. Eliphas Levi talks about it in his book *History of Magic,* Aleister Crowley talks about it in *Magick in Theory and Practice.* It is discussed by Dion Fortune, Israel Regardie, Madame Blavatsky, Franz Bardon, Bill Gray, Gareth Knight, and Ernest Butler, among a host of other authors.[1]

According to all these people, the Astral Plane is the prime key to magical results. It is the secret behind virtually every worthwhile magical enterprise. Those trained in modern Qabalah—the system of Jewish mysticism that underpins so much magical doctrine—claim it is the very foundation of the physical universe, the immediate support of manifestation.

But if you examine the older works, the early grimoires that might, at least in theory, be considered the foundation of modern magical practice, there is no

---

1. The Astral Plane is also discussed by Herbie Brennan and Dolores Ashcroft-Nowicki; in fact, Brennan's first published work was about the Astral Plane.

mention of the Astral Plane at all. It is absent from the *Lemegeton* and the *Clavicula Salomonis*. There is no hint of it in the *Grimoire Verum*, the *Picatrix*, the *Black Pullet*, or the *Grimoire of Honorius*. Even Francis Barrett fails to mention it in his comprehensive masterpiece, *The Magus or Celestial Intelligencer*. These works contain detailed instructions for all the common magical operations—the evocations, invocations, and conjurations, the exorcisms, the creation of talismans, contact and conversation with spirits and angels, scrying, and the rest—but it is as if these things could be carried out without the slightest knowledge of the Astral Plane . . . something hotly denied by practicing magicians in the present day.

Worse still, if you consult the *Sepher Yetzirah*, the ultimate sourcebook of Qabalistic doctrine that underlies much of modern magical practice, there is not a single appearance of the term "astral" anywhere within its pages.

What is happening here? Have all the present-day magicians got it wrong?

The key to the conundrum may be terminology. Although there is no mention of the astral in the early grimoires, there are frequent references to images. The foundation of manifestation in the *Sepher Yetzirah* is the sphere of Yesod, which is associated with emotion and visionary experience. And in the *Archidoxes of Magic,* written by Paracelsus, the foremost magician of the early sixteenth century, there appears this curious statement:

> What powerful operation the Imagination hath, and how the ſame cometh to its hight and exaltation, may be ſeen by an example taken from experience in the time of peſtilence, wherein the Imagination poyſoneth more than any infected Aire; and againſt which, no Antidote, neither of Mithridate nor Treacle, nor any ſuch preſervate, can exhibit any helpe; unleſſ that ſuch an Imagination do paſſ away and be forgotten, nothing elſe will helpe. So quick and ſwift a Runner and Meſſenger is the Imagination, that it doth not onely fly out of one houſe into another, out of one ſtreete into another, but alſo moſt ſwiftly paſſeth from one City and Country into another; ſo that by the Imagination onely of one perſon, the Peſtilence may come into ſome whole City or Country, and kill many thouſandſ of men.[2]

It is difficult to believe this passage means what it says. Does Paracelsus seriously expect us to believe that a single individual could visit a plague on a city simply

2. Paracelsus, *The Archidoxes of Magic* (London: Askin, and New York: Weiser, 1975).

by an act of imagination? Apparently he does, for he devotes an entire chapter of his Archidoxes to the power of imagination. Another (unattributed) sixteenth-century manuscript, the *Regnum Piscator,*[3] is entirely devoted to the training and use of the imagination for magical ends. These sources credit the same importance to the imagination as more recent writers ascribe to the Astral Plane. Could there be some connection between the two?

I (Herbie Brennan)[4] certainly thought so in 1971, when I published my first book, *Astral Doorways.*[5] In that work I reported how, as an occult student, I had been told that "Astral Plane" was an old term for the world of the visual imagination. As I write today, three decades later, I still feel my initial sense of disbelief. I was brought up in an era—or possibly just a culture—that devalued imagination. Children like myself who engaged in daydreaming were accused of "woolgathering" and advised, often with the help of a clip around the ear, to concentrate on the real world. Daydreaming was seen as the ultimate time-waster. As an adult, it was difficult to accept imagination had any value at all.

Yet, when I trained in Qabalah, I began to see things differently.

Jewish tradition holds that the essence of Qabalah was taught to Adam by the archangel Gabriel. A more likely provenance is that it was rooted in the Merkava mysticism that flourished in Palestine during the first century A.D. and drew its own inspiration from the famous vision of Ezekiel in 592 B.C. Ezekiel saw what he believed to be the throne-chariot of God, and the goal of the Merkava mystics was to do the same. They attempted to achieve this by means of a dangerous visionary journey through a series of "heavenly spheres" manned by hostile angels.

Although the Talmud warns that of four men who engaged in Merkava, one apostatized, one went mad, one died, and only one (Rabbi Akiba ben Joseph) had a valid visionary experience, the tradition survived and eventually produced the earliest known Qabalistic text, the *Sephir Yetzirah* or "Book of the Creation," which may date back as far as the third century A.D. and was certainly not written later than the sixth century.

---

3. Unpublished.

4. Herbie Brennan will hereafter be referred to as H. B.

5. This book is still in print and is now published by Thoth Publications, located in Loughborough, England.

The *Sephir Yetzirah* is one of the most fascinating books ever written, and forms the basis of Qabalistic study up to the present day. It describes the creation of reality in terms that would draw sympathetic attention from a modern physicist . . . if modern physicists ever found themselves moved to study Jewish mysticism.

Today, the creation of reality—or at least that portion of reality we experience as our universe—is generally described in terms of the Big Bang theory. This theory holds that sometime earlier than ten billion years ago, there emerged at a point in space, approximately four billion light years from where you're sitting now, a sort of primal atom of such high temperature and density that it contained everything—every speck of matter, every erg of energy—in the universe today.

Where did this primal atom come from? It emerged, say the physicists without a ghost of a smile, from nowhere. What were things like before it emerged? There was no "before." Just as the atom contained all the energy and matter of the universe, it also contained all the time of the universe as well. Before the atom there was no time, so questions about "before" cannot sensibly be asked. Even my statement that it emerged four billion light years from where you're sitting is only relatively accurate. It emerged there only from your present viewpoint. What we experience as space was contained in the atom, so it had no absolute location.

But if the origins of the primal atom are difficult to comprehend, what happened afterward is easy. Sober physics texts maintain that it "expanded rapidly" within a fraction of a second—a polite way of saying it exploded. Scientists think they now know, more or less accurately, what happened during that explosion. Examined in slow motion, this is the picture:

During the first instant of the explosion, temperatures were too high to sustain anything as coarse and solid as an atom. Instead, what you had was a universe, tiny in volume, dense in essence, composed of matter and antimatter particles. Matter and antimatter are antagonistic mirror reflections of one another. If a particle of one meets a particle of the other, both are instantly converted into pure energy, resulting in mutual annihilation. Had matter and antimatter been evenly balanced in the Big Bang, our universe would never have come into being. But they weren't. In the first few microseconds, matter achieved a dominance over antimatter that allowed things to develop the way they actually did. The two conflicting states generated a third that was unlike either. Physicists suspect a great many other elementary particles were formed at this time.

After a few seconds of expansion, the brand-new universe cooled enough to allow nuclei of hydrogen, helium, and lithium to be formed. In about a million years, the cooling process was far enough advanced to convert these into atoms. By this stage, both space and time had been generated. Space was filled with the microwave radiation, discovered in 1965 by the German-American astrophysicist Arno A. Penzias and the American radio astronomer Robert W. Wilson.

But the universe was dark.

In this dark universe there came a time when a cloud of hydrogen and dust grains collapsed inward under its own gravity. As it condensed, its density and temperature increased until it reached incandescence. A star was born, and, for the first time in the history of the universe, there was light.

Stars proved to be the mighty furnaces in which more atoms of various types were forged. Those atoms migrated to form themselves into things we would recognize today—a speck of pollen on the stamen of a flower, a vein of gold, a deep, clear lake. As you read these words, it is surprising—and perhaps a little reassuring—to realize that you are entirely composed of star stuff.

That, in all its poetic appeal, is the scientific picture. The *Sephir Yetzirah,* surprisingly, mirrors it closely. According to this central Qabalistic doctrine, the background to all and everything is the Great Unmanifest, a state of "negative existence," the nature of which is utterly incomprehensible. From our present viewpoint, the Great Unmanifest is so far beyond speculation that it might as well be nothing. We cannot detect it. We can gain no insight whatsoever into its essential nature.

Out of this "no-thing" there emerged an "emanation." In Qabalah, this primal emanation is called Kether. It contained within itself the totality of the universe and is thus associated with the idea of unity. It is also clearly associated with the primal atom of the physicists.

Having arrived out of nowhere, Kether gave rise to two further emanations—Chokmah and Binah. As in the matter/antimatter annihilations of the Big Bang theory, the interaction between these two created the potential for further emanations. Thus, in a series of clearly defined stages, the physical universe came into being.

It is tempting to suggest that the *Sephir Yetzirah* anticipated the findings of modern physics by anything up to two millennia. But while there are eerie parallels between the cosmologies, it would be inaccurate to say they are identical, even allowing for differences in terminology. The *Sephir Yetzirah* describes the principles behind the emergence of the universe, not the process. It is process that is reflected in the Big Bang theory, not correlations.

Once we understand that the doctrines of the *Sephir Yetzirah* refer to principles rather than events, it becomes clear that what is being described is a plan for manifestation. The early Qabalists, like their predecessors of the Merkava, had no problem at all with considering it a plan in the mind of God.

The viewpoint has some benefits. It allows us to see, for example, that God must manifest first and foremost as a Unity; that the Unity always did and always will contain the totality of everything; that the process of manifestation is capable of being understood (albeit with difficulty), while the nature of that which manifests is not. It also shows that we, for all our faults, are a part of, not apart from, a totality that is itself a manifestation of divinity.

But beyond all this, the *Sephir Yetzirah* makes it clear that the process of manifestation (as distinct from the plan itself) is also an aspect of mind. It has purpose and meaning. What is being described is not God's creation of the world as a craftsman might create an artifact, but rather the world emerging out of an idea as God's dream. This dream is not given form. The dream is the form.

We have come full circle to the Buddhist idea of the world as maya created by mind. From one viewpoint, it is your mind that creates your world. From another, it is God's mind. But at root, both are the same thing, since you are part of God's manifestation and your mind is an aspect of God's mind.

In the *Sephir Yetzirah*, the details of this divine plan are embodied in a glyph known as the Tree of Life, where the various emanations are shown as spheres and the relationship between them as paths. The *Sephir Yetzirah* becomes so very helpful because the Tree symbolizes the (divine) psychological process of manifestation, allowing us to see what mindset is necessary to make changes in the world around us. The final sphere on the Tree of Life is called Malkuth, the Kingdom, and symbolizes the physical universe. The second last is called Yesod, the Foundation, which symbolizes the state immediately preceding physical manifestation, the state that gives rise to physical manifestation, the platform and pattern on which physical manifestation rests.

According to Qabalistic doctrine, Yesod is the sphere of God's imagination.

The idea that there is some sort of universal imagination is mirrored in the work of Carl Jung, whose observations as a psychiatrist led him to postulate the concept of a Collective Unconscious—an area of mind common to the whole human race. An eruption of academic interest in shamanism some years after

Jung's death led to the insight that shamanic visions gave conscious access to this level of reality, and that such an access often seemed to produce results on the physical level.

Two things are at work here—the objective, but nonmaterial state of the Collective Unconscious, and the personal, consciously accessible state of the shaman's own imagination. While remaining self-aware and conscious, the shaman—who was, after all, the world's earliest magician—can function within the Collective Unconscious, manipulate its energies, and, in so doing, influence physical reality.

Here, finally, we have the key to the mystery of the Astral Plane. It is not quite an old-fashioned name for the world of the (personal) imagination, no matter what my early mentor had to say. The Astral Plane is the imagination of the universe, that vast substrata of mind-stuff underpinning the dream we think of as physical reality. But human imagination is part of the universal imagination, seamlessly integrated, sharing in its nature, and separate only in that we perceive it as separate.

Thus, my early mentor was not mistaken in his definition. Your imagination and mine are both part of the Astral Plane, an entry point to a greater whole, the tool with which we may control the astral light. In practical terms, an act of astral magic is an act of the trained imagination, and the first step of an astral journey is an imaginary trip.

In other words, work on the Astral Plane involves the manipulation of thought forms.

8 ASTRAL CYBERSPACE

Herbie on: why the United States military called in the Rand Corporation; Paul Baran's Cold War solutions; birth of the Internet; creation of cyberspace; cyberspace and the astral; esoteric cyberspace; a Web experiment for you to try.

IN 1964, THE RAND CORPORATION in Santa Monica, California, published a report few magicians have read, but one that is already having profound implications for anyone with esoteric interests. The report was written by a Rand employee named Paul Baran, and sought to answer some hard questions posed by the United States military.

At the height of the Cold War, the Pentagon was deeply concerned about what might happen to America's communications networks in the event of a nuclear attack. Since 1960 the generals had come to realize that not only would existing networks be rendered useless, but they could not even imagine a network that would survive. They passed the problem over to Rand—a corporation that specializes in problem-solving—in the form of two broad questions: (1) how could the Americans prevent the destruction of its control headquarters during a nuclear attack? and (2) how could the American authorities cope with a communications network that had just been blown to bits?

Paul Baran answered both questions in a most surprising way:

How do you stop the destruction of your control headquarters in a nuclear attack? You get rid of your control headquarters before the fighting starts.

How can you cope with a communications network that's just been blown to bits? You build yourself a network that's designed to function when it's blown to bits.

It sounded bizarre, but Baran made some technical suggestions involving nodes that he hoped would translate his outlandish answers into practical solutions.

A node is a junction where several lines of a communication system come together. Baran's first idea was to make every node of the system do the same basic job as the old control headquarters. In other words, make every node capable of sending messages, receiving messages, and passing on messages.

His next bright idea was to abandon the familiar stream of data used in existing systems and replace it with separate "packets" of information. Each electronic packet would have a target address, exactly like a postal packet, but—and this was the critical point—it did not have to go directly to its destination. If there was a disruption in the network, such as might happen in a nuclear war, the packet could go around the devastated area and get there by another route. Since the packets would be moving at the speed of an electrical pulse, they would not even be noticeably slowed down.

Four years later, the National Physical Laboratory in Great Britain experimented to see if Baran's ideas would work in practice. Although they could only test them on a small scale, results were positive. The American military, which had watched this development with enormous interest, decided to fund a more ambitious program. By Christmas, 1969, they had linked four supercomputers using the principles Baran had worked out.

Nobody knew it at the time, but they'd just invented the Internet.

By 1971, the four original computers had grown to fifteen. A year later, that number more than doubled to thirty-seven. ARPAnet, as the system was called then, was still funded by the military, but was already carrying far more academic and scientific traffic. The pioneers of the system had assumed its greatest value would be distant computing—making use of the capacity of one computer while sitting at the keyboard of another. Instead, the tight little network seemed to be mainly used for the transfer of information.

Because of the way ARPAnet was designed, it could accommodate any make or type of computer. All you needed was the right software, and there was nothing to stop you from joining in. So many people joined in that the military (who theoretically still controlled ARPAnet) surrendered to them and set up a separate, dedicated network called MILNET, which they linked into ARPAnet. Independent networks like BITNET, USENET, and UUCP raced to connect in. So did NASA. So did the United States Department of Energy. So did the various American Health Authorities.

By 1989, the original ARPAnet had been so thoroughly digested by this swiftly-growing monster that it formally ceased to exist. The last remnant of military control disappeared. The Internet, as we now know it, had come into being.

As you will have gathered from the potted history, the Internet is really no more than a number of computers linked together to exchange information over phone lines. But by now it's a very large number. Just two years after the demise of ARPAnet, the new Internet had seven hundred thousand host computers and something like four million linked PCs from thirty-six countries. Between 1991 and 1994, the host computers themselves were approaching the four million mark, and the number of countries involved was more than eighty. By 1996, there were thirty-seven million people with Internet access in North America alone. By the time you read this, even those figures will seem laughably small. As I write, the Internet is attracting ten million new clients every thirty days.

Among the many consequences of the Internet was the creation of cyberspace.

Cyberspace is the great abstract world of computer information, accessible through whatever interface you're using when you log onto the Internet. But that's a little like saying your spouse is three-and-a-half pounds of assorted chemicals and a lot of water. It may be true, but it gives you very little indication of the reality.

The way most people experience the reality of cyberspace is through the World Wide Web, which isn't so much a part of the Internet as a way of communicating with the Internet as a whole. The Web presents itself as a series of interlinked electronic pages stretching right across the Internet. Many of the pages are packed with pictures and color. Virtually all of them have at least some text. In many ways they are like the pages of your favorite glossy magazine. But the Web differs from print magazines in that its pages can include moving images or sounds, and always do include the potential for interaction.

Interaction, more than anything else, is what makes the difference.

What all this has to do with the Astral Plane is best illustrated by one of the most intriguing examples of simultaneous interaction on the Internet—the MUD games. MUD stands for Multi User Dungeon and is a computerized version of the old fantasy role-playing games in which a fictional character ran in a fantasy world. In a MUD, you do just that across the Internet, as—simultaneously—do scores, perhaps hundreds, of others.

The result is that many, perhaps hundreds, of minds are concentrating on the creation of a particular universe. They are picturing its scenery and living in its environment.

MUDs are not the only areas of the Internet where this is taking place. In recent years, Internet "cities" have sprung up across the World Wide Web. The physical reality of these cities is nothing more than magnetic traces on computer disks, but that is not the way they present themselves. Surfers on the Web are encouraged to think of them as actual places. They have streets and districts, houses you can live in,[1] businesses you can set up. Fortune City, currently promoting itself as the fastest growing cybercity in Europe, elects a mayor and sponsors municipal entertainments.

Since no one ever experienced anything of this sort before the development of the Internet, a new word was coined to describe it. The world of the MUD or the skyscrapers of the cybercities are said to exist in "cyberspace."

In my book *The Internet*,[2] I defined cyberspace (rather neatly I thought) as "human imagination driven by the data stream of a computer system." But human imagination is inextricably linked with the Astral Plane. What influences the collective imagination influences the astral. That's why magicians have been warned through the ages to be careful with their visualizations.

In Lodge work, initiate groups often come together to create structures on the Astral Plane in order to generate magical effects. The system they use is easily described. The group will engage in prolonged concentration on a single image vividly visualized, interacting with the resultant astral structure by means of ritual. This type of group work has long been held to be the most potent possible use of human imagination.

Several inventions have influenced human imagination. The printing press (which allowed widespread distribution of literature), cinema, radio, and television all come to mind. But the influence of a specific television program, radio

---

1. I moved into one myself—184 Barney Hill, in the Roswell district of Fortune City—and dedicated it to a particularly interesting text channeled from the Inner Planes: the Way of Laughing. You can check it out for yourself at http://www.fortunecity.comk/roswell/barneyhill/184/.
2. London: Scholastic, 1998.

play, book, or movie is almost always fleeting. It is only in the structures of cyberspace that we have the truly magical prerequisites of prolonged concentration, vivid visualization (permanently underpinned by the data stream), and constant interaction.

While the physical realm will always affect the astral, it is also true that a feedback loop exists by which the astral affects the physical. This effect can be subtle and sometimes delayed—particularly when intent is lacking—but it is very real. Consequently, any structures built in cyberspace will, if left in place for long, eventually reverberate to some degree on the physical world.

When dealing with MUDs and the cybercities, such reverberations are likely to be minimal, since magical intent is lacking. But it is only a matter of time before magicians themselves wake up to the potential offered by cyberspace. The situation is particularly interesting since cyberspace seems to offer something of a shortcut to magical effects.

In this computer age, magical abilities are potentially open to all.

Setting up the esoteric equivalent of a MUD would allow for the creation of cyberspace rituals with a multitude of participants and consequent generation of substantial astral energy. Unfortunately, at this time, anything of this sort requires access to a dedicated server and fairly substantial programming ability. But as the cost of computers drops and server software grows more sophisticated, hence easier to use, the day may not be too far off when experiments of this type are attempted.[3]

Meanwhile, those of you who run your own websites can get the faintest hint of cyberspace potential by setting up the ten interlinked pages coded in appendix A. The html code is simplistic in the extreme, in the hope of encouraging as many readers as possible to participate. It is built around a particularly interesting pathworking created by Dolores and titled the Starborn.

For the links to work properly, the pages must be titled "star1.html" (lowercase without the quotes) through "star10.html." The sequence of pages given are meant to be no more than a skeleton you can customize using your own magical knowledge and creative skills. A few notes have been included suggesting possible approaches, but these, like the pages themselves, have been purposely kept simple.

---

3. If you're attempting one at the time you read this, be sure to let me know. You can write to me at Llewellyn Publications.

Part Two

_____

THE ASTRAL PLANE

9 THE TRIANGLE OF CAUSATION

Dolores on: the Triangle of Causation and its role in the art of thought-forming; desire, emotion, and imagination; the three point location of occult power in the physical brain.

THERE IS ABSOLUTELY nothing that can be done without using a thought form as its basis. Doing something "without thinking" still requires a split moment in time as the thought manifests before the action. We live, act, create, and exist by the power of thought. We feel hungry, we think of food. We look at a golf ball and think about the kind of shot we need to get it off the tee. Reading a document or a book, looking at a knitting pattern or a recipe for a cake, purchasing a new car or a birthday gift, deciding where to put a vase of flowers to its best advantage or what color to paint a wall . . . all require that we think, which in turn means building a mental picture. This creative thought power is readily available to all of us, and we waste it every day of our lives.

The teachers of the ancient mystery schools knew all about the power of thought and trained their pupils accordingly. A few modern schools teach it as an adjunct to visualization and guided meditations, or more seriously as a hidden teaching given to a few. But there is little point in hiding something we all use every day. What is needed is instruction on how to build effective thought forms, and how to apply them in our daily and our spiritual lives. The moment you see the changes you can create around you and within you is the moment life takes on new meaning and purpose.

Once you understand and have acquired the technique and visual data, you can use the power of thought consciously, willing it into a chosen form and molding it to your desire and need. All successful men and women have this power, but most use it unknowingly, ignorant of its origins in the ancient past. They only know it works.

Can *you* build a thought form and hold it clear and true? Can *you* send it out into the cosmos to broadcast its message and gather about itself the building blocks of your desire? Can *you* reverse the power and cut out of your life those things you no longer need? The above sounds like an advertisement for every self-help book ever written. There is a difference. This book will, if used correctly and in sequence, show you how to build a thought form that will (1) be specific in every detail, (2) give you the background of how and why thought forms work, and (3) teach you how to make them persist.

Nothing is achieved without effort, and effort is what you will certainly need. There are too many books on the market offering "short cuts" to your heart's desire. Believe me when I tell you there is no such thing as a short cut. If you want to do something well, be prepared to work, and work hard. (See Herbie's tale of Pema the chela.) The first thing you have to do is understand what makes a thought form effective. My late teacher, W. E. Butler, taught that without understanding, all the knowledge in the world can never become wisdom.

To be successful, occult work must have a strong foundation. The art of thought-forming is no exception. The foundation is known as the Triangle of Causation and comprises (1) desire, (2) visualization, and (3) imagination. The triangle is known in occult work as one of the first and strongest geometric figures. It is associated with Binah, the Giver of Form, and is well adapted for our purposes. But most foundations need a fourth point. For Qabalistically minded readers, the four square figure belongs to Chesed, the sphere immediately following that of Binah and known as the sphere of organization. If you look at the Triangle of Causation (figure 9-1) on the following page, you will see how this symbology works in accordance with occult lore and law.

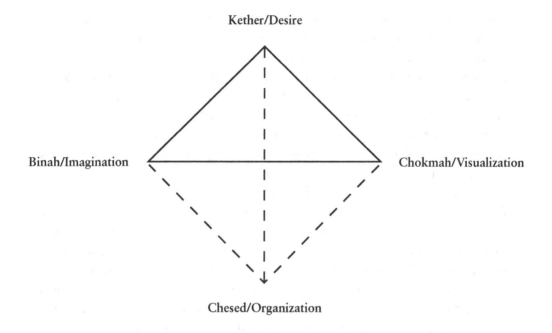

Figure 9-1: The Triangle of Causation

The Triangle of Causation is shown by the solid black line. It indicates that which is needed at the astral level to begin the creation of a thought form. To complete the foundation and bring that thought form down into the physical level, you need one more "point"—yourself, as both recipient and originator. The Triangle of Causation obeys the law of "as above so below" and reflects itself on the lower level, as shown by the dotted lines. You become the fourth point and the whole thing becomes a squared foundation.

Before we leave this intriguing game of geometry, let me point out that once you have this square, you can, by finding the exact center of the square and elevating it, create a pyramid with all that this ancient form symbolizes.

DESIRE

The dictionary defines the verb "desire" as "to long for the possession or enjoyment of a particular object." Usually, though not exclusively, it is used to describe an overpowering sexual need. But as human beings we have many desires and the urge to gratify them. We desire possessions, jewelry, money, houses, cars, beautiful clothes, and so on. We also desire things such as revenge or power—political, personal, religious, and geographical. It is no use denying this—we have all, at one time or another, desired such things. In fact, we are well acquainted with this feeling of desire, an overwhelming need to have or obtain what we want, no matter what the cost. For good or ill, it can bring about a single-mindedness that can and does roll over all obstacles, like the ancient Juggernaut god of India.

It is this single-mindedness of will, this need, this desire, that is the main thrusting-block of the magical thought form—to desire so deeply in mind, heart, and gut that it causes ripples of anticipation strong enough to disturb the placid surface of the astral matter. It also causes (or should cause) warning bells to ring in one's mind. Sometimes we desire things we cannot, should not, or must not have, either at a specific point in our lives or in this lifetime. There are things we are not destined to have, and nothing, no amount of magical expertise, training, emotion, visualization, or desire will bring them to us. At such times we generally blame God, by whatever name we use to designate the One. But we should blame ourselves, for within each of us there is a guardian, an aspect of the Primal Spark, whose task it is to keep us from committing spiritual hara-kiri. We can override it, but do so at our peril.

To deliberately build up desire of this intensity takes practice and common sense, an ingredient sadly lacking in many modern occult circles. First and foremost, ask yourself why you want this particular thing. Is it good for you? Will it cause problems elsewhere in your life or the lives of others? Cultivate self-honesty in your magical work, it will act as a defense against the most prevalent disease in magic—uncontrolled egotism. Ancient Egyptians called it "working with Ma'at."

If you are sure of what you want, and knowing what you want is the hardest part of all this preparation, you can begin to build up the desire within you. Use a magical mirror to talk to yourself about your desire. This will double the input of power because it will reflect the idea, the power, and the impact back and forth. Repeating spells into your mirror makes them work twice as quickly, but only spells you intend to benefit yourself. Remember, you are talking to yourself, after all.

Concentrate on building the desire aspect and leave everything else alone. Do not, at this point, bring in the imagination or visualization. Just "need" it. It will take three days minimum to build up the pressure. Don't stint on time: there is too much of the "hurry, hurry, hurry" syndrome in occult practice today. Concentrate on *feeling,* not seeing. Think of something you own that is important to you, examine the "feelings" you have about that object, and compare them with your feelings toward the desired object. There is a sense of ownership; it belongs to you in a very personal way; without it you would feel bereft. This is the feeling you must try to reproduce. You must feel as if you already have what you want.

There is an example of desire and its role in the building of thought forms that can be very destructive, both to the one who desires and the object of that desire.

The phenomenon of fan worship of stage, film, and television personalities is something that has been with us since the early days of the silent screen. The hysteria over the likes of Rudolph Valentino, Mary Pickford, and Douglas Fairbanks gave way to the same kind of thing over Clark Gable, Jean Harlow, and Gary Cooper. Then came Marilyn Monroe, Rock Hudson, Frank Sinatra, and James Dean. With the arrival of television, things have gone far beyond the worship of actors; now it is the characters in soaps and sitcoms that become the object of affections. These imaginary "people" are the focus of sexual desires for those who watch the dreamworld in which their idols exist.

This is thought formation of immense power. So much power that the screen world has become intensely real to fans. The characters (and not just the actors) get fanmail, receive gifts, love tokens, and proposals of marriage. Immature youngsters battling with puberty and hormonal imbalances find their dreams personified in such idols. They cannot see the difference between the actor and the character. They create in their own inner worlds a situation in which they are the recipients of the love and affection enacted on the screen. If the actor marries in real life, there may be scenes of violent hysteria, tears, threats of suicide, and, in some cases, actual self-destruction. Reality and the world of the thought form has become entwined, and with the advent of virtual reality it may soon become a threat to the sanity of susceptible types.

With the arrival of pop groups and solo rock stars, things have gone from bad to worse. Of course, not all fans go to extremes, but for many the object of their affections becomes a reason for living. Desire is a powerful emotion, but just as powerful is its opposite—jealousy. When the perceived lover takes a wife or husband in real life, some fans may feel betrayed. They project on to the interloper a third emotion: hatred, and the desire to hurt, remove, or eliminate that which seemingly stands between them and their desired object. They daydream of the pair being parted and the loved one returning to them.

This can create actual disharmony between the unsuspecting couple. The spouse begins to feel there is someone else . . . and there is: the neglected, despondent, vengeful fan. As the thought form is fed with these potent emotions, its power grows and the inevitable happens, the couple split up, and the fan once more feels there is a chance for her to become the beloved.

This is one reason for the checkered love lives of people in the public eye. Their inner world is continually invaded by the thought forms of unseen and unknown admirers seeking satisfaction of their desires. To be in the public favor is a two-edged sword. The admiration is, at first, very satisfying to the ego, but it soon becomes a burden. One must be careful not to upset the fickle affections of the fans. They can destroy as quickly as they create. Once out of favor, the supportive power of the desire image fades, and with it, the popularity of the fallen idol.

IMAGINATION

Imagination and visualization always work together, but don't forget that at the same time, the building of desire should continue to be practiced. Use your imagination to create a scenario using symbols, locations, events, and effects, weaving them around the desired object. It's like writing a book; you need a beginning, a middle or climax, and a successful ending.

It's not the spectacular areas of magic that bring success. In real life, the objects, people, jobs, and opportunities that come into your life are often brought about by a succession of small magical events, the seeming coincidences that dovetail into one another. A lot of little things working together can bring about one very big thing. Never do anything of this nature in a hurry—it is all too easy to gloss over a mistake or use the wrong symbol. If a lot of little things can make one big one, a lot of little mistakes can do exactly the same thing, with very different results. A real magician takes time over detail—that's what makes the difference between a magician and an adept!

To widen the horizons of your imagination, read books that offer excursions to such horizons. There are authors whose ability to create images in the mind makes their books ideal training grounds: Joseph Conrad, H. Rider Haggard, Ernest Hemingway, Jules Verne, Michael Moorcock, Gene Wolfe, Isaac Asimov,

Arthur Clarke, Andre Norton, among many, many others. They have the skill to feed the imagination to such depths that one ceases to read, and instead "watches" the action. Reading is another aspect of observation, an art like any other. Those who read only the words miss out on the true enjoyment of reading, which is actually to see, feel, and experience the images presented to you. To read words and to transmute them into scenes, actions, and events is to savor the ultimate skill of an author's talent.

Poetry can also be a useful teacher, as can short stories. Both forms need to create a whole concept, from start to finish, in a small space of time. It requires a special skill to do this successfully. Try writing short scenarios yourself or even a poem. Write about your "desire," and weave a story around it. You are not aiming for the Pulitzer Prize, this is just for your own satisfaction. Soon you will find that writing stimulates the imagination like nothing else.

VISUALIZATION

Visualization is a talent in and of itself. I have only come across a few, a very few, people who cannot visualize. Most of those who say they can't build an internal picture are mistakenly trying to see it externally with the physical eye, or they do visualize but so quickly it doesn't register as a picture. You only have to hold it for a moment for it to register on the astral. Of course, it helps if you can hold it for long periods of time, but try for seconds, work up to minutes, and hours will happen in time. Some nonvisualizers simply do not have a pattern on which to base the picture. I will elaborate on this in the next chapter. Meanwhile, remember, the more detail you add, the stronger the visualization will become, and the more exact a replica will be formed on the astral.

The ability to create or recreate images in the mind's eye and retain them can be classed as one of the most important, if not *the* most important areas of the magical art. Without it, the practice of magic is nearly impossible, though with even a small ability to "see," a fair amount can be attempted. Therefore, it is vital to train the inner sight to the fullest extent.

For that rarity, a person who really and truly cannot visualize, it would be wiser to turn to the practice of mysticism, where it is the art of "feeling" that becomes the most important of the senses. But, for both the expert and the inexpert, the three points of the Triangle of Causation will become the driving forces behind the operations described in this book.

10 THE LOCATION OF OCCULT POWER

Dolores on: the limbic system; the many brains of man; the Third Eye; left and right brained individuals; the triangle— physical, astral, and mental, and how to work with these aspects.

WE NOW COME TO the three areas in the physical brain where we can expect to find attributes, often long disregarded, but pertinent to the use and focus of what are referred to as "wild talents." To see a diagram of the brain, look at figure 10-1 on the following page.

LIMBIC SYSTEM

Speaking personally, I feel we need look no further for wild talents than the mysterious and to some extent still unknown area of the brain referred to as the midbrain or limbic system. Situated in the center and under the brain, this relatively small piece of our thinking mechanism wields a disproportionately large influence over our everyday life and that part we keep hidden away.

Here we find the thalamus and the hypothalamus, the pituitary and the amygdala. Together they form what is virtually a brain in its own right. Human beings outgrow their brains very rapidly, and we have had several of them. The primal brain that we share with all animals is the reptilian or medulla, often referred to as the pons or bridge. This is the stem where the spine

79

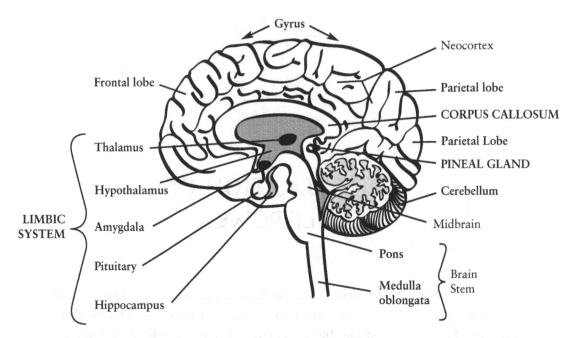

Figure 10-1: The Human Brain

ends and the brain proper begins. It stood us in good stead for millions of years, especially before we actually became "human." Then it no longer served our rapidly increasing needs and enlarging cranium, so we grew another brain. This new one, the cerebellum, took over all the latest things we had to deal with and learn about.

Soon this second brain went the way of the first, and the midbrain evolved. By this time we were making great strides in the civilization stakes and, small though it was and is, this walnut-sized newcomer coped with the concept of memory, the storage and retrieval of information, the mixing and matching of brain chemicals designed to bring about puberty in both sexes, the triggering of labor at the culmination of pregnancy, and the onset of menopause when the physical body could no longer safely cope with pregnancy. The Egyptians knew of this area and saw it as a collection of "Halls," where the various powers or attributes of certain gods might be contacted. They called the pituitary the "Star Chamber of Isis," and spoke of it as "having walls of silver that shone with their own light." The floor of the chamber was spread with "the silt of the sacred Nile." Thousands of years later we rediscovered that the pituitary gives off a slight phosphorescence, and that in about 15 percent of people there is a siltlike residue at the bottom of the gland, roughly the same percentage of psychics in the population (see Colin Wilson's *The Outsider*.)[1]

The thalamus was sacred to Ibis-headed Thoth, lord of books and magic. As it holds memories and learned knowledge, this was a good guess for an ancient people with no modern equipment to help them. Which brings us to the amygdala that controls much of our sexuality and hormonal urges. This was seen as the temple of Hathor, goddess of love, beauty, and music.

It is in this area that the all-important sense of smell connects with the outside world. This sense was, at one time in our history, the most important of all our five senses. Humans relied on it for hunting, recognition, sexual stimulation (we still do), and direction. It is the only sense that connects directly with the brain, there is no junction point, and is still one of the most important senses, despite the fact that at this point in our evolution we only use a minute part of it. We know that smell and memory react to and with one another, and memory itself is found in the midbrain.

PINEAL GLAND

The second point of the three is the pineal gland. This sits higher up in the modern brain, between the right and left lobes. Tucked away and hidden deep in the soft tissues, it has become synonymous with the third eye, the organ of inner sight and seership. It is said that total darkness stimulates the powers of this gland. Although it was once thought to be inferior to the pituitary, it is now seen to be just as important to our mental and psychological health.

Because this book is concerned mainly with the sense of sight on the subtle levels, the pineal will be an important area on which to concentrate and to develop. Seership, clairvoyance, and second sight has always been the most coveted of the higher senses, the rarest in a pure form and the most difficult to train. Often, those born with it need little basic training: they seem to bring into life a knowledge of the main do's and don'ts. What is not always understood is that one must accept the good and the bad. By this I mean that it is not always angels, faeries, and bright spirits that one sees. The subtle realms are full of

---

1. Colin Wilson, eminent author of *The Outsider* and a noted presenter of new ideas, has said, "Humanity in the next two hundred years will take a new and exciting leap forward in the evolutionary sense. That leap may well be the awakening of a new part of the brain."

shells, shades, and shards of things far less wholesome. The pineal is also the point where the internal images that were never meant to "come forward" are sometimes met up with. It is here that the deepest of visions, both religious and secular, can be encountered. This is the mystic sight of the saints. It enables them to see the images that underlie the great healing centers of Lourdes, Chartres, and Monserrat, and inspires the pilgrimages that still wend their way to Compostela, Rocamadour, Canterbury, and Walsingham. It can also be the giver of such visions as tormented St. Jerome in the desert and those we see divulged in the paintings of Hieronymous Bosch.

CORPUS CALLOSUM

The last point to consider is one that has yet to fully manifest its powers. Several years ago, when science discovered the differences between the right and left brains, a plethora of books came out. These ranged from advice on how to stimulate each in turn, to ways in which one might be encouraged to develop at the expense of the other. Much was made of "purely right brained" people and "purely left brained" people. We need both, which is why we have the two of them. Between the lobes runs a deep cleft, filled with closely entwined fibers that act like telephone links between the left and right. This is the corpus callosum, the third point.

It is true that most of us favor one side above the other. Herbie is left brained. He is mainly interested in and conversant with the scientific world. He likes to know the why, how, and where, but he is also, often to his own surprise, a competent psychic. I am right brained, the "fey" one. I go by instinct most of the time, but occasionally I can be quite logical. Together we comprise a pretty good "whole" brain! But, and it is the crux of this matter of the corpus callosum, it appears this bundle of fibers may be an embryonic brain destined to "open up" the as yet unusable percentage of our brain. At this moment, at least a quarter of the human race is beginning to experience this awakening.

The links between the two halves are still fragile. They work, but only on a fairly physical level. Their higher function will entail the complete union of the two halves, enabling humans to see and interact with the subtle levels in a way that seems impossible at this time. But so did fiber optics when they were invented. In each age, what was impossible before quickly becomes commonplace. In the past hundred years we have evolved faster than at any other time in human history. Based on that fact alone, the next hundred years should prove very interesting.

THE PHYSICAL

While on the subject of the triangle, let's consider briefly the nature of our own triangle, that of the physical, the astral, and the mental/spiritual. When it comes to the physical, many people think a psychic is likely to be tall, slim, and fragile, languid in character, and rather woolly-headed. In fact, most psychics tend to be under medium height, stocky in build, forceful by nature, and anything but fragile. Psychism takes a great deal of strength, and the stronger the frame the better the chances of survival!

Dealing with mediumistic talents or magical seership makes demands on one's energy levels that can, if allowed to do so, cause a dangerous lowering of the immune system. Having said that, if the training has been well based, within a few months there should be a strengthening of the physical body that will extend to the immune system, particularly if a personal contact with the subtle levels is made.

Magical work, when conducted properly, can be of great benefit both to mind and body. If there are problems, then 80 percent of the time they will be based on a physical cause alone. Only when the psychic pushes to the limit can a depletion of energy cause problems.

THE ASTRAL

Most people think of the astral body as something that is there permanently. What they are actually thinking of is the etheric. The real astral body is called out of astral matter as it is needed. It is natural for it to return to its own level when not in use.

Later in this book you will be taught how to create a much more effective astral body than ever before. You can even amalgamate the etheric and the astral and create a more solid vehicle, or combine etheric, astral, and spiritual matter to form the kind of simulacrum used by the great masters of the past.

THE MENTAL/SPIRITUAL

Each level is composed of material inimical to its own state of being. As the primal spark descends the levels on its journey to the physical, it collects a casing of matter from each level. This remains with us for a while after birth, but gradually the layers thin out, until only the etheric and a particle of the astral remain active—the others are latent. But because we have known them in our beginnings, they can be reactivated quickly when the right techniques are applied.

You have been given a lot of theory to think about. Believe us when we tell you that it has all been necessary if you are to get the best possible effect from the practical work that follows.

Now, take a deep breath, you are about to enter another dimension.

11 THE ART OF OBSERVATION (I)

Dolores on: recognition and memory; descriptive writing; sources of imagery; storing memories of emotion; observing the world around you; the senses; building a personal library of images; using the World Memory as a source.

THE GIFT OF SIGHT is precious, yet few of us give it much thought. It is not enough to see what is in front of you, you should observe everything there is to see. If you intend to control and manipulate the proto matter of the astral level, then the word "should" will have to be changed to "must." Observation is a vital, basic ingredient for detailed and successful visualization.

We all carry in our personal memory banks pictures and memories of everything we have seen, done, and heard since birth. Nine-tenths of it is locked away and can only be accessed by deep level hypnosis or by sudden, often accidental, stimuli. The sense of smell is an important trigger to memory, as we have already seen, and we often associate people with certain scents. For instance, a perfume or aftershave may bring a particular person to mind because you associate that person with the scent.

We recognize places and people by comparing what we see with the memory images we carry of them. If you see someone you know in the street, your memory banks instantly supply you with all the data you need: name, age, relationship, address, work, family, and so on. Without these stored images we would not be able to recognize anyone, even ourselves, in a mirror. To be able to recall an image, it is important to have seen it in the first place, and not just to have seen it, but to have observed it, understood it, and retained the image.

Take the familiar exercise of guided meditation. Usually students are instructed to imagine an entry point to an alternative state of consciousness, such as a door, a pylon gate, or a landscape of some kind. But imagining a castle with a drawbridge let down, or an oaken door, hundreds of years old, set into a wall of moss covered stones, with rusty iron hinges and locks can be intimidating. Unless you have seen such things (or at least a picture of them) you would have little idea how to visualize them. Photos are better than nothing, but better still is to have walked across a drawbridge or touched the stones, the wood, and the door.

In Durham Cathedral in England, there is an ancient flight of stone steps that sweeps upward in a half-circle (see figure 11-1 for an example). Because of its width, most people climb on the left side, holding the iron rail for support. Over the centuries this has resulted in the steps being worn to a fraction of their original thickness at that point. To see them, to climb those steps, is to feel the weight of centuries. One can imagine the pilgrims climbing them on weary feet. Such an experience arouses emotional links with the past that can make an astral image seem breathtakingly real. But to be able to use such images and memories, one must observe and retain details, seek out the inner feel of the place, and link it to the images—then it can be used to its fullest extent.

It is not only images of objects that are important, but of abstractions also. Can you conjure in your mind the feel of rain on your face or the bite of snow and ice? Can you mentally create the exhilaration that is found when standing on a hilltop in a high wind? Such things count as magical tools, on an equal par with a wand or a sword.

You need to store emotions as well. How does it feel to hold a very young baby in your arms, or walk through the woods alone, at midnight, on All Souls' Night? Is there something you feel passionately about, some cause, some object, some ideal, someone? Remember that feeling, recall its intensity, use that intensity as a guide line when thought-forming.

Can you recall in your mind the scent of freshly cut grass, or the cool, almost liquid smell of mimosa? What does velvet feel like, or fur, or well-used leather? As an exercise, describe these feelings. Write them down. Can you, if asked, create in your mind a knight in armor, correct in every detail? Or, for that matter, can you make it fourteenth-century armor as opposed to seventeenth century?

Figure 11-1: Stone Steps

What did a court lady wear under her outer garments in 1300? How did a knight fasten his sword belt before the invention of the tang in a buckle?

You may ask, "Does all this really matter?" Yes, if you want to build exact replicas in astral material, it matters a great deal. Why so exact? Because this was how such things were made and worn in that time. It is how the World Memory remembers them, how they were patterned into the astral matter at that time. If you can't recall them as they were, the pattern won't match and you won't get the full power behind the image. If you can do it, you will not just imagine it, you will recreate it, or rather, you will remember it. Think about the following sentence and write it in your magical diary, because understanding its meaning is another of those special differences between the would-be magician and the adept.

"Whenever possible, recreate rather than imagine or visualize." Make this your motto in thought form work.

Train your memory to retain images by building scrapbooks of pictures. Once you start, you will find it so useful you will want to amass a library of visual adjuncts. You need several large scrapbooks to start with. Label each one clearly. Begin with buildings of all kinds and from all ages—castles, palaces, churches, cathedrals, cottages and manor houses, towers and museums, opera houses, temples, ruins, and so on. Make one just for doors, steps and stairways, windows and stained glass, another for landscapes both ancient and modern, especially examples showing "then and now" of the same place. Now start on historical and ethnic costumes. Don't forget animals: How can you shapeshift into a jaguar unless you know the difference between it and a cougar? Don't forget the elements—scenes of water, fire, and storms are needed as well, as are caves and subterranean passages.

Don't neglect color. Collect shades of every kind, and especially the many shades of sky, earth, and stone. The pale blue of an early spring day is quite different from the deep blue of high summer. The dramatic thunder clouds that presage a storm or the steel-gray sky that tells of snow are each distinctive in their own way. Search magazines, books, and advertisements for examples. Above all, *read* and *look*. Read books that use descriptive language and use them to help you build images. Read the description, then put the book down and build it in your mind. Later, build it again from proto matter. See the difference it makes.

Wherever you are, *look,* and remember what you see. Take photos, make notes, sketch, or paint. It will all help to store images in the mind. As a catch exercise, whenever you are walking down a familiar street, try to find ten items you have never noticed before—the pot plant in a window, the decoration on a dormer window, the patterns on lace curtains. This will train your eye to find the unusual alongside the commonplace.

I like to walk along a beach in the very early morning after a storm. I look for shells, bones of seabirds, and unusual stones to use when making and decorating staffs, wands, and objects for spellcraft. I fix my mind on what I need as I walk the length of the beach, seeing them in my mind's eye. Then I turn and walk back, visually sweeping the beach before me with intent. Within minutes the shells and other things will show themselves plainly. Having patterned my desire in astral matter, I simply allow them to reveal themselves.

Try linking the images you already have with those you can see around you. Pair them, change them, or shift them around. Look at one of the pictures you have of a castle, and picture it as being on your street or road. Now enter the picture in your imagination and explore the castle.

Imagine you are decorating a film set, a room set in the mid-1930s. How will you "dress" it? What will you use for floor covering? What kind of ornaments, china, pictures, or furniture would be suitable? What about the actors—how should they be dressed and what do they actually look like? If you look at portraits painted in the last three or four hundred years, you will find that human features, and our whole idea of what constitutes beauty, have changed considerably. Very few could walk around in our time without looking out of place.

After a while, one of the oldest of magical rules will begin to take over. Your visualizations will become second nature and appear at will. When you take the trouble to do something time and again, doing your best each time, suddenly you no longer need to make an effort. It is there. But you have to go through all the hard preparatory work in order to be able to tap the World Memory within you. The same thing happens with temples, tools, and rituals. One day, after years of work, you will no longer need all the usual trappings: they have internalized and you have them at your command. That is the day you become an adept.

If you want to give form to your thoughts rather than just visualize, it is up to you to decide if it is worth working for. To build with power needs hard, concentrated effort. It is not my job to coax and cajole, only to show you how to do it. The rest is up to you. But, visualization is just one part of thought-forming. You have to have something to form them with, like astral matter. But what is astral matter?

12 THE COMPOSITION OF ASTRAL MATTER

EXACTLY WHAT IS astral matter? The answer is so simple that very few people understand its importance. It is sentient proto matter, primal building material, the molding clay of the Elohim . . . the mysterious beings who made man in their own image (see Gen. 26). The fact that it is *sentient* material enables it to reproduce the mental patterns we imprint on it. Calling it astral matter, while basically true, does not go anywhere near explaining what it really is.

What we know as physical life, in all its myriad forms, is really a manifestation of imprinted sentient proto matter—in simpler terms, a thought made into reality. But imprinted by what? Or, more to the point, by whom? Again, the answer is simple: by a mind or minds infinitely more powerful than our own.[1]

In order to get a firm hold on this idea we must return to basics—the beginning of our universe, in fact—and offer a hypothesis. Take a look at figure 12-1.

---

1. The opinion expressed is that of Dolores. Herbie believes that while the action of minds "more powerful than our own" may well be involved in the universe as a whole, our immediate environment results from an imprinting of astral matter by our own minds, usually at an unconscious level.

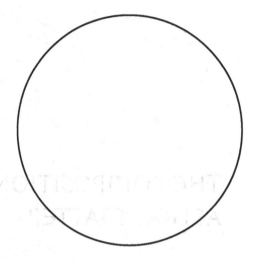

Figure 12-1: Unmanifested Nothingness

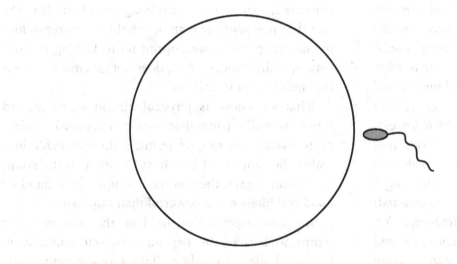

Figure 12-2: Intelligent Entity

It depicts an area of unmanifested nothingness, a space of inert and nonsentient matter. Bearing in mind the axiom of "As above, so below, but after another fashion," look at at figure 12-2.

This shows a familiar symbol approaching an area of uninhabited space. The newcomer is an Intelligent Entity. We have no way of knowing what it is or where it comes from, but we may surmise that it is looking for a place in which it can become itself. (Asher Eheieh Asher.) It enters the proscribed space, and realizes, to coin a phrase, that the space fits and takes it over.

Through untold eons, it broods and delves into itself and its reasons for being. Finally, realizing that true fulfillment cannot be achieved alone, it acts, and thus causes a reaction. This "act" is the sending out, or sloughing off, of part of it's own substance, and the reaction it causes is the *first* wave of creation.

It has no other image on which to draw for inspiration but its own. Therefore, what has now come into existence is, like itself, capable of self-realization and the creation of other forms. But they are like children in school, and are without the knowledge of the precosmic existence of the Parent. They are the Elohim, the First Children of what is now and forever will be, the One (figure 12-3).

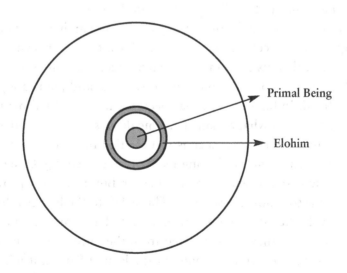

Figure 12-3

Figure 12-4: The Four Holy Creatures

But this is not all. The One has a grand plan for its universe. Now comes a second sloughing of primal substance. Like the first, it has the capability to understand and reason, but experience has changed it. This second wave produces beings with a specific task: to channel the will of the One—the Chaoith Ha Kadesh, the Four Holy Creatures. (See figure 12-4: the Winged Lion, the Winged Bull, the Eagle, and the Winged Human Being.)

A third and fourth birthing brings about the archangels and the lesser angelic groups. Now, successive waves of Primal Matter are thrown off, and each one, as it moves further away from its Primal Source, is less in power (see figure 12-5).

Now comes a pause while thoughts, ideas, and plans are prepared, adapted, and refined. In light of what has been learned, the final plan of the universe is determined. And what a plan. The One desires to know, understand, and experience reality, but its substance is too rarified to become that dense, so another way has been found. Still using its own substance, the One sends out a succession of increasingly dense layers of matter. But it can only provide the substance. It is unable to follow its progress. This is left to the beings it has already created. Each level takes it down as far as it can. These are the dimensions, and they grow denser as they are separated from the influence of the One. But, because this matter comes from the body of the Primal Parent, it inherits a sense of self and the ability to create, though much diminished. In fact, it can create only if provided with a pattern. (See figures 12-5, 12-6, and 12-7.)

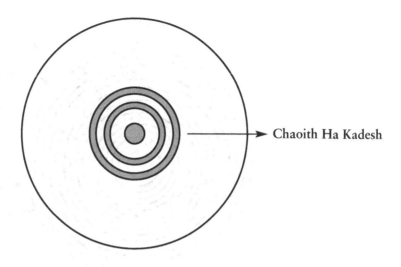

Figure 12-5

The last level of all has three basic instincts—to survive, to keep close together, and to reproduce. Although separated from the Primal Parent, it obeys the law and creates its kind time and again. It is this level that the One intends to use as a vehicle for its plan. That plan is intelligent life, through which it can experience its own universe at the densest level. To bring this about, the matter particles of the last level have each been provided with a particle of pure mind, the greatest gift of all, for it includes free will, given for the first time. Remember, the beings created in the first waves are not human, although they live in the sense that we know and understand life. Great in power they may be, but they do not have free will.

The word of the One goes out to those created to channel its will: "Give me life forms to inhabit. Give these forms the gift of sound. Let them feel desire, joy, hope, and anger. Let them live, grow, and die. They will return again and again until all has been experienced, then they will return to *me*."

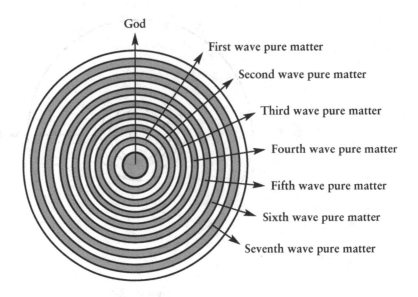

Figure 12-6

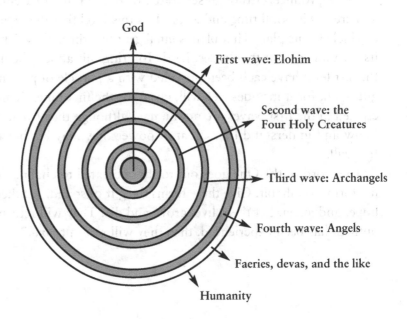

Figure 12-7: Archangels and Lesser Angelic Groups

So the Elohim and the Holy Creatures came together and consulted long and hard. "Let us make man in our own image," said the Elohim. And they did, using the proto matter of the existence level just above the physical. The thought forms thus created descended through the astral into the physical level. How many times have you read that early humans were more ethereal in form than those of later models? Perhaps it was because the pattern needed long eons of time to gather the layers of astral and etheric substance about itself to protect the divine thought form at its core. Because of our divine descent, we possess the same capability to create forms, both physically and astrally.

All dimensions are capable of being imprinted by the combined power of desire and imagery, but the higher dimensions are difficult to reach, and more difficult to hold onto long enough to imprint. However, the astral is close to our own level, and responds well to strong and sustained thought from the physical level, and from the higher mental and spiritual levels once the mind is trained.

Anyone can build an astral thought form, but without training it will disappear as soon as the form is no longer held in the mind. When it is held by many minds and over long periods of time, a semipermanent form is achieved. This is how God forms are built, how the ancient Egyptians built tomb guardians, and it is the reason why images that catch the public's eye, mind, and heart become real on this level. Examples are King Arthur, Mickey Mouse, *Star Trek, Star Wars,* Teenage Mutant Ninja Turtles, Power Rangers, and their spinoffs, along with other television, literary, and movie images. However, once they cease to enthrall the human mind and are forgotten, they revert back to astral matter. It is as well that few people have the mental strength to build and sustain such images. This is *not* a game to amuse or titillate one's senses. Building thought forms at high levels can be very dangerous, a warning we will repeat throughout this book. On the other hand, you will probably only need to make a mistake once (well . . . maybe twice) before realizing the truth of this statement.

Having learned the basic structure of the material with which you will be working, we can now proceed. You have already learned the value of collecting photographic images as patterns for your visualizations. Now we take it a step further. As I have already explained, the astral world has no natural landscape of its own. It is simply an all white or smoky-gray expanse of unstructured proto matter. To enable you to experience this, procure a cardboard box about ten inches deep, twelve to sixteen inches long, and ten inches wide. Cut away one side, and paint the inside with brilliant white matte paint, as shown in figure 12-8.

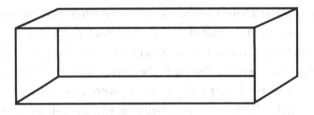

Figure 12-8: Cardboard Box

When the paint is dry, hold the box close to your face and imagine this as an entry point into the astral level. The effect will give you an idea of what an all white world would be like and help you to visualize it with the inner eye.

Silly? Yes. But it works. Until you can "see and feel" the effect of a totally white terrain, you cannot really imagine it. Think of it as an Arctic wasteland without the cold. Take some time (one or two days) to fully experience the effect and internalize it, because this is what the astral plane is like in its natural state. The total "whiteout" can be a little disorienting in the beginning, like being lost in a blizzard. When walking on the surface, it gives slightly and feels a little rubbery to the touch.

Approach the astral world with care, and at first just take in the flat whiteness and enjoy the effects without even trying. You will find that every passing thought will cause a form of some kind to materialize out of this basic matter, usually without much color, symmetry, or detail. Then it will flow back just as quickly as you let go of the mental image. Some of the shapes may be distorted or unfinished; this is because the thought form was not specific enough to be reproduced exactly.

Once you can build this white world clearly in your mind, you can take the next step, which is understanding the structure and purpose of the astral level. What surrounds you is *living matter* one step away from manifestation—a kind of solid fluid! A paradox? Yes, but the world of magic is full of them.

Proto matter obeys thought, any thought, detailed or not. It *needs* to manifest, and will take any and every opportunity to do so. It is constantly in motion, though so slightly it can scarcely be felt. In its natural state, it will manifest whatever you think of in exactly the way you think of it, including faults and flaws. The latter are not what you want or need when working magically.

Figure 12-9: The Magician

Most visualizations don't work very well because the thought matrix is faulty. The clearer and more accurate the thought pattern, the stronger and more effective the form on the physical plane. This is why you need to observe things in detail, collect examples to help you visualize, and have precise data in your mental filing system. Slap-dash images will be reproduced as slap-dash manifestations. Never rush into a visualization—map it out so you know what you need and how you need it to look, work, and behave.

If you aim to control proto matter, you must first learn to control your thought images. This is one of the inner, hidden meanings of the tarot card named the Magician. (See figure 12-9.)

He is oblivious to everything but the task in hand. Before him on the altar lie the building blocks of manifestation, the symbols of the four elements (the Four Holy Creatures). The upraised hand symbolizes the will (working in accordance with the will of the One), directing the future shape and form these elements will take. The other hand indicates the earth, where the manifestation will take place. The Hebrew letter associated with the card is *Beth*, meaning house, a symbol of solidity, form, and protection. The Magician is in total control.

When a pebble is dropped into a bowl of milk, or a drop of water falls from a height onto a hard surface, the slow motion result shows the liquid erupting upward into a coronet formation. In the same way, a trained and controlled mind can "pull up" from astral proto matter a shape that can then be refined into other shapes. The only "magical" tool needed is thought.

This is how all thought forms are manipulated. There is no quick way to learn it—you must go through the whole sequence while in the early stages. Neither is there a way in which the actual "mental pull" can be conveyed in words—you must try it, hit or miss, for yourself.

EXERCISE ONE

For this exercise, you will need the following supplies:

1. A sheet of white polystyrene ¼-inch thick.

2. A block of material thick enough to make a 2-inch cube, a pyramid shape with a 2-inch base, a sphere 2 inches in diameter (or use a table tennis ball), and a 2-by-1-by-4-inch rectangle.

3. A sharp knife or hot wire cutter.

Cut a hole in the sheet just large enough to allow the cube to be pushed up through the polystyrene, as shown in figure 12-10. Do the same for the other three shapes.

Retain the pieces you have removed to cover the holes; you will need them later. Take a good long look at the sheet of white material; this represents the astral world.

Remove the square cover and fit the cube into the hole from below. Gently push it upward until it begins to show, as shown in figure 12-11.

Stop and look at it. This is how you pull up astral matter from its matrix. Look at it closely for a few minutes and carefully memorize it. Push the cube up farther, then stop and look at the result. Do this until the cube is fully exposed. Do the same with the other shapes, each in turn. As the form rises out of the base, it will give you a clear idea of how to make a shape from astral matter. When you have done this with all the shapes, you are ready for the next part of the exercise.

Remove the shapes and replace the covers over the holes. Place the cube on the base and observe it for a few minutes. Next, insert a long pin or needle into

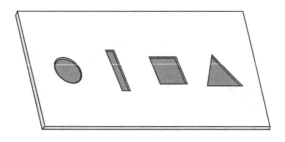

Figure 12-10: Box With Shapes Pushed Through

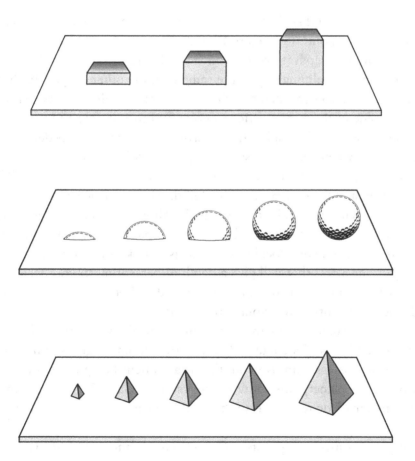

Figure 12-11: Astral Matter Pulled Up From Its Matrix

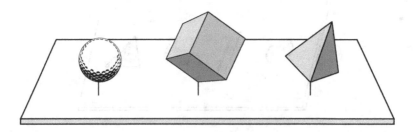

Figure 12-12: Shapes Standing on Point

one of the corners, and stick the other end into the base. Your cube should now be standing on its point. (See figure 12-12.)

This is how you separate your form from the matrix. Turn it slowly so you can observe it from all angles. Do the same with the other shapes. With the aid of sharp needles, you can make each shape display itself in many ways. Now, make each side of the cube a different color and turn it around again. Observe the colors along with the angles. If you have the patience and the determination, you can actually make a second set of shapes and color them.

If you wish, make shapes out of other materials and observe the difference between them and the matrix. Try using all the shapes displayed at different distances from each other and from you as the observer. Note how perspective is needed even on the astral level. Place another shape in the center and put the others around it to give a focal point. This is a trick you will find useful when working on the astral that will give a depth of perception to your visualization. All this will take time and effort, but the reward will be a razor-sharp image and a high degree of control over your astral work.

While on the subject, something students of magic who train and study outside the higher levels of a contacted school are seldom taught is that each plane or dimension possesses an oversoul that is a sentient being in its own right. In our world (this planet), we know the oversoul as Gaia. The astral world that we call, in Qabalistic terms, Yetsirah, would be conscious of itself by the name of Levanah.

In medieval times, alchemists and magicians found and used ways to trap and imprison portions of astral matter. Because its nature was designed to create forms when stimulated by thought, the superstitious and fearful ideas present in the human psyche at that time gave rise to horrific forms that were mimicked by the entrapped proto matter. The hapless form was then cursed, threatened, and damned for displaying the form it had been given to copy. The nightmare figures painted by Hieronymous Bosch are a prime example of such folly. It all goes to prove that if you find monsters in your astral world, you've brought them with you!

So much for playing with shapes on the physical. Now for the real test.

EXERCISE TWO

Prepare yourself as you would for a guided meditation. Build up the white landscape and contemplate it as background for at least three to five minutes. You should begin every building session with this preparation time. Why? Because (1) it gets the inner eye attuned to the shift, both in perspective and dimension, in the same way a physical eye takes time to adapt from light to darkness, and (2) it allows the astral world to recognize and adjust to you. Remember, this is *living* matter; it reacts not only to your thoughts, but to the signature of your personality.

Standing in your white astral world, fix your inner eye on a point about five feet in front of you, and form in your thoughts the shape of a cube, but much bigger than your polystyrene one. (Make it about four feet square.) After a few seconds, you should begin to see the edges of your cube emerging from the astral matter. Concentrate on pulling the cube up and out of its surrounding matter until it is complete. Now add the detail. Sharpen the edges and corners and separate the whole cube from its matrix. Now walk up to it, walk around it, examine it from all angles, and strive to make it as perfect as you can. To give more substance, add shadow. Now lift it away from its matrix and hold it suspended; there is no weight to it as yet. Turn it, stand it on end, color each face differently, then place it to one side and order it to "stay" as you would when training a puppy.

Try it with other shapes. Draw them up slowly, making them much bigger than those in the first exercise. Separate them from the main base. Lift them, color them, twirl them around. Try other letters, numbers, symbols, whatever you like. This is a game you can play on long journeys, while waiting in airport lounges, walking the dog, or lying in the sun while on vacation. Just a few minutes each day will make a 300 percent improvement in your ability to visualize—and that's a promise. Always give the command to "stay" if you want your shape to persist.

Try even more shapes—diamonds, hexagons, isosceles triangles, or cylinders. These are the easiest forms with which to begin your training and gain entry to the fascinating world of the astral. Once you have mastered the art of creating simple forms, go on to try double shapes, a sphere within the cube, a pyramid atop an inverted pyramid, a series of interconnected shapes, one inside the other, twisted columns, or stairs and steps that meander in all directions, until you can achieve an Esher-type landscape on the astral level.

While working on shapes, try changing textures and materials: striated marbles, granites, porphyry, lapis, or alabaster, for example. Color must also be a part of this exercise, which should be practiced daily until you can create any shape or form, in any texture, material, or color you wish. Once you have reached this point, you can begin to add "weight" to your program. Hold a pound of sugar in your hand for a few minutes, then try to emulate that weight on the astral.

There will be a temptation to hurry through these exercises, especially if you've already had some magical training. However, repeating something you already know never does any harm; it reminds you that skills lose their sharpness when familiarity turns to smugness. A month spent on daily practice of just five minutes will prove invaluable. I know this is not what you want to hear. I'll bet you are already telling yourself you don't need to do it, that you are competent enough to skip this chapter. I am also willing to bet you are wrong. *Nobody* is so good that a refresher course of hard practice cannot make them better. It can and will.

During the month's work you must involve all your senses in the routine. It is not enough to see, you must also listen. Tap the cubes, rectangles, and so on, and listen to the sound they make. If you can't hear it, repeat the action on the physical level until you can remember it on the astral. Experiment with sound. When tapped, a hollow cube makes a different sound than a solid cube.

Associate color with scent when you change your shapes from white into colors. Recall in memory the smell of a red rose and apply it to a red sphere. Associate a golden cube to the cool scent of mimosa. A green rectangle might take on the smell of freshly cut grass.

Touch can be lined up with the smoothness of polished wood, or the roughness of granite, the cool feel of glass and the warmer feel of leather. Remember, your senses rise on the planes with you and become more sensitive until, at a stage somewhere between the higher mental and the lower spiritual, they will amalgamate and become a single sense. When this occurs (rarely) on the physical level, it is referred to as synesthesia, a condition where the senses become scrambled and begin to intrude upon each other. It can be a debilitating and depressing, even dangerous, affliction. On the astral, however, especially on the higher levels, it has the effect of expanding the consciousness.

Next comes taste; you might ask how one can taste a shape. With reference to the syndrome of synesthesia mentioned previously, try reading Richard Czytowic's book *The Man Who Could Taste Shapes*. Remember, you are not working with the limitations of the physical world here. Your red sphere can become a large tomato combining shape, color, smell, and taste, plus weight when you pick it up. Your shapes do not have to remain large—you can make them small enough to be held in the hand.

Then there is the sixth sense. It is this sense you use when you are recalling shape, form, color, and so on. This extra sense has a connection with time and memory, for memory takes you back in time to past events. You have to recall from your memory what a sphere or a triangle looks like, what blue or green looks like, what a certain flower smells like, or the difference between the feel of velvet and glass. It is this sense that can warn you of events to come, or enables you to perceive events that have happened in the past. You can see there's a lot of work to be done with this exercise.

Something I found helpful in training was to build a row of shelves out of astral matter and stock them with my attempts at shape-forming. This helped me to retain them when I returned at a later time. The subconscious mind is your greatest ally here. It recognizes symbols and accepts them as real. A shelf stores things; thus, it is a storage symbol. My shapes remained in situ because my subconscious mind believed that a shelf is a place where things are kept until needed.[2]

Another tool, or, to be more accurate, a prop, for this stage of your work is the "central point." This is invaluable as a means of focusing on the various images and shapes. I use a Doric column, building it some eight feet high with a solid ten-inch pediment to give the effect of strength. This became my focal point immediately upon entry into the astral level. I could orientate myself right from the start, something that can be difficult to do when in a one-color environment.

---

2. See Herbie's chapters on the Memory Palace later in this book.

Shapes and forms can be grouped around the central point according to height, or color, or using identical shapes in different colors and materials. The column gives perspective and adds a lot to the overall effect. Give it a strong color that will stand out against the background. I used black for the first one, then as I progressed I added another in moss green some distance away.

It doesn't have to be a column. Try a pyramid, or a wide curving stairway on which your shapes can be set. The latter can be attractive *and* good practice. Satisfy your taste for beauty and take pleasure in what you build. Follow this rule in all astral thought-forming, no matter how expert you become in the future. All your work should be the best you can do. Dion Fortune taught that "only the best is good enough for the gods."

Remember, you are still using the plain white background, but you will soon change that for a more interesting and colorful landscape. But there are still a few things to try before we move on. Have you thought to look up? Yes, the same whiteness! On the physical level, such a color might mean snow. So, fill your mind with the idea of falling snow, and . . . here it comes. You have been pulling thought forms up from under your feet, but in the astral, the matter with which you work is everywhere: below, above, and on all sides. You're surrounded by dreamstuff, not just for your use in magical work, but also for your pleasure.

The snowflakes have stopped because you stopped thinking about them. Begin again, and enjoy a real snowfall without cold hands and feet. Pile it up against the shapes you have built, or build a snowman. You don't even need a shovel. Think it into being. Had enough? Shut off the snow and try for rain. Remember rain on the physical level, the feeling of wet clothes and wet feet. Make this rain soft and warm, as it is in the tropics during the rainy season. Revel in it. Rain is just as wet on the astral as it is on the physical. Make both worlds real to you, let them reflect each other, and, above all, learn to create on the inner what pleases you on the physical.

EXERCISE THREE

Create a stone circle based on a picture from a book or photo. Do it slowly, making one stone at a time. If you have a clear photo, try for an exact replica of each one. Pull it up from the matter matrix as you've been taught, in an approximation of the original. Refine it, altering texture, color, size, and so on, until it is as near as you can get it.

Do the same with the next one. Work on one or two stones a day until the circle is complete. Now work on the ground creating grass, turf, or shale. When this is done, you'll find that the rest of the landscape appears with little effort on your part. Remember, creating things on both the physical and subtle levels is something you were programmed to do. You are a living part of the One Creator, with the same powers, albeit on a much lower level.

With this exercise, you have completed the present part of the training.

13 THE ART OF OBSERVATION (II)

YOU NOW HAVE all the basics. You know what astral matter is and what it does. You can pull it out of its matrix to create shapes and geometric templates. You have learned to observe, retain, and store images both mentally and actually in the form of photos and pictures. You have explored the depths of your desires and learned to use feelings like the magical tools they really are. Now is the time to start stretching your talents even farther.

Let's begin with static images. Look for a picture of a statue among your reference scrapbooks. Choose one that is simple and uncomplicated. An Egyptian statue is ideal; its lines are simple, strong, well defined, and unfussy. Move into the astral landscape and pull up an undefined column of proto matter, center it and adjust for preferred height, then give it the "stay" command. Recall from memory the chosen statue and hold it still, mentally. Standing before the pillar of the undefined matter, recall the memory image. Begin to build up a desire to see that image created from the astral matter. Allow yourself to become curious about your ability to do this. Let the curiosity become stronger until it turns into a real need to prove that you can do this.

Imprint the mental image of the statue onto the matter. Don't try to keep it steady; allow it to flicker on and off. Gradually exert your will to control the flicker, and in a few minutes the column will begin to reshape itself into a replica of the statue. As soon as it is complete, order it to stay. At this point it will not be exact. You need to refine and define it from here according to your mental image. At this point you can make it larger or smaller. Try to recall the kind of stone, its color and grain, and imprint the image over the figure. Mentally push it into the matter. It will dissolve into it and within seconds the aspect will change, adding the new instructions.

To your "stay" command, you can now add others, such as "prepare to change," "back as before," and "completion achieved, stay and save." The statue can now be allowed to go back into its natural form. Henceforth, you will only have to recall it from your memory by saying: "Reform statue of Amenhotep III," and it will rise out of the matrix just as you patterned it before.

Try several different types of Egyptian statues, and "save" them for future use. Why bother to save them? Because your brain works like a computer, enabling you to file, save, format, and edit. These commands have become a living part of our language. The brain instantly comprehends what they mean and proceeds accordingly. It saves the pattern and files it without the need for you to go through complicated thought processes. The proto matter is able to do this because, like us, it is living matter, it has a memory, it can think and act as you do, but in a different way. It also stores the memories of every "pattern" it has been asked to reproduce since the first imaginative thought woke it up like some sleeping beauty. When you work for long periods of time with the astral level, you begin to understand that it is an "it" and should be accorded courtesy and appreciation. In fact, each level has a sense of itself, something not often taught to modern students of the occult, but known to the alchemists of old. Dr. Dee may have used Kelly as a medium to delve into the secrets of the subtle levels, but he also contacted the thought processes of the Astral Plane itself, and from it retrieved the prediluvian knowledge of the Nephilim, which we now call Enochian.

One of the worst things a would-be magician can do is to think of himself as being above the rest of creation. All is one and one is all—never forget that. Make a friend of Levanah, the oversoul of the Astral Plane, and you will find magic a lot easier to cope with.

Now try your skill with the more precise, flowing lines of Greek statuary. Here the emphasis is on a true copy of the human form. Nowhere is this skill seen to better advantage than in the superb form of Praxiteles' *Hermes* in the museum at Olympia. Set in a small room on its own, it seems to float just above the floor; such is the skill of its maker. Blue walls and a white ceiling give the impression of a spacious sky from which vastness the larger-than-life figure has just touched down.

Originally, Hermes held in his left arm the child Dionysius, while the uplifted right arm held a bunch of grapes just out of the child's reach. The gentle smile on Hermes's face and the caring expression for his little half-brother speaks well of him. Every movement is beautifully defined, and the balanced grace of the whole body creates the lightness of a winged being. But the skill of the artist does not end there. One can see beneath the marble "skin" the faint outline of deeper musculature. The figure is nude and has been carved with such delicate skill that the slight pull of the skin emanating from the upraised arm and flowing down the whole side of the body can be clearly seen. Along with Michaelangelo's *David* and the *Venus de Milo,* it is one of the greatest representations of the human form ever made. Making one of these is your next task. Proceed in the same way as before, taking it slowly and trying to reproduce the figure as exactly as you can. When you have achieved this—and it may take you several tries—save it in the usual way.

You may think all this practice is very tedious and unnecessary, but each time, you are perfecting your technique and ability to observe and recreate an original piece. Remember that it was on the astral level that Praxiteles first grasped the final concept of his work, long before he took chisel and hammer to a block of marble. Soon you won't need to put in as much effort, because observing minutely what you wish to create will become second nature to you.

Now try for a multiple image. Again, begin by choosing a simple Egyptian image. The one I have chosen is of Ra Hotep and his wife. The uncomplicated lines will be easier to construct. Pay attention to the outline and the edges of the picture you choose, for they are the areas most likely to "fade out" and become distorted. The brilliant colors of the original should be left until last. Begin the whole thing in white stone. Pull up a rectangular block of proto matter and make it solid, adjusting the height and width if needed. Give the block the stay command, then begin to impress a mental image of the original onto the block. You will see it slowly begin to reform, shifting and moving almost like a liquid until the outline becomes clear. Now you can refine it. Give the "stay" command and rest for a while. When you return, bring back your work just as you left it, using the "open file" command. It should rise up out of the basic matter as if appearing out of a sea of white. Now add the colors and final detail. If you have done your work well, what you now see should be three-dimensional and in vivid color.

You can now attempt a more ambitious project. Try *The Three Graces*, sculpted by Antonio Canova. This is a very complex piece of art, and may take you a while to achieve. However, you may, if you have been practicing and have a natural flair for visualization, get a surprise. There comes a point in this type of work when the oversoul of the astral begins to anticipate your desire, having already connected with your thoughts on the matter.

As you move into the astral, the white surface ripples and churns, and out of it rises the original concept of the piece in question. Allow it to do so until fully revealed. When this happens, you can congratulate yourself: You have made a definite and lasting contact with the oversoul. From now on, unless you are creating something entirely new, you can contact the oversoul with an image of what you want and it will do the work for you. It may not happen every time, but it will happen most of the time.

Why couldn't you have done it like this before? For the simple reason you didn't know you could. You have to make the contact by doing things the hard way. You are beginning to reuse ancient techniques that few human beings have used for centuries. It takes time for the oversoul to realize that it is being contacted again. Anything that has ever been made, built, constructed, put together, painted, sculpted, written, or designed remains here, locked into the memory of the oversoul of the astral. Why else do you think it is called "The Treasure House of Images?" This is "The Place of the Hall of Records," "The Machinery of the Universe," "The Cosmic Library of Creation."

But don't let it go to your head! You still have a lot of work to do and techniques to master.

Architecture is next on the list. What you do with statues you can do with the Parthenon, St. Marks in Venice, Windsor Castle, the Prado in Madrid, the Hanging Gardens of Babylon, or the original Troy. However, before you try rebuilding Ninevah, take a look at pictures of the other buildings. The complexity of design will be your greatest challenge yet. To hold such images in your mind takes intense concentration. So, take it in small pieces and build slowly, saving frequently, as you would if writing a book on a computer.

Anything no longer extant in our world must be retrieved from the oversoul's memory. You may not have the slightest idea what building material was used in Babylon, Persepolis, or Ur of the Chaldees, so you need to research such things before your visualization can provide true images. Only then will the oversoul be able to show you what you want to see in a way you can understand. Unless you know what you are looking for, the oversoul cannot locate it. Where architecture is concerned, the best way to go about it is by using the theater scenery idea.

Many of you have likely seen the miniature theaters that were popular toys many years ago. Only scale really separates them from full-size theaters and, indeed, from huge film sets. So the next exercise is to create your own scenery on the astral. Go to the local library and get some books on theatrical scenery. These "sets" are the product of a fertile and creative mind, and they can create a "magical" world out of wood, paper, canvas, and paint. Set designers for both the stage and films must have an eye for detail in addition to a well-trained imagination. You can use their expertise to extend your power to create thought forms.

All sets begin as drawings, then progress to small-scale models, some of which are very elaborate and pay meticulous attention to detail. Choose an illustrated set and study it, then draw it. (You don't have to be good, just make it recognizable). First, build it in your mind's eye to get its design fixed, then move onto the astral and build it from proto matter. Take your time, and build it like a theater set at first, flat with nothing behind it. Then scrap it and do it again and again, until you can raise it with no effort in a few minutes. When you get it down to sixty seconds you can go on to the next set. Remember, you can "set" these scenes to stay until you return, but it is better to rebuild them each time for the first seven to ten days so you can get used to doing it from scratch.

When you feel you have the hang of it, stop making it two-dimensional and go for three-dimensional. You do this by stepping into the "scene" and exploring what is behind the facade. At first try not to anticipate, but allow your imagination to provide whatever it wants to create. Do you remember Obi-Wan Kenobi's advice to Luke Skywalker? "Let the Force do the work, allow it to control your actions." That was damn good advice—follow it.

Now you have the scenery. Add the actors one by one. A word of advice here: never, ever, build an image of a living person. I cannot stress this too forcefully. If you have built a *Star Trek* scene, the ending of *Casablanca,* or even the Yellow Brick Road sequence from *The Wizard of Oz, don't* simulate the original actors.

Why? Because the power being fed through the simulacrum can affect the living person. It might cause an accident on the freeway, a heart attack, or a momentary lapse of attention that could be fatal. If the actor has passed on, there should be at least two to three years before the persona is used. This allows the spirit to assimilate its life lessons, evaluate them, and set that life aside and begin to prepare for a new one, without being hauled back for a rerun.

Build the figures as you have done before, pulling up the astral matter and molding them. Build them one at a time and in the place you want them to be, and, of course, make them life-size. Preferably, the placing should be part of the action of the scene. Try for some real differentiation among your characters. Combine features to make each one a type of person. Use racial types, coloring, gender, voice patterns, heights, shapes, and ages to make your figures as diverse as possible. Animation of the figures can be done by using some of your body heat to jump-start them. But first let's look at what you have created out of the astral matter. You have a scene illustrating a moment from a chosen play, film, or book. The landscape around you matches the action, season, time, and place. In a very minor way you are playing at being a god. You have created all this and now you are going to bring it to pseudo-life. Like wind-up toys, the figures will slow down, stop, and have to be reenergized.

Why do you want to go to all this trouble? Because it is all part of learning to control, create, animate, and build using the sentient proto matter that makes up the "body" of Levanah, the astral world.

I have no illusions that every one who reads this book will (a) take it seriously, or (b) do the exercises as they have been set out. Twenty in one hundred will read it and pick out what they want to use, and disregard the rest. Most will think they know enough already. Fifteen in one hundred will begin to work through it with enthusiasm, then give up when it gets boring. Ten in one hundred will stick at it and make it halfway through. Five in one hundred will slow down and amble to the end in fits and starts. One in one hundred will see the core of it, understand it, and use it as a stepping stone toward their adepthood. All the work is worth it for that one person.

Standing amid your creations, begin to call up heat in your physical body. Concentrate on the solar plexus until you can feel the heat. Feed that heat into the astral self at the same point. Pull it up to the shoulders and down the arms into the hands. Cup them to create a ball of white heat. Lift this to fifteen or twenty feet above the "scene" and spin it. Tendrils of light and heat snake down to contact each figure and cause a burst of electrical power. Try to make it simultaneous and your scene will come to life. Because of the effort and detail put into it, it will become a virtual reality and, with you to guide and direct the action, will continue to work while the charge lasts.

You will find at first that if you have too many figures, some will slow down and freeze. This is because your attention has been tightly focused on another figure. It is difficult to control more than two or three at a time. As an exercise in control of proto matter, concentration, and visualization, this is without peer and can, if practiced on a regular basis, bring startling results.

14 THE TRAINING OF THE TROUBADOUR

WE ARE SO USED to television, films, videos, radio, and computer games we forget these entertainments have only been part of our lives for a very short time. Before that there were theaters and, earlier still, strolling players, mummers and street performers, jugglers, singers and dancers. But if we go back to when there was little in the way of amusement, when the day's work was done we could find the professional storyteller, the street singer, the wandering musician, and the troubadour—all highly trained users of the imagination and all with the ability to weave pictures and images through the medium of the voice and project them into the minds of their listeners.

In the Middle Ages, each village, hamlet, or small town had an overlord or thane—someone who owned the land and/or a title. He would have lived in a large hall or manor, which would have held sleeping quarters and communal dining and living quarters. Once a year—twice if they were lucky—a Bard, Skald, or Seannachie (they are all storytellers in one way or another) would arrive. Often he would be accompanied by a young boy, an apprentice who would carry the harp and the few belongings they owned. Their arrival would cause great excitement, and within minutes everyone would know about it.

Such a visitor would expect to be housed in the great hall. First he would be offered the best food and wine to be had, then water to wash his hands and feet free of the dust of travel. He might then, wishing to prolong the anticipation, sleep until the evening meal. The owner of the hall would invite friends, neighbors, and family to dinner and feast them while the poorer folk would crowd into the stifling hall and sit wherever they could find room.

Finally the great moment would arrive. The Bard would rise to his feet and ask his host what he would like to hear: an epic hero story, a tale of battle and glory, perhaps a story of a magician with powers over life and death. Maybe one of the old legends of the area, or, to please the ladies, a romantic tale of unrequited love, Deirdre of the Sorrows, Tristan and Isolde, Gawain and the Green Knight. Any of these would do, or he might offer a new tale of scandal and intrigue set in London or Caerdyffyd or Dubh-linn.

When the choice had been made, he would take his harp (or if the apprentice was advanced enough he might accompany his master); silence would fall on the crowded room. As the story began, the heat and smoke of the central fire, the stale smell of human sweat along with dogs, ferrets, beer, and whatever was lying under the week-old floor rushes would be forgotten. The walls fell away, the wind and weather outside were ignored, the aches and pains of the elderly would be forgotten as the trained voice of the Bard began to weave its spell.

More than likely, the Bard was the only person in that gathering who could read and write. Even if they could, the only books would no doubt be locked in the library of the local priory. This was a time when, if a monastery could boast of a library of ten or twelve books, its fame would travel the length and breadth of the land.

Few, if any, of the listeners would have traveled more than twenty-five miles from their birthplace. The lord and lady of the manor may have made the long and dangerous journey to Winchester, Salisbury, Canterbury, or maybe even London just once in their lives. The Crusades were still a hundred years away, so the Eastern lands were virtually unknown. The noise, bustle, sights, sounds, and smells of a city were things of which they had no concept. But through the magic of the Bard they could catch a rare glimpse of another world. The magical voice, the mastery of words, and the hypnotic power of the harp combined to lift the listeners to another level of being. The names of the great Bards, troubadours, and Skalds such as Taliesin, Amergin, Llewarch Hen of Wales, Senchan, Coipre and Aithirne of Eire, Snorri Stursluson, the master of the Skaldskaparmal, or poetic diction of the Norse kingdoms are still available to those who wish to research them.

It took many years to train as a Bard, for they were more than simply tellers of tales. They were the guardians of the history of their time and place; they were also illusionists and magicians, weavers of spells and enchantments. Prodigious memories and quickness of wit gave them an enormous advantage over their fellow men. Most of what we know about these distant times has come down to us in their epic poems. As apprentices, they studied *Clasarch* by way of the harp, *Ben shene,* and *Ballach,* which comprised many different kinds of music. They could make you laugh or cry, sing and dance, or fire up your spirit for battle.

Twelve long years it took to make a Bard, and then he had to win his fame, or not, as the case might be. For those who wish to follow this fascinating subject further, you can do not better than to read *The Bardic Source Book,* edited and compiled by John Matthews, published by Blandford Press. I cannot praise this book too highly. In the introduction we are told: "[It is] the two poles of verse and vision that define the Bardic Mysteries. Indeed the two are inseparable since verse without vision is dead and vision itself is best expressed in verse. In fact, the poets are shamans of a kind, entering the other world through trance and returning with the fruit of their vision."

Skalds of Scandinavia and Seanachies of Ireland were, like the Bards, wanderers and purveyors of the mysteries of the aforesaid verse and vision. *The Edda, Beowulf and Grendel,* and the *Kalevala* are the great epic poems of Scandinavia; *The Mabinogion, The Battle of the Trees, The Gododdin Poems, The Black Book of Carmarthen,* and *The Red Book of Hergest* can all bring ancient Wales to light, even read in translation.

We first hear of the early "tales of chivalry" in France. They were the *chansons de geste* composed by the minstrels to flatter their patrons. Often the tale of a great battle was eked out over many nights, leaving the audience in suspense until the next episode. They were not songs in the sense we understand, but were more like rhythmic chants to specific meters that lulled the listeners into a state of near-hypnosis so visions might arise in their minds. But it was not only battles and deeds of daring that interested those in the great hall—the ladies had to be catered to as well. The courts of love provided a way for them to have their cake and eat it, too. The minstrels and trouvères were in demand to compose poems and songs that praised the current lady's beauty of form and face. The ideal was to "worship from afar." To court her in secret, in the mind, but never to consummate that love. To do so would destroy its purity. In effect, this was a way of siphoning off the excess energy when there was no war going on!

All this notwithstanding, there was a serious side to the troubadours. They held contests that were fiercely fought for the best song or poem. You can see and hear what this would have been like by listening to the opera *The Mastersinger*. But, like the Bards and the Skalds and the Seanachies, their skill lie in the ability to raise pictures and images in the minds of their listeners, to lift them into the world of astral imagery. Now let's try a little astral imagery ourselves.

> We are back in a little Saxon manor house in 783 A.D. Lit only by rush lights and the firepit, the usually noisy room is now hushed and still with all eyes upon the tall, spare, white-bearded Bard as he slowly makes his way to the center of the hall. He turns and looks at those present, deep-set eyes taking in every face and committing it to memory. He has already taken note of the quality of sound in the building and has adjusted his breathing rhythm to compensate for the extra resonance he will need. He lifts his elaborately carved staff and every eye follows it, as he intends them to do. The tiny shards of crystal set into its surface reflect the flames of the fire and serves to focus their minds. With the skill his years have given him he begins to fill those minds with images, images that he has painstakingly created over many years and which now maintain their own reality in the realms of faery. They will see what he wishes them to see, listen with rapt attention to his voice, get lost in a world he is creating specially for them with no other thought but the imagery wrought by the voice, tone, and music of a true Bard.

There are still Bards, but alas, not like those of ancient times. The nearest we have is Robin Williamson, who almost single-handedly has kept the ancient way of harp and voice alive. Look for his tapes, and listen to his magical sound.

All of which brings us to the use of astral sound. Is there sound on the Astral Plane? Yes, but it is an astral sound and can only be heard on the inner levels. You may have heard the term "clairaudient," meaning a psychic who hears rather than sees. What they are hearing is astral sound. We all hear on the inner level, but do not realize its significance.

We've all experienced those irritating times when a tune gets stuck in our heads and we cannot seem to get rid of it. That is an astral sound loop. When you lift your head suddenly, convinced that you have heard your wife, husband, or mother call your name, that is astral sound. Many students record having heard the sound of a bell. This phenomenon is often referred to as the Bell of Isis. It usually indicates that your attention is being called to an Inner Plane message.

With practice, sound imagery can be developed to the point where it is possible to replay on the inner levels any piece of music, listen to any favorite singer or song, bird song, or environmental sounds from the howl of a wolf to the roar of Niagara Falls. As with visual images, the data must be acquired first. Learn to listen to voices of the people around you; close your eyes and try to catch the cadence, timbre, accent, and pitch of the voice. When alone, sit quietly and try to recall the voice of someone you know well. Hold a conversation with that person in your head, and try to get an exact replica of the voice as you do so.

Take a favorite piece of music and play it several times, continuously. Listen to the words, if any, and to the phrasing and intonation. Listen for the way in which even a modern song, tune, or orchestral piece is divided into several different areas. In the case of a classical piece, this may mean three, four, or more quite distinct sections. When you think you can do it, sit quietly and begin the piece in your head. Listen to it intently, following each part, listening to the words, voice, and the instruments.

To my mind there are three important, informative, and pleasurable areas to musical imagery. The first is the ability to identify each instrument as it makes its appearance, and to be able to tune out others and listen to each one in turn as it makes its musical statement.

The second is to listen and allow the music to induce a mood or emotion, and to follow that mood or emotion through the piece as it changes. At the end you will find you have made a journey through a veritable landscape of sound via emotions and feelings. You can also do this with color in exactly the same way that Disney's *Fantasia* did many years ago.

The third area of audial imagery is exactly that—imagery. Many classical and semiclassical pieces offer a series of pictures that arise in the mind as it is played. Some are geographically evocative. Roderigo's "Aranjuez Concerto" and De Falla's "El Amor Brujo" could be nothing but Spain. The brooding overture to Bizet's *Carmen* heralds tragedy even if one had never heard it before. Greig's "Piano Concerto" and "Peer Gynt" suite, and one of the most magnificent, Mendelsson's "Hebridean Overture," are further examples of evocative pieces.

With audial imagery, you can either replay it inside your head if you have memorized it thoroughly, or listen to it physically but allow the sound to offer images, colors, or emotions.

Exercises for this part of your training should include playing several vocal tracks of singers whose techniques and quality of timbre and phrasing are very different, then replaying those tracks on the inner level. Three voices will give you a good range. One might choose Frank Sinatra, Janis Joplin, and Loreena McKennitt—an almost frightening mix! Another trio might comprise Nat King Cole, Jim Reeves, and the late John Denver—very different voices and styles, but all instantly recognizable.

Holst's "Planet Suite" is ideal because each piece is so very different. Look for any music described as a "Tone Poem," because it is just that—a poem set to music. Respighi's "Fountains of Rome," "Tintagel" by Clifford Bax, and "Till Eulenspiegel" by Richard Strauss are perhaps the best known. For individual instruments, you cannot beat Benjamin Britten's "A Young Person's Guide to the Orchestra," which introduces each instrument and allows you to listen to its tonal qualities. Saint Saens' "Carnival of Animals," Mussorgsky's "Pictures From an Exhibition," Ravel's "Bolero," and Debussy's "La Mer" will show you pictures, colors, and images as you listen. Even modern music will do it— Andrew Lloyd Webber's "Memories" from *Cats,* "With One Look," from *Sunset Boulevard,* or "Bring Him Home," from *Les Miserables.* "America" and "Tonight" from *West Side Story,* or even the amazingly evocative "The Stripper!"

What I am asking you to do is listen to music!

Try environmental tapes of sounds such as thunderstorms, rain, ocean sounds, water sounds, whale music, wolf song, and bird song. In the thirties, a composer named Ketelby wrote a series of very evocative musical pieces: "Bells Across the Meadow," "In a Monastery Garden," and "In a Persian Market"; although they will draw gasps of horror from the purists and the rappers, for the purpose of this experiment they deliver the goods. All have recently been rereleased. They evoke the images of the title very easily. Play them a few times, then listen to them in your head, and see how close you can get to the original.

Part Three

USING THOUGHT FORMS

15   BUILDING OCCULT FORMS

Dolores on: building God forms and angels; prayer as positive thought-forming; prayer and ecstacy; the adoration of saints and icons; the exercises of St. John of the Cross and St. Teresa of Avila; visions; the revelation of St. John the Divine.

BY NOW YOU SHOULD have acquired fairly good control over astral matter, so we can look at other aspects of its use in various areas of magic. One of the most important, both in guided meditations and ritual, is the building of God forms.

The rule of knowing what you need to build applies here as much as collecting pictures of places, doors, stairs, and the like. You need to "know your gods and goddesses." You must also know mythology as well—the tales, legends, attributes, symbols, and appearance of the gods you want to thought-form. Back to the scrapbooks! Start collecting pictures and list them by pantheon. You don't need to have a lot of pictures—one or two will be enough—but they must be acceptable to you. In other words, they must suggest the God form to you in a pleasurable way.

Look through books on mythology, colored plates, and paintings to find what appeals to you. Try to get or make a copy or a color print and use it as a basis for your thought form of that particular god or goddess. Learn about the places, powers, and symbols that belong to them. In my book *The Ritual Magic Workbook*

(Dolores Ashcroft-Nowicki),[1] I wrote that those who study magic must have an adequate grasp and knowledge of at least two pantheons of gods. Gods have always been humanity's way of externalizing its own inner powers. Look at a god and you look at your true, divine self. It is important, therefore, that you build God forms that are pleasing to you as a person.

This kind of thought-forming is different from any other because you have two options open to you: You can build them and then observe them as they interact with both the astral and physical at your command, or you can build them, then assume the form you've built and, for a short space of time, become what you have built. We call this second procedure the "Assumption of God forms."

Angelic forms are created from proto matter in the same way, although it is not advisable to assume them as you might a God form. Why? Because in the mind of human beings, angels have become synonymous with religion, God, the afterlife, and variations on the symbols of the Christian faith. You may or may not profess to believe in them, but at some level of the subconscious mind there will be an uneasy feeling that this is a no-no. Such forms are extremely powerful on their own level, and it is best to admit that there are some things it is wise to leave alone. (This will not deter some of you, but it will certainly be an interesting experience!)

Gods and angelics have their own level of beingness that belongs to a level that came into existence long before that of the astral and the physical. They had and have a reality beyond our understanding that has nothing to do with actual form. They do not need forms. They just *are,* and have *been* since the first waves of creative effort made by the One. The forms we, as humans, give to both gods and angels are only how we think they should look. In their own reality they are abstractions, and the closest we can get to this is to "see" them as geometric forms, equations, concepts.

We can build a God form or an angelic form from astral matter according to how we think they might look. God forms, because they are lower on the scale of power than angels, can be assumed for short periods of time during ritual or guided meditations. Angelics are a different thing altogether. As soon as you build an angelic form, there is a tendency for an angelic power essence to indwell it. This is another reason for not assuming them: it can get overcrowded and overpowered! The same can be said of elementals, elemental Kings, and other

---

1. Weiser, 1998. Dolores Ashcroft-Nowicki will hereafter be referred to as D. A. N.

assorted denizens of the subtle levels. The rule of thumb is: If you don't know what it is, or what it does, don't assume it.

Let's backtrack now and look at the building of a God form.

First decide what god or goddess you are going to form. I am assuming you will have looked at different pictures and decided on one as a pattern. Hopefully you will also be conversant with their attributes, symbols, and powers, and, above all, because you know what those powers are, you will be prepared for any phenomena that may or may not occur. For the sake of argument, we will use the God form of Hermes, since he was used to illustrate an example in chapter 13.

BACKGROUND

Hermes was the son of Zeus, the ruler of gods and men in Greek mythology, and Maia, a nymph. He was a precocious child, walking and talking only hours after his birth. He showed an early talent for thievery. (He is the god of thieves and pickpockets!) At the age of two he stole, killed, and ate his half-brother Apollo's cattle. Understandably, the sun god was upset and complained to Zeus, their mutual father. Hermes' silver tongue placated his father and soothed Apollo's ire, especially when he made him a gift of a turtle shell fashioned into the first lyre. This later became one of Apollo's best-known symbols, for he is the god of music as well as healing and prophesy.

To keep him out of mischief, Zeus made Hermes the messenger of Olympus and gave him a pair of winged sandals, a winged hat, plus the baton of authority known as the caduceus. The new appointment didn't make a lot of difference to his disposition. Hermes remained a mischievous, cunning, and light-fingered rogue, but everyone loved him anyway.

In appearance he is a tall, slender, but well-muscled young man seemingly about twenty-five years old. His has the classical Greek face—straight nose, large eyes, fair curling hair (the early Greeks were fair of skin and hair; modern Greeks are of mixed Scythian and Turkish descent). Hermes is often portrayed nude or seminude, with a light cloak thrown over his shoulder. His winged sandals have a life of their own; they are sentient and are magical symbols in their own right, as is his winged hat, which represents thought.

Use the same technique you used to create figures in a landscape. On entering the astral level, set up your focal point, a pillar of some sort. This gives you a sense of size and perspective. Now draw up from the astral material a column of matter. Make it taller than life, since most accounts of the Greek gods speak of them as being larger than humans. Holding the picture of Hermes in your mind, mentally throw it onto the shapeless matter and allow it to reform into the image you have given it. Slowly it will take shape. Don't try to hurry it; let it go at its own pace.

At first it will look like a statue, white and lifeless. To give it more substance you must will it to assume a skin tone, giving it a slightly golden hue. The hair is a light honey-blonde, the eyes are gray and full of humor. Think of the head turning toward you, and watch as it does so. Because you have a mental link with it, it will obey your thoughts. You now have a choice: You can either will your consciousness into the form and animate it in that way, or you can invoke the abstract essence of the original concept that was the beginning of "Hermes" to indwell it. This is done when you wish to make a contact with the Hermes energy for ritual purposes. You can then direct it to a temple or sacred space of your choice and invite it to participate in the ritual. Or again you can infuse the form with a small amount of your energy and use it for a guided meditation or as a companion, guide, or informant. The same format is used with any god or goddess.

We have already discussed the inadvisability of assuming angelic forms, but they can certainly be built and used in magical work. Their main use is as focal or quarter points in ritual, as guardians for temples, sacred spaces, children, carriers of prayer thought forms, or simply as companions for those who have need of their particular energy, each angel or archangel having a different attribute or power. When you feel alone, hopeless, have been bereaved, injured, or are facing the more serious tests of life, an angelic companion can be of great comfort. In such cases, one should build the form with extra care and then invoke the essence of the angelic being itself to indwell the form. From that point you need to build a rapport with the inner essence of the being and seek strength, love, support, healing, or companionship directly from that essence. This has been the way of mystics and saints down the ages.

As I have said elsewhere, the true form of angelics bears no resemblance to the Victorian idea of robes, curls, and feathers. They are closer to primal geometry than anything human. Even geometric shapes are merely signatures of what they really are. This goes double for the highest levels such as the Four Holy Creatures. Having said that, it should not deter you from creating thought forms for the powers to indwell. After all, human beings having been doing it since the Bible was written, and long before.

In Judaic belief, each letter of the Hebrew alphabet is an entity in its own right, with a built-in knowledge of its own inner power and meaning. Not an angelic being, but one that is of a high level of creation. This means the Hebrew letters can also be recreated via astral matter and a mental link established that will enable the magician to draw on that particular letter's internal store of wisdom. A thorough knowledge of the correct shape and meaning of each letter is essential for this. The idea can be taken much further. Each letter is also an image (and a number), and with these images a whole scenario can be brought into being on the astral.

Take the letter *BETH,* meaning house, building, edifice, or shelter of any kind. It can be broken down into images like this: B = House, T = Tau/Cross, H = Heh/Window/Source of Light. By astrally building a stable (shelter) with a tau cross inside it and adding a small window through which a light from within shines outward, you will get a symbolic Christian link with Christmas, the Light of the World shining through the small window of a stable to the world outside, and Easter, with the symbol of Christ's birth (the stable) and his death (cross), and the Light of Sacrifice. Both will connect the mind with the town of Bethlehem, the meaning of which is "the House of Bread," which again takes the mind and thought forms on to the sacramental wafer.

Every letter of the Hebrew alphabet can be extended in this way, astrally manifested and used as a method of study. The above example is not, of course, purely Christian symbolism since it has Judaic beginnings, but for those whose preference lies in Esoteric Christianity it can be a very powerful path of mystic imagery that leads to the visions of people like St. Teresa of Avila and St. John of the Cross, among others. Equally, one can find images from other faiths running parallel to that of the Christians that will apply and serve the same purpose. Mithras, for example, born of a virgin mother and an unknown father on December 25 in a cave surrounded by animals, fits into the same scenario.

It is important that the magician in training realizes the sheer scale, usage, and importance of thought-forming in all areas of magical work. Without sufficient expertise in the manipulation of sentient proto matter on the astral level, the way forward will be almost impossible, and only the lower levels of magic will be open to you.

PRAYER

"My prayers fly upward, my thoughts remain below. Prayers without thoughts never to heaven go." So speaks the king in Shakespeare's *Hamlet,* praying for forgiveness and watched by the brooding Hamlet himself. Certainly the play-wright's words hold the truth. How often I have heard people say, "I prayed so hard, but nothing happened. God cannot be real." For some people prayer is a way of life, a living part of their faith; for others it is something to fall back on when all else fails. But do we pray in the right way? What is a prayer anyway?

When we pray, we petition a power much higher than ourselves for help, something we need, something we desire, something outside our own ability to manifest. Occasionally, but far too seldom, we offer a prayer of thanks, gratitude for what has been received. Another kind of prayer, offered usually by those whose lifestyle and spiritual dedication requires it, is the prayer of pure worship and praise. Where the layman is concerned, a prayer is often interspersed with promises to do things, go without things, or to stop doing things as a kind of bribe, hoping that God will listen and act accordingly.

But God is beyond bribes.

So, what if we looked at prayer as a thought form communication between the One and humanity? What if we stopped using words and returned to the ancient ways of using symbols, shapes, forms, and minipathworkings instead? Thought came long before words both spoken and written. *It* was there in the very beginning. In fact, thought was the beginning.

It has been said that if you want to pray, put yourself in the attitude of prayer and it will happen. It has been done in this way for hundreds of years, but now, with the new millennium upon us, it is time to affect a change.

In fairy tales, the gift of three wishes usually brings about disaster because the recipient cannot decide what to wish for. Prayer often has a similar effect. You may know what you want, but not how to express it. So don't try, simply picture it.

EXAMPLE ONE: THE TOWER

Are you asking for forgiveness for something you've done? First of all, recall what it is you have done. Go over the incident in your mind and look specifically at your part in it. Were you the only person responsible? Did you do it deliber-ately? Are you really sorry and want to make amends? Can you make amends to the person(s) affected by your act? Is this a cosmetic act or do you truly want to be forgiven?

If you truly want to be forgiven, then proceed to the astral plane. This is a location now familiar to you so you know how to go about things. Don't think you are going to be let off lightly! From the astral floor, draw up a tall column of proto matter and imprint it with the pattern of a tower of gray stone. It's very high and looks forbidding. It has a door at the bottom and at the top you can see a small window. Open the door and enter. Right before you is a staircase that obviously twists its way to the top. Every now and then a narrow window slit lets in some light. Each step is roughly four inches high, and there are 365 steps, which, if one adds the tower room at the top step, makes the tower about one hundred feet high. Visualize this clearly and in detail. When you have done so, start climbing.

Not the kind of prayer you are used to, I imagine! Hundreds of steps, and you will climb each and every one of them astrally. As the steps turn, you will catch glimpses of a landscape from the slit windows. But mainly you will concentrate on why you are doing this. You are going through an expiation—you *must* experience every one of those steps. Don't run, just climb, and as you do think about why you are asking for forgiveness. Go through it over and over again until every part of it is burned into your consciousness.

Done correctly, you will arrive at the top in a state of astral exhaustion. There is a door here that leads to the tower room. Open it, cross to the window, and look out. Look at the landscape and into the distance where you will see a line of blue-gray hills. Without words, open your heart center and send out a request for forgiveness. Keep looking toward the hills, and soon you will see a bird winging its way toward you. Watch it as it comes nearer, and now, hold out your hand. The bird alights on it, and you see in its beak a small twig of olive leaves. This is your symbol, your proof of forgiveness. Now comes the hard part: Can you accept this symbol and allow yourself to be forgiven? Because you have worked with images and symbols, your inner self has communed with the most ancient part of yourself, a part that is extremely powerful and capable of altering your perspective on life and your place in it.

There is nothing to say that a prayer must be couched in words. A prayer may be danced, or sung, while standing and watching the sun come up over a mountain. A garden can be a prayer. If you want to ask a favor or for help, support, or whatever, learn to build a prayer into a scenario similar to the theater scenery you were taught to build earlier in the book.

EXAMPLE TWO: THE PRAYER GARDEN

This is something you can set up and "keep on file" to use in similar circumstances in the future.

Create a walled garden on the astral level using the techniques you have been taught. Look at examples of such gardens and select ideas, plants, trees, and colors, accordingly. Remember, you are building from the inside to the outside. Arrange a covered arbor of something like vines, roses, wisteria, or similar climbing plants. Within, there should be a wooden bench.

Arrange pathways leading through scented flower beds and aromatic herb bushes. Place seats here and there, a fountain or even a small stream to freshen and cool you in the heat of the day, fruit trees that peek over the walls, willows that sweep the ground and hide secret places of rest. You now require two doors. One will be for you to enter the garden, the other will be the entrance from another level and will be the door used by those who will help you when you need them.

Your door is narrow, arched, and made of plain beech wood. It is unlocked and has an old-fashioned latch closure. On both sides at eye level is a carved wooden symbol that you must devise for yourself. Before lifting the latch, either going in or returning, you must touch this symbol.

The other door is wider, made of solid oak and always locked.

You can use this garden for relaxation, for peaceful moments when you feel rushed or stressed in the real world, and for prayer and help from the higher realms. If you like, you can make the touching of the symbol also a signal for you to become dressed in a simple robe of light wool or cotton with leather sandals. Now you need to create a form for a being from a higher level to indwell.

It may be a man or a woman, a religious recluse or an ordinary human being. Create the form as you have done before, adjust it to what you will feel comfortable with, maybe someone older than yourself, or the same age. It is your choice. Build it with care and attention to detail, then offer it to the higher powers for their indwelling and use.

Suppose you have a problem that has been worrying you, or something you have been praying for. It is important to you and you would like to talk to someone about it, and you decide to go to the prayer garden and discuss it with the guardian, friend, companion . . . whatever name feels right.

After passing through the door, you walk along the scented paths, breathing the air and relaxing in the peaceful atmosphere. You reach the arbor, and there you find your friend. Sit down and say what is in your heart. Hold nothing back—you know it will never go farther than this garden. Ask for advice, but don't expect cut-and-dried answers to everything. They may ask you to return after they have given thought to your problem. They may tell you what you do not want to hear. They might even remain silent, or tell you that this time you must make the choice. They may lay hands upon you and give you healing, or pray with you. You can ask them to take your personal prayer with them when they leave and to send it "on" to the One who should receive it. You can send this by a token, a small bouquet of garden flowers or a single bloom, a fruit, or a bird's feather found on the path.

You will never be banned from this garden. Your friend will never refuse to meet you. You will never leave without an infusion of strength to face the physical world. Oh yes, you might find it useful to talk to the gardener occasionally. The gardener changes from time to time. He may wear the green turban of a Haj, or the yamulka of a Jew, the beard and turban of a Sikh, the habit of a Poor Clare, or the saffron robe of a lama. He may wear the cotton *schenti* of an Egyptian, or the chiton of a Greek. Sometimes he is just a gardener, until you see the scars on his hands and feet. The saviors have been many and there will be many more.

What if you are in church and cannot build such elaborate locations? Fold your hands in prayer and ask yourself what or who you want to pray for. Don't think in your head, but try to create feelings in your heart center. Imagine what you want or need as an object and surround it with emotion. If it is for a loved one, you might visualize their face within the heart of a rose. For a child, you could use the form of a dove. Whatever it is, try to link the subject of the prayer with something of this nature and hold it in your heart. Build up the emotion until you cannot contain it within you anymore. Then release it and allow it to be drawn upward into the light.

Words can lead to confusion when praying because they do not accurately convey the thoughts and feelings surrounding the object of the prayer. So don't try; fill the heart center with love and gratitude for the possibility of success. Always add the corollary "and it be thy will," because sometimes we ask for something we cannot have; perhaps it is not time, not allowable, or not right for us to have it, often because the reaction to it might cause damage to others. Remember the Universal Law of cause and effect, for everything is both the cause of, and the result of, an effect. Words are seldom needed; just open the heart and allow those beings whose work it is to carry communications between levels to sort out what is needed and take it where it needs to go.

Prayer is a beautiful thing no matter what faith is involved or by what name the One to whom it is addressed may be called. Take time to offer a prayer of thanks and gratitude for what you have and what has been given to you.

Prolonged and concentrated prayer occasionally results in a state of ecstacy. This is linked with chemical changes in the brain, but whether the ecstatic state causes the changes or vice versa is a matter for conjecture. When it happens, it brings about a heightened state of mind that opens the senses to a finer, more subtle level. This usually involves the visual and audial centers resulting in visions and voices reaching farther into our physical world than is normal. Atmosphere is also a part of this. The quiet, enclosed, and highly spiritual ambience of a monastery or convent, especially in earlier times, would have been very conducive to such events. St. Teresa of Avila, St. John of the Cross, Bernadette of Lourdes, Therese of Lisieux, Francis of Assisi, and Joan of Arc all have left records of what they have seen and heard when in such states. Levitation and physical stigmata are often another aspect of such states of mind.

But as I have pointed out in the earlier pages of this book, the mind has to have some cache of images on which to draw. In the case of saints and religious visionaries, they can draw on paintings, statues, records, and descriptions of those who have gone down the same road, as well as symbols and icons. Once the precursory state of mind is approached, the "image file" in the mind opens up and the relevant images and symbols are released, along with a flood of emotions and often long-repressed sexual feelings. One only has to see the Bellini statue of St. Teresa of Avila with the angelic arrow embedded in her heart, or read the spiritually erotic poetry of St. John of the Cross to understand the symbology buried within their visions. The eroticism does *not* detract from their spiritual message, but enhances it, for it underlines the power of love both sacred and secular.

Icons, religious paintings, and statuary all have their beginnings in a thought form. If you want to see the birth of astral creations emerging into the physical, look at the notebooks of Leonardo Da Vinci. These scribbles, doodles, sketches, and detailed line drawings are clear examples of someone whose mind is existing on a plane higher than his body. His thought forms of a primitive helicopter and submarine were so vividly imaged that they persisted on the astral and eventually, hundreds of years later, became fact. (The same thing happened with Jules Verne's books, *20,000 Leagues Under the Sea* and *Journey to the Moon,* as with the stories in the early science-fiction magazines. The ideas, regarded as ridiculous nonsense by scientists then, have come true in the last fifty years with amazing speed.)

Painters more than most have been responsible for giving us thought imagery. From the incredible cave paintings with their vivid colors and amazing ability to convey movement, to the majesty of the Sistine Chapel, we have a legacy of images so rich in its variety and complexity it boggles the imagination.

Many of these paintings have become focal points for concentrated thought and prayer, but none more so than the religious icon. Stemming mostly from Eastern Europe and the Orthodox Churches, these highly specialized representations of saints, Jesus Christ, and the Virgin Mary have become the "household idols" of their time in much the same way that Terah, father of Abraham, valued his household gods so much he took them with him on the journey from Ur of the Chaldees.

Some icons are extremely old and valuable, and have become the center of pilgrimages and cults. One of the most famous is the Black Madonna of Chesztohowa, located in the small Polish town of the same name. Slashed by the swords of invading Turks, the image is said to have bled profusely. The defilers fled, leaving behind them a legend that persists to this day. Thousands flock to see the miraculous picture and to pray at her shrine. The picture is protected by a steel, silver-embossed shield that is raised only when the pilgrims are in place.

Montserrat, outside Barcelona in Spain, is the mountain monastery of the Black Virgin visited by over a million people every year. Her statue is the focal point of veneration and prayer. We see the same thing at Chartres in France, and there are many others throughout the world. All are places where a specific statue or painting has caught the imagination of humankind and woken us to such an extent that its primal astral form has become a reality in our physical world.

It is not just the Christian world. Islam has its sacred symbols, usually expressed in its flowing calligraphy and mosaic. The Buddhists have statues, relics, and sacred edifices; and the same goes for all faiths. These objects, whether paintings, statues, books, abstract symbols, or locations are all representations of sacred thought forms and form part of the worship and religious fervor of humanity. Concentration and focused prayer on them will release the power and imagery built up, over hundreds of years in many cases, by the thoughts, hopes, and dreams of those who have gone before. Never underestimate the power of prayer.

For those of you who think guided meditations are something new, try reading the *Spiritual Exercises* of St. Ignatius de Loyola. They are not exactly the kind of pathworkings you will be used to, but they are proof this kind of training has been in existence for a long time. Jesuit priests still use visualization and thought-forming today, which may be the secret of their success in many areas, for they are the "magical mystics" of the Roman Catholic Church.

THE REVELATION OF ST. JOHN

The Bible, especially the Old Testament, is incredibly rich thought-forming material. It needs a book to itself, and I have already begun work on such a book.

The visions of the prophets show clearly that their inner level experiences were taken seriously and acted upon when it concerned the welfare and guidance of the people. From the ecstatic and mind-blowing visions of Ezekiel, Elijah, and Samuel to the divinely inspired spiritual contact we know as Revelation, the ancient world was full of thought forms so powerful that they could be seen, walked with, and spoken to. Humanity was not so skeptical then, and accepted that angels and their like walked among them.

This seems to be the right moment to explain that so far we have been looking only at the ability of human beings to create thought forms from astral matter. It is not usually explained that the beings who inhabit the higher levels of existence have the same ability. They use them to encapsulate minute portions of their superior mental energies. The resulting forms can then descend to the physical level for short periods of time, something such beings cannot do in their natural state of existence.

These are the forms we see, mostly with the inner eye but sometimes with the physical sight, and tend to refer to as angels or, in the ancient world, as gods. The oft-reported ability of Tibetan lamas of high degree to send simulacrums of themselves to visit other lamaseries is well known. Such "temporary" beings appear to be solid, can hold conversations, and can teach disciples.[2] This would explain a great deal of the phenomena reported in both the Old and the New

---

2. A British schoolteacher told me (H. B.) of a personal experience of the phenomenon. She decided reluctantly not to go on a school trip into the mountains because she had a class to attend. During the event, she spent the time regretting her decision and daydreaming about the mountains. The following day, one of her colleagues insisted she had been on the trip . . . because he spent the afternoon talking with her.

Testaments—events such as the encounter of Tobias and the angel, the visitation of Lot by the three "angels of the Lord," the annunciation, and even, though no doubt there will be a howl of disagreement and denunciation, the transfiguration and the appearance of Jesus to his disciples after his death. Remember, Jesus said, "Touch me not, for I am not yet come to the Father."

If the "body" he was using was made of proto matter, it may well have been unstable carrying such a pure energy. To touch it might have destabilized the whole thought form and released an energy wave that could have killed them all. By warning them, he could hold the body of astral matter together long enough to pass on final instructions. Then and only then could that interim body be discarded and the pure energy that was the Christ ascend to its proper level.

There is much more that could be discussed and considered along these lines, but that is for another book. For now we must return to one of the most spectacular visions in recorded history, the Revelation of St. John the Divine. Setting aside the modern argument that it could not have been written by St. John himself, let's look at the text purely and simply as a visionary experience.

What does the word "revelation" mean?

It means "some knowledge or information that has been hidden up to this moment is now made clear and explained to all."

Who is doing the revealing?

Well it wasn't John—he was only acting as a postman. It was his job to deliver the message to others. We are told this is the Revelation of Jesus who got it straight from God. Jesus "sent and signified [signed] it" via an angelic being to John.

To whom is the new knowledge to be revealed?

John addresses it to the "seven churches in Asia." He tells them it is from he who is, was, and is to come (the Creator), and also from the "seven spirits before the throne" (the Elohim?). Only then does he add, "and from Jesus Christ." John then tells us that "I was in the spirit on the Lord's day and heard behind me a great voice as of a trumpet."

"In the spirit" clearly tells us he was in an alternative mental state, and underlines it by saying that he not only saw clairvoyantly, he heard clairaudiently. He is instructed to write what he hears and sees in a book and send it to the seven churches in Asia, churches actually named. Now comes a flood of visions, one after the other.

It is not my intention to interpret these. Better scholars than I can ever hope to be have spent years of their lives doing just that. What I want to do is to show just a little of the immense scale of the vision and its diversity of imagery and to prove that what you have read and learned in this book is not just waffle: it is an inherent talent for between-the-worlds communication that lies in all of us to a greater or lesser extent. Thought-forming is not new. It is an ability we share with all beings. Indeed, I would go so far as to say that all life in this universe, not just this galaxy, but in the universe as a whole, share this ability, no matter what form it inhabits. It is life's birth-gift from the One, the Creator, the Matrix of all universal matter. We have tended to reject and ridicule it for hundreds of years, and now is the time to reclaim it and use it, or perhaps lose it for good.

One of the things that all visionaries have in common is their tendency to see living forms and symbols as a mixture. For instance, a writer in the Bible describes an angel as having legs like pillars, a cloud for a body, and a face like the sun. Albrecht Dürer made an engraving of this; he followed the description exactly and it looks weird. But remember that in the days when those words were written, they had, overall, perhaps one thousand working words in their vocabulary. This makes it difficult to describe things that are beyond your understanding.

Perspective was unknown in that time, so if the vision was much taller than the observer, those long legs may well have looked like pillars. The only thing the observer knew to be that long or tall were the pillars in the temple. If the visitation had been created from astral matter, its body may well have had a pale, cloudy appearance, and the blazing intelligence inhabiting the insubstantial astral form would stream from the eyes and dazzle the unfortunate receiver of this unearthly visitor.

So when we read of John seeing seven golden candlesticks (not, notice, a menorah or a seven-branched candlestick), we can assume they were seven beings radiating golden light. We may also assume these were the seven spirits before the throne mentioned earlier. This is underlined by the following sentence: "In the midst of the seven candlesticks was one like unto the Son of man."

From the center of the universe come the seven before the throne and Jesus in glory. In his right hand he holds seven stars, another reference to the seven; this time they are stars, however, not candlesticks, but they are still described in terms of Light. The reference to the right hand tells us these are important, highly placed beings. His "right-hand advisors" are, without doubt, the Elohim.

The explanation given in the text is that they are the angels of the churches and the stars the churches themselves. I offer a different viewpoint. The seven churches are the seven levels of existence and one of the Elohim is set over each level. There is little reason for the churches of Asia to be picked out as the only receivers of this knowledge—there were many other churches as well. All this is taking place on a much higher level than the physical. Knowing the divine seer-ship of John, we might hazard that it is takes place in Atziluth, which might be why John fell down, as if he were dead, for the pressure would have been unbearable at that level.

Hold in your mind the fact that when interpreting ancient symbology, not every word is original and much must be discounted.

Each "church" is addressed and praised or admonished, but in the middle, this God of Love says, "But this thou hast, that thou hatest the deeds of the Nicholai-tanes, which I also hate." Hardly the gentle forgiving Lord of Love we expect.

The visions now come thick and fast. In Rev. 4:2–6, John sees the One upon the throne at the center of the universe, surrounded by the twenty-four Elders, or hours of the day and night, and attended by the seven lamps that are the seven spirits/archangels/Elohim before the throne. He also sees Ezekiel's winged Beasts: the Lion, the Bull, the Eagle, and the Man. In descending order we now have the four, the seven, and the twenty-four.

Please remember that these are my own interpretations and are not to be taken as "gospel." As an exercise, try to unravel the symbology of Revelation for your own satisfaction; this will extend your ability to observe and see beyond the immediate landscape. It is very tempting to go on and delve further into something that has occupied the minds of scholars for almost two thousand years, but this book is a finite thing in a finite universe, and there are interesting things to investigate still before us.

But before we leave this area, let me say this: It is not just saints and highly spiritual human beings that see visions and experience ecstasy. Think of the chil-dren and the vision of Fatima. One could hardly be more down to earth than Bernadette of Lourdes. Modern mystics abound, and you should certainly read the books of Teilhard de Chardin, and at the other scale of things, those of Arthur C. Clarke. Both are visionaries in their own way. Both have changed the way we look at what we believe in. Abstract paintings may look like a heap of dislocated and meaningless shapes to the untutored eye, *but it is what the painter saw*. That was his vision, and we cannot see what he saw unless we try very hard, and maybe not even then.

16 THE MEMORY PALACE

Herbie on: the occult importance of memory; Simonides and the banquet disaster; the creation of the locus; testing your memory and improving it; Hannibal Lecter, the unlikely occultist; the Inner Castle and the Memory Palace; building your palace.

ONE OF THE OLDEST APPLICATIONS of thought forms in the formal practice of magic was the creation of the Renaissance Memory Palace. This structure, built entirely of mind-stuff, nonetheless aided generations of occultists who were convinced that a single slip in the ponderous litany of their rituals could lead to their being carried off by demons. These men (and the few women who practiced magic in fifteenth-century Europe) needed an excellent memory, and the Memory Palace gave it to them. It can deliver the same benefit today, but more recent developments indicate it can also be used as a potent tool for self-development and spiritual progress.

The foundations of the Memory Palace long predate the Renaissance. The technique on which the palace is built seems first to have been discovered by the lyric poet Simonides in the sixth century B.C. Simonides studied music and poetry on the Aegean island of Ceos, but left as a young man to live in Athens. Noted for such epigrams as "painting is silent poetry and poetry painting that speaks," he was a popular guest of the aristocracy and his name is associated with the tyrant rulers of Athens, and Crannon and Larissa in Thessaly. On one occasion he was invited to a victory banquet that ended in tragedy when the floor of the hall collapsed, plunging guests to their death in the chamber below.

Simonides missed the disaster by a stroke of luck—he was called away just before it happened. He returned to a scene of horror with hundreds dead and so disfigured they were unrecognizable. Simonides was asked to help identify the corpses. At first it seemed an impossible task, then he discovered that he could remember the names of the guests by visualizing where they had been sitting.

The experience got him thinking. He began to wonder if he might be able to turn his discovery into a full-scale memory system. His basic idea was that if he could visualize a place in detail—as he had with the banqueting hall—he might be able to remember items that he set around the place in his imagination, exactly as he had remembered the guests. He began to experiment. At first, for convenience, he visualized locations around his own home, placing objects in imaginary versions of his cupboards or on imaginary versions of his tables. Then, when he wanted to remember, he would visualize the particular (imaginary) location and examine what he found there.

By trial and error, he discovered that the system worked. He found he really could remember more effectively. From visualizing just a few specific containers, he progressed to visualizing locations as a whole, starting naturally enough with his own home, but soon advancing to other familiar buildings. Eventually he shared his discovery with some colleagues, who found it just as effective as he did. Soon the Simonides technique had spread through the intellectual elite of Greece. Not all of them used it, of course, but a great many educated people at least knew about it.

From Greece, the method spread to Rome, where it became popular with orators, who discovered that if they visualized the main points of their speeches (symbolized by concrete objects) in imaginary locations, they could mentally move from one to the other as a powerful aid to their oration. The practice became so widespread that it gave rise to the habit, still used by many public speakers, of prefacing their remarks with such phrases as "In the first place" and "In the second place." In Roman times, the "places" were literal, if imaginary, locations.

With the fall of Rome and the advent of the Dark Ages, much of the knowledge of classical times was lost. But the Simonides technique seems simply to have gone underground, preserved by occultists who appreciated its practical value.

Simonides was not, so far as I can discover, a magician, so it is unlikely that he knew anything of the Astral Plane. Nonetheless, he was engaged in an astral operation, whether he realized it or not. As Dolores has already pointed out, the astral reflects the physical. Although any aspect of the physical requires an astral "idea" before it can manifest, the idea itself requires physical manifestation for stability. This sets up something akin to a feedback loop. Anything that exists on the physical plane has its astral counterpart. The longer the physical item has existed, the more stable its astral image. This means that by using an image of his own home, Simonides chose something that was already reflected on the astral and was consequently that much easier to visualize. (You can put the characteristic to the test by contrasting the ease with which you can visualize the Great Pyramid at Giza—which has existed by orthodox dating from more than four thousand years—as compared to the problems you might have in visualizing, say, the Empire State Building, erected in 1931.)

In some cases, the "objects" Simonides placed in his locus—as the imaginary house came to be called—had their physical plane counterpart as well, which gave them an additional astral stability. Small wonder they became easier to remember. They really did take on an existence at another level.

You can begin your own experiments in the technique exactly as Simonides did by using your own home as the basis for an astral locus. Building on the fundamental techniques for creating astral imagery already given in this book, try to see it as clearly as possible in your mind's eye. Visualize yourself standing outside the front door, then imagine yourself entering the building and entering each interior room in a particular sequence. Repeat the process several times, making sure to keep to the same sequence, until you are very familiar with the technique. Then try the following practical experiment.

First, read through the list on the following page. Concentrate as you do so, because I'll be asking you how many items you can remember when you've finished.

Cat | Television set
Door | Crescent moon
Light bulb | Blackbird
Rose | Sailing ship
Bottle | Newspaper
Table | Saucepan
Lion | Broomstick
Star | Beachball
Buddha statue | Plate
Parcel | Mirror
Telephone | Handbag
Suitcase | Chair
Spectacles | Cocktail shaker
Standard lamp | Bird's nest
Cardigan | Laptop computer
Fried egg | Deck of cards
Tree | Paperclip
Baby's rattle | Paint brush
Book | Stetson hat
Cushion | Pair of trousers
Window |

It's a long list—more than forty items—but I'd like you to turn the book over now and write down as many items as you can remember. And while you're at it, try to remember them in the order they appeared in the list.

When you've finished, don't get too depressed by the gaps, because however poor your natural memory is, you'll find it will improve through the use of thought forms. Try the experiment again, but this time instead of just concentrating, visualize your locus, your home, and visualize yourself walking through it as before. But this time, set down the various items on the list as you go.

Unless you live in a bigger house than I do, chances are you don't have forty-one rooms, so you can't leave an object in each. What you can do is leave several objects in each of the rooms you do have—one just inside the door, one by the window, one in the middle of the floor, one on a table, one in a cupboard, one on a mantle, and so on. If, again, you follow a set sequence in placing the objects, it will allow you to recall them in the order of the list.

There is no need for you to try to remember the various items as you place them. Your concentration should be on visualizing them as vividly as possible. Once you have done this and set an item down, simply continue to the next item on the list.

When you have finished placing all the items, it might be fun to make life a little difficult for yourself by taking a coffee break. Then, when you have finished your coffee, you can test yourself by using the locus to remember the list.

Here again there is no need for heavy-duty concentration. Simply walk mentally through your home, taking the same route you did before, and note the items you find there. Chances are you won't be able to recall every object on the list since this is the first time you've used the technique. But I can promise that you will recall far more than you did before—and almost all those you do recall will be in their correct order.

As you become more accustomed to using your locus, you will find your score improves until perfect recall becomes commonplace. You might also entertain yourself by "memorizing" your lists backward—a feat accomplished simply by reversing the order in which you walk through your imaginary rooms.

Many occultists—and quite a few people with no esoteric knowledge whatsoever—have used the locus purely as a memory aid. But its initiate use goes well beyond this.

Curiously, the clearest description of locus potential so far published appears in Thomas Harris's thriller novel *Hannibal,* which topped the best-seller lists in 1999. In an earlier book, *Red Dragon,* Harris introduced his most disturbing fictional creation, Dr. Hannibal Lecter, a psychopathic cannibal who achieved even greater prominence in a second novel, *Silence of the Lambs,* which was subsequently filmed and stars Anthony Hopkins and Jodi Foster.

In both of these novels, Lecter was a monstrous figure who hovered on the edge of the action like some hideous bogeyman hiding in the shadows. In Hannibal, by contrast, Harris set him center stage and allowed readers insights into the character's background, personality, and psychosis. At least one critic (writing in Britain's *Sunday Times*) thought this was a mistake, on the grounds that the most frightening monsters are those that remain hidden. But regardless, the approach taken by Harris introduced the concept of a locus to the general public at a remarkably sophisticated level. For in creating Hannibal, Harris decided his character had survived his own madness through the use of a Memory Palace.

The Memory Palace (as distinct from a simple locus) seems to have been developed by a select group of fourteenth-century initiates, almost certainly working in Italy. In place of their humble homes, they began to familiarize themselves with public buildings as their loci, then trained their minds to build imaginal equivalents of the greatest, most elaborate mansions in the land. Thus the true Memory Palace was born, a complex astral structure of labyrinthine corridors and hundreds, sometimes even thousands, of apartments.

The given reason for this monumental creation was that some magicians had a lot to remember. The real truth lay deeper, and Thomas Harris came so close to it in his novel that one has to admire the extent of his research. In *Hannibal,* he explains how Dr. Lecter controls his most destructive memories by locking them away in an imaginal oubliette—a secret dungeon in his Memory Palace accessible only by a single trapdoor. The novel also showed how the not-so-good doctor lightened his moods by "replaying" memories of pleasant experiences stored in his palace. At times Lecter escaped into his astral creation in order to endure torture. It's all a far cry from remembering lists.

The book *Hannibal* is, of course, fiction, and Lecter's Memory Palace is used by a murderer certified insane, so emphasis is placed on control and criminality. Nonetheless, Harris's description of a Memory Palace and its initiate use is accurate, at least as far as it goes.

Used to its full magical extent, the Memory Palace shares its essential nature with another astral structure sometimes created by magicians as part of their fundamental training—the Inner Castle. The Castle, in turn, appears in the writings of the mystics—notably the sixteenth-century St. Teresa of Avila—where it is described as a visionary building that the individual can explore in his search for God.

Jungian psychology, with its emphasis on deep mind states, maintains that where a building of any sort appears in dreams, it may be interpreted as a container of the psyche. Examine the building and you have clues to what is currently happening with your inner processes. A small, cramped cottage suggests limits to mental activity, while a university might indicate a more expansive outlook with lessons currently being learned.

Magical philosophy, which stands somewhere between the psychological and the mystical, sees the Inner Castle as an astral analogue of the body, the mind, and even, properly constructed, the spirit. Typically, a spiral staircase winds around the central pillar of the spine, and glyphs in certain upper chambers may be used as a control center for the generation of certain desirable results.

Unlike the mystics and the Jungians, who tend to seek out an Inner Castle that has arisen spontaneously out of natural psychological states or been generated in the course of a religious life, magicians like to build their own. It is frequently patterned on a mythic structure, such as King Arthur's castle at Camelot, thus allowing it to draw energy from the associated myth.

The Memory Palace combines elements of a simple locus with an extended Inner Castle, and in so doing creates a magical tool that supercedes them both. To create and make use of your own Palace, this is what you have to do: First, select a physical building to use as the template for your Memory Palace. This should not be your own home. This building should be much larger than your home, and one that you have never actually entered. An old, well-established structure is better than something recently constructed. You may be lucky enough to have a suitable building in your locality. If so, pay it a visit and familiarize yourself with the exterior (but only the exterior—you should not enter the building). Walk around it to get an impression of the overall size. Take photographs or make a sketch of the major features, particularly the main entrance.

If there is no suitable building near you, it is perfectly acceptable to use an architectural reference or even tourist board photographs. The world is full of wonderful buildings, from the Potala in Lhasa to the Doge's Palace in Venice.

Now set aside some time each day to visualize the outside of your chosen building until you can see it clearly and in detail in your mind's eye. Don't try to "enter" your new Memory Palace at this stage. It is only at the stage of construction and it is quite important that you do not have any preconceived ideas about what is inside—the reason why you're using a building you have never actually entered.

Once you have a clear picture in your mind of the outside—which should not take long—you can begin to create the kernel of the interior. But before you do, I want to explain the theory.

Your use of an actual building as a template creates the initial linkage between the astral and the physical worlds. The building already exists on the physical, and thus has an astral reflection. Your visualization of the exterior connects you with this reflection, allowing you to easily construct a second, similar astral building of your own. This point is important. You will not be using the actual astral reflection of the physical building you selected, but rather your own astral counterpart of that reflection. It's as if you saw a house you liked and decided to build something similar for yourself.

But the external appearance of your Memory Palace is its least important aspect. In the next part of this exercise you need to make the structure personal to you. This you will do by placing an analogue of your physical body inside the Palace. (I'll tell you how in a moment.)

The body analogue automatically generates a second analogue inside the Palace. This is an analogue of your psyche, which includes such areas as your deep unconscious, your higher self, and, even though it can be difficult to find, your personal point of contact with the Collective Unconscious.

The second analogue arises out of the fact that your body and psyche are not separate. Your body is something generated by your psyche in order to function in the physical realm. By creating an analogue of one, you automatically create an analogue of the other. And since you are almost certainly more familiar with your body than your psyche, it makes sense to create the analogue that way around.

The simplest way to create the body/mind analogues is to tape-record the following short script and play it to yourself while in a state of relaxation. If you don't have access to a recorder, ask a friend to read the script aloud to you. Either way, you will need to repeat the process until the structures described become so completely familiar to you that you can mentally visit them with ease. Here is the script:

> You are now stepping through the main entrance of your Memory Palace. As you pass across the threshold, you find yourself in a large, wood-paneled hallway with marble tiling on the floor and marble statues ranged around the walls. You can examine this hallway in more detail at a later stage, but for the moment, walk directly across to the door in the opposite wall.

> When you open this door, you will find yourself in a second hall, this one with a polished wooden floor. There are doors leading off the hall, but once again you should ignore all but one of these for the moment and walk directly to the opposite door.

> On opening this door, you will find yourself in a third hall, substantially larger than the other two. In the exact center of this hall is a spiral staircase in stone, leading, as far as you can determine, upward into a turret and downward into some lower chambers of the Palace. Once again you should ignore the doorways for the moment and concentrate your attention on the spiral staircase.

Cross to this staircase and begin your clockwise climb upward so you can explore the higher reaches of the turret. As you climb, you will notice two doors set in alcoves leading off the staircase at an upper level. You will soon explore what is beyond these doors, but for now continue to climb until the staircase leads you into the highest chamber in the turret, a library room with two large windows allowing you to look out across the rolling countryside in which your Palace stands.

Through these windows you can see the neatly cultivated and familiar gardens that surround the Palace. Beyond them are the woods and fields of your estate, and beyond these wilder, less familiar countryside.

If you turn your attention to the books on the library shelves, you will quickly discover that pride of place goes to the multiple volumes of your personal biography, numbered one for every year of your life. Take one down and examine it and you will discover it contains information—pictures and text—pertaining to your life at that specific age. But there are gaps and blanks in its pages, as if some information has been lost. You will notice these gaps increase in the earlier volumes and decrease in those that deal with your more recent life. But all volumes, including the most recent, have at least a few gaps.

Should you examine the most recent volume, the one marked with the age you are now, you will note that the text is unfinished. But you will see, too, that there is an ornate quill pen and a plentiful supply of ink on the writing desk beside the shelves, so you can continue the record at your leisure, for it is clear by now that each book of your biography is in the form of a diary record kept by yourself.

Leave the multivolume biography now and examine the other books on these shelves. You will quickly discover they are all works on subjects that interest you greatly. Later you may enjoy examining some of these books in greater detail, although you will discover they seldom contain anything you do not already know.

Now that you have familiarized yourself with the upper room, return to the spiral staircase and begin to descend until you reach the two recessed doorways you passed on the way up. As you enter the first of these, you find yourself in a large chamber almost filled by a pair of mighty leather bellows driven by massive machinery so that they inflate and deflate in a steady rhythm.

Through the second recessed door off the spiral staircase, you enter a very similar chamber, but in this one the machinery drives a giant pump attached to a series of pipes containing a red fluid. Like the bellows in the other chamber, this pump maintains a steady rhythm. If you pay close attention, you will discover that the pump follows the rhythm of your heartbeat, while the bellows follow the rhythm of your breathing.

If you now follow the staircase downward, you will return to the hallway from which you started, but continue farther into the basement area of the Palace where you will find a furnace room. The furnace itself is well stoked, but controlled so that the heat it generates is carefully contained.

Now return to the room in which you started, and leave the Palace by the same route you entered, then open your eyes and end your visualization.

You will need to return to this exercise several times, striving to add reality, tone, and detail each time you do so, until you find you can visualize the areas described without strain or effort. When this is achieved, try the exercise entirely from memory and continue to practice until the trip into your Memory Palace becomes second nature to you. When this point is reached, you can safely assume you have constructed the astral analogue of your physical body—which means that an astral analogue of your psyche is now in place as well and your Palace has become a tool for some serious psychospiritual work.

17 USING YOUR PALACE

IN 1909, WHEN CARL JUNG was thirty-four years old, he went on a trip to the United States with his mentor, the founding father of modern psychiatry, Sigmund Freud. Over a period of seven weeks, they were in each other's company every day and fell into the habit of discussing their dreams.

In one of the dreams he shared with Freud, Jung found himself in the upper story of a two-story house, which, though unfamiliar, he somehow knew was his own. This level of the house consisted entirely of a salon furnished in rococo style and with a number of precious old paintings hanging on the walls. It was all very much to Jung's personal taste and he was pleased he owned the house, but suddenly realized he did not know what the lower floor looked like.

Jung went downstairs to discover that the ground floor was much older than the upper story. The floor was of red brick, the whole place dark and gloomy, the furnishings medieval. He felt this part of the house must date to the fifteenth or sixteenth century.

As he walked from one room to the other, Jung felt a growing conviction that he had to explore the whole of the house. He arrived at a heavy door that opened onto a stone stairway leading down into a cellar. Jung descended the stairs to find himself in a beautiful vaulted room that looked very ancient indeed. When he examined the walls, he concluded that they dated back to Roman times.

Excited now, he looked more closely at the floor, which was paved in stone slabs. One of them had a metal ring in it and when he pulled, the slab lifted to reveal a flight of narrow stone steps leading down into dark depths. Again Jung descended, and this time found himself in a low cave cut into the bedrock beneath the house. There was dust on the floor, scattered with bones and pieces of broken pottery, like the remnants of some primitive culture. He found two skulls, very old and half crumbled away. At this point he awoke.

Freud seized on those skulls when he heard the dream, suspecting that they represented hidden death wishes. To humor him, Jung ventured that he might harbor unconscious malice toward his wife and his sister-in-law, but did not actually believe it. Instead he realized that the house in the dream represented his psyche. The salon at the top was his consciousness concerned with the present moment, the day-to-day business of making a living and surviving in the modern world.

But below the threshold of consciousness, there were traces of humanity's historical inheritance—attitudes, interests, and ideas developed in previous centuries. The ground floor stood for the initial level of his unconscious, which, in the dream, he decided to explore for the first time. But the deeper he went, the darker and more alien his environment became. By the time he reached the cave, he had found the remnants of primitive humanity within himself, a world difficult to reach or illuminate with the light of consciousness. This area, he felt, bordered on the animal soul: caves, in prehistoric times, were often inhabited by animals before people laid claim to them. Later, Jung was to see in this cavern, with its fossil remnants, a substratum common to humanity as a whole, our remotest ancestral heritage, which he dubbed the Collective Unconscious.

The entire dream provided a model of the human mind that has proven useful to generations of Jungian analysts. Although it arose spontaneously, it seems to have universal application. Explorations of this sort of "inner house," using a Jungian technique known as "active imagination," will often enable patients to gain fresh insights into who and what they are.

Active imagination has much in common with the spiritual techniques of meditation and pathworking. It involves penetrating an imaginal (occultists would say astral) world, then noting and interacting with whatever is discovered there. Sometimes entities are discovered, prepared to enter into discussion with the individuals concerned. Analysts, by and large, consider such entities to be personified aspects of the patient's mind. A few accept the implications of Jung's Collective Unconscious and see at least some of the entities as objective, but continue to explain them in psychological terms. An appreciable percentage of occultists, by contrast, think of the entities as spirits.

None of these ideas is entirely correct. The "entities" one encounters in dreams, active imagination, meditation, or pathworking are all, without exception, thought forms. Some of them, as the psychologists believe, are personified aspects of your personal psyche, astral puppets created by your unconscious mind as a means of self-expression. Some of them—called archetypes by Jungians—seem to be the same creatures ancient people thought of as gods, an insight that was not missed by Jung himself. Some of them, as occultists postulate, are manifestations of spirits.

All of them may be encountered in your Memory Palace.

Before using your Memory Palace, it is wise to examine your essential nature. Just as the world around you is something other than it seems, you are very different from what you appear to be.

Whatever our philosophical stance or religious belief, many—perhaps most—of us identify the body as our ultimate reality. We can see, hear, feel, taste, and touch it, and it hurts when somebody drops a heavy object on its foot. There is a mind attached to the body, but it cannot be touched, sensed, weighed, or measured. The body seems to be the main man, so to speak. We would not be the same without it, and we fear its disappearance when we die.

Yet this touchstone of personal identity is an impermanent illusion. If you took the trouble to examine your body with a microscope, you would discover that you were shedding skin cells all the time. As you move through your day, you are, on the microscopic level, a constant snowstorm. It is a disturbing fact that a major constituent of house dust is human skin . . . and a menagerie of tiny creatures that eat it.

Your skin is not the only thing you're changing. Your liver is entirely replaced every six weeks. The remainder of your vital organs renew themselves more slowly, but just as inevitably. Even your bones, which seem so permanent, are in a state of flux. There is not a single molecule in your body that will still be there in seven years. At the atomic level, you are in a constant state of exchange with your environment, shedding an atom here and taking in an atom there in a continuous process, which means the eyes you were using at the beginning of this paragraph are not the same eyes you have now.

Yet for all this juggling of your atoms, something holds the pattern. You may be in a constant state of change, but I will still recognize you as an old friend when we meet next week. I will even, barring accidents, recognize you in seven years, even though not one single atom of your body will remain the same. Something—some immaterial thing—will manage to keep the whole whirling interchange of atoms in their correct shape.

Whatever you wish to call it—mind, soul, spirit—that immaterial thing is the essential you. It is this essential you that the Memory Palace will allow you to explore.

But unless you are a great deal more saintly than I am, the odds are high that your essential self is well hidden under years of accumulated mental garbage—hopes, fears, aspirations, and ego patterns that can (and will) be symbolized, sometimes personified, within your Memory Palace. Consequently, it is a good idea to carry out a little spring cleaning before you enter.

One of the best ways to do this—which, coincidentally, also uses thought forms—is a simple exercise I've used frequently during workshops. It brings results out of all proportion to the energy invested, but has one small drawback—you will need a friend to help you. Here's how it works.

Select a room in your own home that you are going to clean. It must be an actual room and it should preferably be a room you use fairly often. If you have very recently moved into a new house, you may select a room from your old home rather than your new one. It is also acceptable to select your office, or workplace, if you find you spend more time there than at home. Explain to your friend that you are going to clean this room mentally and that you require his help.

Decide what equipment you are going to use. You can have anything you need—buckets, sprays, detergents, soap, step ladders, and so on. Explain to your friend what you will be using. Then, in your imagination, begin the cleaning process. Describe to your friend in detail exactly what you are doing as you do it.

Your friend's job is to listen and encourage the process by asking questions designed to ensure you are visualizing the room as vividly and in as much detail as possible. You might, for example, say you were cleaning the light-fixture on the ceiling. Your friend should ask you to describe the fixture and what equipment you were using to reach it. If you mentioned that you were cleaning a book, he might ask the name of the book, its color, or what picture was on the cover.

Do the cleaning in the following sequence:

Start with the ceiling, then go down the walls. As you reach pictures, bookcases, and so on, clean them and move them so you can clean behind them. If necessary, move furniture into the center of the room. Clean the contents of cupboards or bookcases, item by individual item. Try to visualize each one clearly as you do so. Take as much time as you need.

As you clean, decide which items you are going to keep and which you are going to throw out. Move those you plan to throw out immediately outside the door. Small items should be placed in a packing case, larger items can be piled in a heap.

Clean the carpet, then roll it to one side and clean the floor. When finished, double-check what you want to throw out. Go outside and either burn the lot in a bonfire, or take it to an imaginal lake and dump it.

The results of this exercise are quite startling and are usually felt at once as a sensation of relief. An interesting side effect for some people is that their dreams become very vivid for a night or two afterward. If you enjoy the process—and many people do—there will be no negative effects should you decide to repeat it. But having completed the exercise at least once, you can move on to the use of your Memory Palace.

At this stage, it may be wise to alert you to a particular and somewhat peculiar experience that sometimes arises with the use of a Memory Palace—and, indeed, similar structures like the Inner Castle. This is the experience of being filled with bright, white light. Although the light is not the light to which we are accustomed in the physical world, it is distinctive and unmistakable—a flooding of brightness within your inner space. The sensation is so dramatic, and often so unexpected, that there is a tendency to panic; or at least that was my tendency when it happened to me. You need to know before you begin work with your Memory Palace that the experience of the inner light, if it happens, is not harmful. If anything, it is an indication of progress and, as such, should not be resisted. If it happens to you, relax and enjoy.

Your first step toward the use of your Memory Palace is simple exploration. In the instructions on setting it up, you will have noticed there were several doors mentioned that you were cautioned to ignore. Now is the time to stop ignoring them. You are free to enter any door you find. Indeed, I would urge you to search carefully for doors not mentioned. (There is, for example, a secret doorway concealed in the wood paneling of the entrance hall. You will find it on your left immediately you enter. And there may well be other secret doors and passages throughout the Palace.)

Despite the preliminary head-cleaning, you will almost certainly discover areas of your Memory Palace that are dirty—walls and ceilings covered in cobwebs, litter on the floor, and so on. When you find places like this, it is important that you clean them. Do exactly what you did in the preliminary exercise,[1] bringing in whatever equipment you need and carting out the rubbish for disposal. If you do nothing else at all with your Memory Palace, regular cleaning will still bring you enormous benefits in terms of your well-being and emotional state.

Alongside dirt and litter, it is also likely that you will find areas of your Palace where the air is stale and musty. It is as important to get rid of this stale air as it is to clean out the rubbish. Throw open doors and windows, or, if all else fails, bring in an extractor fan to suck it out. Stale air seems to be closely associated with negative thoughts. Removing it from your Palace has the interesting result of increasing the optimism of your outlook.

Although Memory Palaces are unique to the individuals who construct them, they do tend to have features in common. It would, for example, be quite surprising if you did not find a temple or chapel somewhere during your explorations. This is, in fact, one of the most important Palace areas for those of you interested in spiritual evolution, since it represents your contact point with the divine and/or your own higher self.

The inner temple can be used in a variety of ways. The simplest and most obvious is prayer, which may be verbalized or left as a written petition on the altar. Be careful what you ask for. The Memory Palace is a genuinely magical structure with a distinct tendency to generate concrete results. So consider the wording of any request to make sure you are asking for exactly what you want, and, even more importantly, consider the implications of getting it. Magical practice is littered with horror stories in this area, and while most of them are lit-

---

1. Or, take the shortcut suggested by Carol K. Anthony in her book *The Other Way* (Mass.: Anthony Publishing Co., 1990). In exploring her own "inner house," Anthony discovered a cosmic vacuum cleaner that she could pull down from the ceiling. It was about the size of an elephant's trunk, but had such amazing suction that it could cope with anything and cleaned out littered or dirty rooms in double-quick time.

tle better than urban myths, they are driven by a genuine concern. It is not, for example, a good idea to ask for fame if you value your privacy; and many other apparently innocent requests carry hidden timebombs. The advice to aspirants seeking entry into the Greek Mysteries was "Know Thyself." It holds good when you pray for something as well. Should you find it difficult to get the wording exactly right, a good safeguard is to make your prayers conditional. Adding a phrase like "if this be to the greater good of others and myself" can go a long way toward defusing unexpected problems.

An altogether safer—and in many ways even more beneficial—use of the inner temple is for sacrifice. You can use the altar to sacrifice negative attitudes and emotions, desires, grievances—anything, in fact, that you feel may be hindering your spiritual progress. If you picture yourself placing the particular element of your personality on the altar, it will disappear at once. Don't be surprised if the altar transforms itself into a trash can (or even a builder's dumpster) if you have a lot of things to sacrifice. They will still disappear, and after a while, as you have less to get rid of, the altar will revert to being an altar again.

Dungeons are also commonly found in Memory Palaces. You will recall from the last chapter that the fictional Hannibal Lecter used the dungeons of his Palace to imprison bitter memories, thus preserving what remained of his sanity. I can't say I recommend this practice to those readers who are neither fictional nor psychopathic. Imprisoned memories tend to cause trouble sooner or later. If anything, your attention should be focused on releasing and healing those aspects of yourself that have become trapped in these dank regions. But this is a tricky area generally, so tricky that the dungeons are best left alone until you are well experienced in the use of your Memory Palace and, ideally, until you have met up with your Inner Guide.

Esoteric tradition has it that when the pupil is ready, the teacher appears. But it is less widely appreciated that the teacher may not actually be in incarnation. While chatting about gurus, Carl Jung asked a friend of Mahatma Ghandi if he was prepared to divulge anything of his own guru. The man, an elderly cultured Indian, said he was being taught by Shankarcharya, the Vedic commentator who had died centuries before. When Jung asked the obvious question, the man confirmed his guru was Shankarcharya's spirit. Your own Inner Guide may be your higher self, an historical personage like the guru of Jung's friend, another type of spirit, or an archetype (that is, God form). This Inner Guide will, when necessary, use your Memory Palace as a convenient vehicle for communication.

It's quite important to realize that you should not try to visualize any particular Inner Guide. Creating a suitable astral vehicle for a specific spirit is a legitimate magical technique, but it is an advanced form of practice, properly looked on as evocation, and should not be attempted in the context of your Memory Palace. (Or at all, until you are well versed in the esoteric arts.) Rather, you should continue to explore your Palace, secure in the knowledge that the tradition is correct in suggesting your Guide will appear when you are ready. Paradoxically, letting go of expectation will tend to speed up the process of contact.

Another common aspect of the Memory Palace is the pleasure garden, an area of rest and relaxation (often with running water) where you can go to recuperate and regain your strength.

This is not meant to be a definitive list of what you might expect to find in your Palace. Most Memory Palaces will contain a chapel, dungeons, a pleasure garden, and, potentially, an Inner Guide. But they will contain much more as well, some or all of which will be unique to the structure you have built. Early explorations of my own Memory Palace, for example, led me to discover a small clinic staffed by two irascible Greek doctors whose advice on matters of healing proved remarkably sound.

Exploration of your Palace will bring you information on its further uses. (This is particularly true if you manage contact with your Inner Guide.) While you are waiting for guidance, you could do a great deal worse than enhancing your pleasure garden with memories of pleasing incidents and people you might otherwise forget.

If nothing else, it will prepare you for the forbidden territory Dolores wants to lead you into next.

18   HOMUNCULI (I)

Dolores on: the imagined dark areas of thought-forming; raising forms in the Middle Ages; familiars and guardians; cartoon characters; taught with care, used with ethics; dangers; how to create and program.

THIS IS WHERE WE begin to tread on toes, ruffle feathers, and disturb hardline Christians. Those of a nervous or sensitive disposition should perhaps call it a day and put the book back on the shelf!

Still with us? Good.

Human beings of both sexes are notorious for their curiosity and their ability to gallop into places where angels fear to tread. Having said that, we are told in the Bible that "man is above the angels." Presumably this means we are entitled to explore beyond the limits placed on the angels. We are about to do just that.

Herbie and I are assuming that if you're reading this book you have a reasonable amount of magical knowledge, the same amount of common sense, and can recognize ethics when they stand in front of you. We have come a long way since the Middle Ages. What scared the breechcloth off aspiring magicians then merely makes us pause to polish up our wands now.

The creation of homunculi and the raising of forms was seen as the darkest area of magic in days of old . . . and with good reason:

159

- it could get you burned by the church;

- it could get you killed by what you had called up;

- if what you called up didn't kill you, it could drive you insane because you were incapable of understanding its nature;

- what you called up wouldn't go away again!

This did not deter everyone. Some brave souls soldiered on, and from their experiments (and in rare cases, their records) we have learned a great deal. Moreover, we now know much more about the nature of the universe around and within us. Concepts they couldn't handle without danger to minds and even lives, we accept with no problem. This enables us to venture further into what was once forbidden territory and understand that not everything is as black as it has been painted.

In the Middle Ages, magicians and alchemists worked under great difficulties. They had to maintain utter secrecy, could trust no one, and had to battle very real fears concerning the unseen worlds. Remember, these unseen levels exist within as well as around us. When, as primal entities, we were pushed down the cosmic birth canal of the multiplanes, we collected a layer of matter from each plane, thus ending up with a "coat of many colors." The color of the planes we bonded with most often manifest as a basic aura color. These internal layers of dimensional matter are inextricably linked to the external layers and interact with them continuously throughout our many lives.

Raising astral thought forms and bringing them into manifestation was considered the pinnacle of adepthood in the Middle Ages. The very real danger was the state of the magician's mind! It is how you perceive a form that controls how you conceive it on both the astral and the physical. In other words, you get what you think of, and if you think an angel is something with Doric pillars for legs, cumulus clouds for a body, and a smiley sun for a face, that is what you are going to materialize.

The attitude of the church concerning anything other than angels (on the astral) was that it was demonic and therefore resembled something akin to a Hieronymous Bosch nightmare; this included elementals, nature spirits, anything that was not obviously angelic. This was common thinking because it was the only thinking. Paintings, drawings, teachings were all the same—angels were angels and everything else was twisted, ugly, and obscene. So when a magician prepared to invoke to visible appearance, be it astral or physical, what appeared would inevitably be influenced by what he expected to appear.

One can imagine the dismay, disgust, and downright indignation of an elemental King conjured by the great Names of God, who found himself in a thought form body that had horns, a tail, a second face in its stomach, and everything else filled in with scales! And that would not be the worst visualization. Not surprisingly, the denizens of the subtle realms were not keen on working with human beings.

This said, there are beings of the Qlippothic realms that are devastating to the human mind. They are best left alone and, believe me, I am not kidding or being alarmist. As a teacher of ritual magic I see many types of magicians, and the ones most at risk are those who think reading a couple of books makes them an adept. To paraphrase an old saying, "A fool and his soul are soon parted."

Alchemists tried to create forms in glass retorts. They tried mixing all sorts of messy things together to imitate life. But the real homunculi are made by impressing creative proto matter with a thought pattern. Forget those engravings of little men and women in glass bottles—leave that to the biologists and geneticists.

Taught and used in an ethical manner, there is no reason why thought form homunculi cannot be made. They will not last—thought forms don't—but they can be made.

Once into the astral dimension, you will need to draw up from the matrix something that looks like Casper the Friendly Ghost. *Never, ever* use a real human being as a pattern. It is dangerous for both you and the other person, and can result in a mirror image running amok. And *never* use yourself as a pattern for the same reasons.

With the astral matter, build a rough outline of a figure, then flesh it out. If you have the knowledge to underpin it with bone, muscle, and such, then do it— it will help enormously. At this point, stop and look at it critically. Adjust where you need to do so. Add the flesh and give it tone and color. Do not add features or hair at this point. Freeze it, then "save" it like a program, giving it a file name. If it will help, use the idea of *Star Trek's* holodecks and give the main computer (your mind) an order to freeze and save holodeck program *Animation 1*. Now go back to your own level. You need to do this slowly.

When you come back to your program in a few days, you will no doubt be full of ideas. Call up your program (for example, "Computer, run holodeck program *Animation I*"). Simple, isn't it? Look at your thought child and change it here and there if you feel the need. Now, slowly and with detail, begin to build up the figure the way you want it to be. Add hair to head and body, and adjust flesh tones. Add nails to fingers and toes. Add details such as nostrils, ear lobes, wrinkles and hair lines, and color of eyes. When you have gotten this far, get it walking up and down. Make it run and jump, sit and lift things. Adjust the finer motor skills.

No doubt you are thinking that all this will take too long. Why can't you do it more quickly? You can . . . but it will not work as well because the pattern will not be finely tuned. If you want to be a magician, cultivate patience—lots of it. Freeze your program and return. During the next few days, consider other things you can do to make the form better. Face the fact now that your first six or seven tries will be failures. But you will get better. Try not to think ahead to its completion, this can begin the animation process too early.

Now you can begin to program the form. Make it simple: protection for your house, family, or business, or simply a companion you can talk to . . . but not in front of the neighbors!

As you get better at building forms, you will be able to program it to do other things. Remember, as an astral creature it has access to that level and can take messages and bring back answers. You have already been told how to use body heat to animate, and at this stage it is all you need. Do not attempt to go further than this for a while. You can teach later "models" to speak by giving them a larynx, vocal cords, and tongue and teeth.

At first your form will last only a few hours, but as you refine your skills it will last longer. Never try to extend this longer than a few days. After that time it will run out of energy and take it from the nearest source . . . you. You may, if you are lucky and have the physical and emotional nature of a materializing medium, find your form coming to visible appearance. If it does, it will be for a very short while—only a few minutes, if that. It can be scary and can deter you from making forms for life. It happened to my father. Sometimes a psychic can see your forms, especially if you get to the point where they persist for many hours. When this happens, you will know you have made it as a magician.

ASTRAL GUARDIANS

Almost every sacred space has an Inner Plane guardian. Often they are raised and set in place at the time of consecration. In ancient times this was often accomplished by the sacrifice of an animal or a human being. If and when that space is deconsecrated, the guardian must be summoned, thanked, blessed, and dispersed. If the space or temple is to be raised in another place and at a later date, the guardian can be temporarily housed in a flame, or in a suitable container, ideally of glass and made for the occasion. This is closed with a suitable talismanic seal and hidden away. It is from this practice that many of the stories of a genie in a bottle can trace their origin.

If a guardian is not placed deliberately, one is often drawn to the place of its own accord. This happens in two ways.

- A small portion of the spirit of someone intimately concerned with either the location or the power source behind the location will remain there after physical death. Often this is the first person to die after the setting up. The living person forms a great attachment to the location/power source and is drawn to stay with it at death.

- The location becomes so empowered by use that it attracts an angelic being who joins with those who worship and work there and increases the spiritual reservoir of power. Or it might be an entity that moves in to feed off the power supply. If the sacred space falls into disuse, the guardian slowly weakens and fades until it is no longer strong enough to remain with the location and returns to its original level, or, if it is an angelic, it returns to its own spiritual level.

This is often the case when a psychic becomes aware of the faint outline of a guardian or guardians, such as Roman soldiers who remain at their posts, unaware they are dead. They may have been killed on duty and, not having been formally released, are still there. Hadrian's Wall, separating England from Scotland, is such a place, though most have now been recognized and released. During World War II, I remember walking with my father along the Roman wall surrounding the city of Chester. We passed one of the small sentry stands built into the wall itself and the nebulous figure of a Roman guard sprang to attention, giving the correct salute. My father, a remarkably fine psychic in his day, stopped and said quietly, "Good work son, but its time to go off duty, you are blessed and released."

A startled look went over the young man's face, and for a moment his form became perfectly clear, then he smiled and vanished. My mother and grandmother strolled up smiling, and my grandmother said, "Well spotted Leslie, the lad will be glad to get home." And we all walked on.

Sometimes a weak guardian can be strengthened if there is a need for it. A friend and I went walking along an ancient towpath some years ago. It had once, long ago, been part of a Neolithic complex about a hundred yards away. The guardian was so faint we walked through it before we realized it was there. It drifted about, sending out ripples of weariness and distress at its inability to do its job, for the river was polluted and full of junk thrown there by vandals and the whole area needed to be cleaned.

We returned the next day with a bag full of fresh chicken heads, courtesy of the local butcher, and buried them by the path. This, along with half a bottle of wine and some honey, was enough to fire up the guardian. Some weeks later the council decided to clean up the river and the vandalizing stopped. Perhaps the guardian was flexing its muscles again!

If your sacred space is worth consecrating, it is worth protecting, and guardians of this type are easy enough to raise and set in place. Older guardians of places such as stone circles or Druidic groves—even those that have been decimated—can remain extremely powerful, and their guardians can be unpleasant if they think you should not be there. Remember, they have been thought-formed by experts and set in place with very specific instructions. Never walk into such a place without mentally approaching its guardian for permission. It may ask for a sign, symbol, or password, but even if you do not know it or cannot make a guess, open your hands, build a thought form of an appropriate god or goddess, and ask for permission in their name to proceed. You will be surprised at the difference it makes.

Guardians can be met in many places, some of them unlikely. There is a lady in a sunbonnet and a starched white apron in a northern England village who maintains a watch over an old stile that is still used as a shortcut over fields by the local people.

Churches always have guardians, usually ensouled by the essence of the saint to whom they are dedicated. Pre-Reformation, this ensoulment often came from a holy relic of the patron saint himself. Many of the old churches have or had a stone phallus encased within the stone altar—a symbol of the fertility of the land and of the church's faith spreading far and wide.

Old pubs built on the site of ancient meeting places are often said to be "haunted," and indeed they are, by their guardian who still keeps a watchful eye on the comings and goings. In England, many such pubs were built on or near "Tumps" or "Toots," two of many English names describing witches' gathering places. When such a place became well-known over a period of time, it was inevitable that sooner or later a place to eat and drink and stay overnight would follow. Things have not changed a great deal between then and now.

By the same token, every country has its guardian, which should be recognized and greeted as you approach its territory. A small gift to the land during your stay is appreciated, such as a packet of seeds sown in a suitable place, some food laid out for the wildlife, or flowers on the altar of a church. When you leave, an expression of thanks and a blessing will make sure you are recognized and welcomed on your return.

Building the right kind of guardian by means of thought-forming is an art, and one that needs careful attention to detail and strength of purpose to install. First off, what do you want to guard? A house guardian needs less programming than one for a Temple, which has to guard against many different dimensions. A personal guardian for a child is often a Dream Companion, usually an animal based on a favorite toy or even the family pet. Begin by visiting places you think may actually have a guardian, and see if you can sense them. Churchyards and cemeteries always have one, the older the better, but they are not always nice to look at. There is a tradition that the last person buried in a churchyard does guard duty until the next burial. This is fine as long as you are not the very last person buried there! I will recount an Irish tale about a graveyard that had only two vacant lots: Two old men died on the same day, and after the service the families raced along country roads dodging each other and trying to find shortcuts so their coffin would not be buried last. Finally one cortege arrived at the gate and were overjoyed to find the others nowhere to be seen. What they did not know was that the other group had not bothered to go in by the gate but instead had pitched the coffin over the wall into the churchyard directly opposite the grave and had already gotten their coffin into the ground.

Old houses often have a family chapel that may hold a family guardian. Ireland is famous for its banshee, the wailing woman who sits in a bush by the front door and wails loudly when a member of the family is going to die. If the family leaves the country the banshee will go with them. I have heard this wail only once in my life, and have no wish to hear it again. It begins low and harsh and lifts higher and higher until it pierces the eardrums and fills the head with pain, then slowly dies away.

But back to the building of a guardian.

Think about the form you wish it to take—animal, human, or angelic. Think about the kind of ensoulment you will need. Dogs, horses, snakes (especially cobras), dragons, miniature and full size, lions, jaguars, unicorns, bears, and "fetish" animals are the usual nonhuman choice. Roman or Greek soldiers, samurai, monks, genies, Nubian guards, Amazons, and so on, come high on the list for human forms. Usually, angelic shapes are the tall, beautiful, curly haired, androgynous, and, frankly, boring ones.

If you want to be original, try a series of geometric shapes in varying colors superimposed on one another. The true form of angelics is more of a cipher or mathematical equation than anything else. Once you get used to the idea, a red triangle (Michael) around a sea-green ovoid (Gabriel) that contains a rose-colored, six-pointed star (Raphael) will seem quite normal.

Once the form has been decided, the next step is to list the duties you want it to perform. These must be explicit. "To guard the temple" is not enough. Guard from what, whom, and which direction? What you might think is obvious needs to be made unquestionably clear to the guardian. Remember, this is a form made from sentient proto matter. What ensouls it does not have your human ability to make decisions. Angels are messengers only; they are, for the most part, programmed for one or two tasks but cannot go beyond their instructions. *We*, as humans, have free will. *They* do not. Even the Elohim, the Four Holy Ones, and the archangels can only do so much and must work within the parameters set for them, and, what is more, they cannot help humans unless humans *ask* for help.

Their guardianship must include such instructions as: "You will guard this sacred space and those within it from all dangers, be those dangers human, elemental, demonic, or from the outer and inner dimensions. You will stand guard to the east, to the south, to the west, and to the north, from above and from below, from without and from within. Your strength you will draw from the Lords of Light, who stand against that which has no Light. Your power you will draw from the anointed altar and the angelic force it contains. The safety of those within the temple is your prime task."

Add whatever other tasks you may think fit: assessing the character of those entering for the first time (which will weed out those who would not have fitted in anyway), or alerting the physical plane guardian to outside danger, such as fire, for example. These may be added to the programming over a period of time.

You have a form, you have programmed it, now you must animate it. There are several ways to do this. Whether you are working as a solo magician or with a group, the process is the same. You animate an elemental guardian with pure elemental power. Likewise, an angelic guardian with pure spiritual power. You may choose to work in the ancient or modern ways. Both require positive physical input from you.

To form, program, and animate a thought form requires data, knowledge, practical know-how, courage, and, most importantly, a particle of life to act as the spark.

THE ANCIENT METHOD

This is one I do not recommend. It is here purely for your information. First, a small model of the guardian was made out of beeswax or clay. This was softened in the hands, and the maker kept kneading it while holding the finished form in his mind. He thought about the image, what it would look like, its color, its scent, its fur, claws, and type of teeth. In the old days the blood of a real animal would have been used and the vital parts that housed its spirit, heart, spleen, sexual organs, and brain would have been dried in the sun, then cut into pieces and pounded into a powder. This would then have been mixed with the material during the first stage.

Now the model was laid aside for twenty-four hours to allow the mental image and the model itself to come together. The shaman, priest, or Pattern Master would sing to it, talk to it, tell it tales of its physical counterpart, all the while identifying one with the other. He would take great care to enlarge the mental image so it would look threatening to a stranger. If the image was to be in human form, he would often model it on a real human being (this is a real no-no in modern magic, so be warned . . . it can backfire on you). From this person he would take blood, hair, a tooth, nails, and things like spittle, semen, urine, and excrement, all of which contain special magical powers in that they are personal and hold the vital ingredient of life, having been a living and working part of a human being.

All this was dried and powdered, and each lot added to the model as a separate part of the ritual. Often the parts of the body, human or animal, that were of most use, such as eyes, ears, claws, teeth, and tongue, were added. This part took several days, as each ingredient was added and then chanted or prayed into place. The underside of the model was hollowed out, and each day one type of powder was added with great ceremony, usually at night. Then the form would be asked to use that particular part to enhance its usefulness as a guardian:

O thou terrible one, great is thy making and great will be thy task. Behold, thou shalt see beyond the farthest star, even unto the end of eternity shall thine eyes see. Terrible are these eyes, for they blaze like the sun and shine in the darkness of the night. To the wrongdoer they shall be as twin bolts of lightning. Let these, thy new eyes, be as weapons for the guarding of (name). I (name), Priest of Osiris, say this.

Listener in the Dark, thou who dost not sleep throughout the eternal night of millions of years. I give thee ears to hear the whispers of the Gods. The Lords of Amenti in their palaces shall be heard with these ears. The smallest footstep shall alert you to your task. The sound of a fly breathing shall be as loud in these ears as a trumpet.

With these ears shalt thou hear the stars sing and the sun speak praise to Atum-Ra. Take these ears, and use them. They are for the guarding of (name). I (name) say this.

With these lungs shalt thou draw thy breath. That breath is terrible and like to the fire of the sun at noon. With it thou shalt slay the enemies of the king and strike terror into the hearts of those who come against you with evil in their hearts. Thou art brave, thou art invincible, thou art strong in thy power. Thou art the guardian of (name) from now until eternity.

Now thou art set into thy place. Unto eternity this is thy place. Guard the heart of the king, guard the stomach and the lungs of the king, guard the intestines and the liver of the king. Stand thou in this place and look into the eyes of those who come to rob and desecrate the king's resting place. From the bowels of the underworld thou shalt look and he that cometh to rob shall wail and beat his breast. He shall fall down and his bowels shall turn to water. Blood shall come from his mouth and his ears and his body decay while still living. All this because you look upon him with thy power.

When all the powder had been used and prayed into place and all the instructions given, the hollow was closed with fresh wax and a sacred seal. Finally the priest would name the guardian, and emphasize that naming with his own blood smeared on the model.

After this, the model would be taken and buried in the place it was meant to guard. This type of guardian was most favored by the Egyptian to guard the royal tombs, for it used all four elements: water = urine; excrement = earth;

blood/sexual organs = fire; and lungs = air. All this would have been done during the forty days allotted for the preparing of the mummy. When the body was laid to rest, the guardian would also have been buried. Then at night the priests would have returned and called out the name, alternating with chants and invocations until the astral form stirred and rose to take its place for all time.

MODERN METHOD

If you are using an animal guardian, try to obtain a piece of real fur, a claw, or a tooth—a taxidermist can often supply this. It works well, and often zoos will have important animals stuffed to put on show. In this way nothing is killed unduly, and you can work with a clear conscience. If even this disturbs you, you can use the Magical Change Ritual. Take a piece of fake fur or patterned material such as a leopard print, and a sliver of bone from a chicken, and chant over them. Use you own words, for it is *you* who is working the change. Tell them that they are reborn into the form of (*name*). Speak of the attributes of this new form and how it will serve your purpose. This is not ideal, but it will work, though not strongly. When this is done, grind the bone into powder, then burn the material and use the ashes. Gradually work this into the wax or clay. Now lay it aside and leave it for twenty-four hours. During that time think about it and picture it in your mind. Move into the astral plane and build your animal or elemental guardian out of the proto matter; look at it and try to hold that shape in your mind, and keep projecting it down into the wax/clay image.

When the shaping is complete, it is time to do your part. Hollow out the underneath of the figure to the size of a thimble, and put a flake of flint into it to represent fire.

> Let this flint become the fire within thee, that the qualities of that element shall be yours until the end of your task, which time shall be appointed by me.

Now take some soil (a few grains will be enough) and put them into the hollow to represent the element of earth.

> Let these grains become the earth within thee, that the qualities of that element shall be yours until the end of your task, which time shall be appointed by me.

Take one drop of water and put them in place.

> *Let this drop become the water within thee, that the qualities of that*
> *element shall be yours until the end of your task, which time shall be*
> *appointed by me.*

Do *not* follow on with air until you have completed the next task.

Take one drop of semen or menstrual blood. If you have gone through the menopause, then use saliva, one drop of urine, and one fleck of excrement, and mix. (Yes, I know its messy and disgusting, but one of the things they seldom tell you about magic is that it is not all sweetness, light, angels, and honey. If you want to be an adept, then get in there and do it and stop fussing!)

Now separate this mixture from yourself, like this:

> *This came from my body; this is of myself and I acknowledge this,*
> *but now it is gone from me forever. It has a task to do that it must do*
> *alone. Go from me with my blessing. Be separated from me and be*
> *blessed in your task.*

This is so you do not become identified with the guardian of its task once it has been set in place. This is important, and you *must* separate yourself in this way.

Put the mixture into the hollow, which by now will be full:

> *These gifts of life I bestow upon the guardian to be set in a place that*
> *shall be appointed. With the power that is in them, let the guardian*
> *be raised up and given the name of (name).*

Take a straw and have ready a piece of wax or clay. Place the straw just barely into the hollow and blow into it. Seal it at once.

> *Let this breath become the air within thee, so that the element of air*
> *shall be yours until the end of your task, which time shall be*
> *appointed by me.*

You are almost done. You have a model filled with all four elements, plus those elements repeated but from your own body constituents. It has been named and given breath, and now it must be put in place and "raised up."

This is a basic "recipe" for an elemental guardian. It can be adapted for a place, object, or person. A personal guardian is a comforting thing. The higher you go up the magical ladder, the more enemies you will make and the more likely you are to become a target. Until then you are more or less safe, except, of course, from your own ignorance, but that is a learning tool, and we *all* learn from mistakes. If you are just starting out, you will not need a guardian . . . you won't have had time to make enemies . . . but you will!

THE RAISING

Decide where you want it to be based. Wrap the model in pure cotton, as you would a mummy, and place it in a box bought or made for it. If your sacred space is outdoors, bury it in the north, the place of greatest power if you are Wiccan, or in the east to greet the sun if you are Druidic, Pagan, or Hermetic. If your space is indoors, attach it to the wall just inside the door. If you use the room for things other than ritual, then it must be kept somewhere safe where it cannot be discovered and put into position when needed.

Seal the temple or sacred space in your usual way, and call in the elemental Kings at the quarters. Take the box to each in turn, and "present" it to the King by name, asking for a blessing on the guardian. Finally, bring it to the altar and place it in the center.

Your invocation to raise the guardian must include a definite time of service—a year, or three years plus one day. It might be five or even ten years. Personally, I think that is the limit to a term of service. Build into your invocation a request to the Creator, God, or Goddess, and ask for a blessing "to the amount it is able to receive." This will mean that the elements will return to their own place with a reward greater than they could otherwise hope for, something that will keep them at their task with diligence. When time is up, open the box and destroy the model to set them free.

It goes without saying that you should take at least one person into your confidence so, should anything happen to you, they can take on the care of the box.

Take the box to the sacred place. Make a mental link with the guardian and your body essences within it. Call the guardian by name three times. With the inner eye, watch it emerge from its resting place and grow until it reaches the size dictated for it. Welcome it as an essential member of the group, and put milk and honey on the altar. Eat and drink the milk and honey (if you're in a group, all may do this), then offer the rest to the guardian. It will take up the essence of the "communion." Now it may be set in place. Close down, and as you depart, bid the guardian goodnight.

ANGELIC GUARDIANS

Build a form of astral matter as you have been taught, using a specific pattern; for example, wings and a halo and robes, or a pillar of Light either white or multicolored. Use an idea from a painting if you like, or use a small painting or a carving as a receptacle, but you don't need to fill it with elements. With the other guardian you drew on the four elements around and within you; with this you will call on different powers.

You need to make the astral form twice that of human size to enable it to hold the power safely for you and those working with you. Build the form daily, increasing the detail until you feel it is ready. This usually takes a lunar month. In the meantime, decide upon what type of angelic being you wish to invite. Will it be one of the great choirs that gather about the seven archangels, the warriors (Michael), the healers (Raphael), the builders (Gabriel), or the keepers (Uriel)? Or you can choose one of the angels of the hours, or of the seasons. Consult Gustav Davison's *Dictionary of Angels* for further information.

An angelic guardian needs less input than an elemental; it does not need as many safeguards or specific ingredients. Once the form has been finalized, the "Calling" may begin.

The spiritual levels of the "Seven before the Throne" mean working at a very high level, one you will only be able to endure for short periods of time, so the work is best done on a weekend when you have time to concentrate. Prepare yourself for the ascent by fasting for twelve hours prior to the calling, and drinking only water. Bathe and put on freshly washed clothes. Then make sure you will not be disturbed (this is important).

Calm your mind with deep breathing, then settle into a meditative state; after a few minutes, begin to breathe deeply again to induce a deeper state. Hold the mind steady for another five minutes, and then breathe deeply again, going deeper still. Continue to alternate deep breathing and meditation until you cease to be aware of anything around you.

Set your mind free to float with the idea that it is going to rise upon the levels, like a bubble of air rising to the surface. This may not happen the first time or the second, but it will happen. You'll begin to feel as if you are floating. Allow it to continue, but hold the name of the angelic being you wish to contact firmly in your mind, and the thought that you want it to spare some of it's essence to ensoul a guardian.

An archangel is a being of almost pure spiritual vibration. It exists not just in its point of space, but pervades the whole of it. It exists everywhere in that space by reason of the fact that every particle of its being is a conscious whole. Thus, one minute particle, and it is made up of billions of them, can indwell a form and *be* there as a whole. But it will not do this unless it can be convinced of:

- the purity of what will contain its essence;
- the dedication of those making the request;
- the quality of the work of which it will be a part.

You must make your request with a sincere heart and be prepared to answers questions that will come to mind about your aspirations. Sooner or later you will get a sign that will tell you *yes* or *no*.

If *yes*, you may go ahead with the work. Now, when you go into meditation, hold the carving or painting in your hand and offer it as a "form" to the angelic presence. This is one of the most fascinating spectacles in magic. Watch the angelic being gather about itself layer upon layer of matter and gradually move down the levels toward the astral form you have built. It will surround it like a spiral of pure energy and begin to meld with it. The spiral will become translucent in the process, then change, becoming clearer and more solid. The astral form will reappear, glowing with the inner light that now indwells it. The physical form you are holding is now a manifested reflection of what is on the astral, and the astral form will be a reflection of the physical.

You need do nothing more now than present the physical to the four quarters and then to the altar, where you will state the length of time you need it to be with you, and ask for a blessing upon the angelic being when its work is done.

This leads us on to a very different kind of guardian, which we will now tell you about.

19 CURSES AND FAMILIARS

IN FEBRUARY 1923, when the archaeologist Howard Carter opened up the hitherto untouched burial chamber of the Egyptian Pharaoh Tutankhamen, his sponsor, Lord Carnarvon, asked what he could see.

"Wonderful things!" replied the awestruck Carter.

But as the two men entered the packed chamber, it appears they may have encountered something Carter could not see. A hieroglyphic inscription above the tomb seals had warned that death would slay "with his wings" anyone who disturbed the pharaoh's rest. No one took the curse seriously. And yet . . .

On entering the tomb, Lord Carnarvon was bitten by a mosquito. The bite became infected, complications arose, and the man who funded the Tutankhamen expedition died in a Cairo hospital on April 5, 1923. As he did so, a power failure put out the lights across the city, while back on his English estate at Highclere, his favorite fox terrier dropped dead, too. It was the beginning of a long series of oddly connected deaths.

Carnarvon's friend, George Jay Gould, traveled at once to Egypt when he heard about the death. Carter showed him the Tutankhamen tomb. The next morning,

Gould was running a fever, and by the afternoon he was dead, apparently from bubonic plague. The American archaeologist Arthur Mace, who had removed the final piece of wall blocking the main chamber, complained of growing exhaustion, then fell into a coma and died in the same hotel where Carnarvon had been staying.

Tutankhamen's mummy was taken from the tomb and x-rayed. The man who carried out this work, Sir Archibald Douglas Reid, promptly died as well. A Colonel Herbat, who was at the tomb when it was opened, died unexpectedly. So did Jonathan Carver, who was with him. Richard Bethell, Carter's archaeological colleague and secretary, died suddenly. His father, Lord Westbury, committed suicide, and the hearse carrying him to the graveyard ran over a small boy. Around the same time, Lord Carnarvon's wife also died . . . as the result of an insect bite. The British industrialist, Joel Wood, visited Tutankhamen's tomb while archaeological work continued.[1] He was returning home by ship when fever killed him.

Within five years of the opening, thirteen of those who had participated suffered premature deaths. In the same period, the death toll of those directly or indirectly involved had risen to twenty-two. Even Howard Carter's pet canary died. It was swallowed by a python, emblem of the Royal House of Tutankhamen.

The sequence of deaths gave rise to the legend of a "pharaoh's curse," and, on reviewing the facts, one is certainly left with the uncomfortable feeling that what happened stretches coincidence to breaking point. Yet as skeptics have rightly pointed out, the main desecrater of the tomb, Carter himself, was entirely unaffected—he died peacefully in London in March, 1939—while others present at the opening lived into ripe old age.

So was there really a curse on Tutankhamen's tomb?

The answer is instructive. Ancient Egypt was a culture with two great obsessions—magic and the afterlife. According to Sir E. A. Wallis Budge, former Keeper of Egyptian Antiquities at the British Museum, magical interest and practice permeated the entire social structure. Belief in the effectiveness of spells was universal, and so, as the entire thrust of modern Egyptology attests, was belief in an afterlife. And it was a very literal belief indeed.

---

1. The archaeological work took nearly ten years to complete.

If you visit the tombs in Egypt's Valley of the Kings, the thing that strikes you first about the tombs is their size. (That of Tutankhamen is an exception, but this is because the boy king died suddenly and was entombed in the only space available.) Typically, you walk along high-ceilinged passages into a complex of massive chambers made of rocks, their walls carefully plastered and decorated with cheerful scenes from the pharaoh's life. Even lesser nobles spent enough money to create tombs that could easily accommodate a party of a hundred people. It was as if in death they wanted lots of living space; which, in fact, they did. Egyptian tombs were known as Halls of Eternity, because it was accepted that the souls of the deceased would inhabit them forever, and thus they needed to be made as comfortable as possible.

They also needed to be guarded against robbers.

The problem of robbers was particularly acute, since concern did not end with the loss of grave goods. If the mummy was desecrated, the whole foundation of the pharaoh's afterlife was destroyed—the exact equivalent of murdering his souls.[2]

Many Egyptologists believe the country's enormous pyramids were built in an attempt to foil grave robbers, but if so, they did not work—no intact burial has been found in any of them. Orthodox theory has it that later pharaohs settled for secrecy, creating unmarked subterranean tombs they hoped the robbers would never find. A strong local tradition, backed up by some—though not much—archaeological evidence suggests that as a second line of defense, some tombs were trapped.

Although the traps could be physical—one writer[3] has suggested poisons, bacteria, and even the natural radioactivity of uranium were all used to deter intruders—the widespread interest in magic ensured some of them were more subtle. Texts like the *Book of the Dead* speak of "divine forces of the city of Bubastis that come up from their crypts," and there are several other papyrus references suggesting the use of "secret powers" to punish robbers and other wrongdoers.

Records of how these "secret powers" were generated are less easy to find, but modern esoteric practice would point to the use of thought forms. Certainly a guardian could be created in an Egyptian tomb in the way Dolores has just described.

---

2. Egyptians believed there were three—the *ba*, the *ka*, and the *ib*.

3. Philipp Vanderberg. See his book *The Curse of the Pharaohs* (London: Coronet Books, 1977).

But such a guardian would not last. As Dolores says, the guardian of a sacred site draws from the power source at that site—the power of ongoing ritual practice in an ancient cathedral, the geodetic and stellar power tapped by the great megalithic circles. Even places like the Roman wall at Chester, where Dolores' father released the guard, absorb energy from visitors and passersby. Few guardians are above a little mild vampirism to sustain their substance, and can endure in this way for centuries.

A tomb guardian is in a very different position. The whole point of a secret burial is to prohibit visitors. The tomb cannot be located on an existing sacred site (which would be too obvious). Consecration of the tomb and, perhaps, the sacrifice of an animal could generate enough energy to keep the guardian active for a time—long enough to deter any tomb workmen from profiting from their knowledge of its location—but after a period measurable in decades at most, it would fade away.

Almost certainly, one or more guardian thought forms would have been set in Tutankhamen's tomb. But the pharaoh died in 1323 B.C. His tomb remained sealed for more than three thousand years. What could have made the guardian endure so long? The surprising answer may be Tutankhamen himself.

There is substantial historical evidence that King Tutankhamen was murdered by a blow to the head. Sudden violent death with its consequent emotional charge will sometimes lead to an earthbound spirit. In such cases, the ghost tends to haunt the scene of its death, but in the case of Tutankhamen, cultural factors would come into play. The pharaoh was little more than a boy—perhaps as young as seventeen and certainly no older than twenty—and would certainly have accepted without question the doctrine that his physical mummy was the basis of his afterlife. Thus, he would have remained with his embalmed corpse, following it to the tomb in the Valley of Kings.

A thought form requires an energy source to persist, and the spirit of the king provided it. Tutankhamen survived as he believed he would survive, established in his Hall of Eternity, not realizing he was in fact earthbound and feeding the thought forms with his obsession to maintain the security of his mummy and his tomb until Carter became the instrument of change.

When the tomb was opened in the twentieth century, the guardians struck out indiscriminately at those he would have seen as grave robbers.[4] Some, like

---

4. Perhaps correctly. The morality of reopening tombs in the name of Egyptology is rarely questioned.

Carnarvon, were particularly susceptible to attack. Others, like Carter himself, proved immune. (And it must be admitted that some of the listed deaths may well have been coincidental.) Perhaps, too, their programming had become confused over the long period of time. Perhaps Tutankhamen's disordered thoughts influenced them.

Ironically, the release of Tutankhamen himself may well have come when his mummy was removed from its sarcophagus. The x-raying and subsequent unwrapping would have been seen as a desecration, and the spirit of the dead king would have been forced to progress beyond his long earthbinding.

FAMILIARS

In medieval times, every witch, male or female, had a familiar, a companion, which was usually a small animal, often a cat, toad, spider, mouse, rat, ferret, or weasel. More rarely it was a nature spirit—a gnome, house goblin, or brownie. These were the witches' confidants, often their only friends, and a bastion against the loneliness of their situation.

You seldom hear the term today, or hear of a modern witch having a familiar. They have cats, dogs, and other pets, but they are pets, not part of the rituals as were the familiars of old.

Animal familiars were obtained when young and brought up like a child. If the witch had young children, it was suckled at the breast or fed on saucers of breast milk, and meat was chewed and fed to the animal, thus furthering the bond between them. They slept in the same bed, were talked to and treated like a human being.

At some point—usually when the animal was a year old—the final bonding took place. Having been deprived of food and water for a day and a night, the animal would be lightly drugged and placed in a prepared circle. Sometimes a small amount of blood would be drawn, sometimes a piece of the ear or tail would be sacrificed and placed in a container beside the animal. Into the same container the witch put a drop or two of her own blood. Now the rite began.

Remember that at this time the witch would have it ingrained in her mind (by her upbringing) that she was in league with the devil and his imps. Whoever had taught her would have instructed her in the names and attributes of these beings. She would have already chosen a particular imp/demon and now called on it, casting herbs and meat into her cauldron as she did so. As it came to a boil, she cast in the blood and flesh from the container. Breathing over it, she stirred the mixture and conjured her chosen imp, willing it to appear in its true form. As some of the herbs used would have been hallucinogenic, there was a fair chance that, in her altered state, she soon begin to see what she wanted, the form of the imp rising in the steam and smoke from the cauldron.

Lifting the pot from the fire, she placed it in the circle beside the animal. All the while she chanted the imp's name and powers and rocked back and forth until, in the early hours, the mixture would cool. Within it would be, she believed, the essence of the imp. During these hours she would also have received its true name.

By dawn the animal would wake up, hungry and desperately thirsty. It would thankfully drink the meat-flavored liquid and, in doing so, imbibe the essence of the imp, who would now indwell the animal until death when the imp would return to its master. The witch also drank the mixture, bonding even more with her familiar who now received its new name. The animal was accepted as a physical form of the imp and treated as such. It was consulted, petted, and took its place in ritual. If the witch died a natural death, which was not often, her familiar, if still living, could be passed to a younger witch, or it might be killed and buried with her. Much of the success of this ritual depended on the thought form of the imp being clear enough for the witch to see it. If not, it was taken as a sign that the animal had been rejected and another one would have to be sought.

CARTOON CHARACTERS

We all have our favorite cartoon characters, and our children seem to have a daily diet of them. From the moment Mickey Mouse stepped onto the world stage we were awestruck. Donald Duck, Goofy, Pluto, Bugs Bunny, Tom and Jerry, and Tweety Pie followed in quick succession. All these little figures with their four-fingered hands and pseudo-human forms are the result of thought forms carefully crafted with exceptional skill by their makers.

Then Walt Disney moved the whole cartoon industry into the future by giving us *Snow White and the Seven Dwarfs,* and we were hooked. Other cartoonists came along, some of them very good, but it is to the genius of Walt Disney that we owe the fact that every day we can switch on the television and see the result of someone's thought-forming.

Some of these images have become so powerful that now they cannot be discarded. For those of you who are computer junkies, think about this: sometimes when you trash something then try to empty the "trash can," your computer will tell you it cannot be done because that item is "in use." Exactly the same thing happens with these cartoon thought forms. They have been "in use" for so long and are so deeply imbedded in our psyches that they can no longer be erased. Think of Snow White and it will be the Disney image that pops into your head. Even if you read the original story in Grimms collection, no doubt the images in your mind will be those of the film. *When this kind of thing happens, the thought form ceases to be just a thought form and becomes an archetype.*

It has happened with Superman, Batman, Teenage Mutant Ninja Turtles, Wily Coyote, Mr. Spock, *Star Trek,* and Fred Flintstone, along with Mickey, Donald, Goofy, and a thousand other cartoon characters, both on the screen and as seen on advertisements.

Laughter is one of the most powerful forces on this planet, along with love. Whatever makes us laugh or cry, we love, and we tend to perpetuate what we love in images. This not only happens with cartoons, but also with company logos and advertising characters.

Everything begins with the thought. The art of advertising began in the latter half of the twentieth century and will undoubtedly rule the twenty-first. We are bombarded by these thought forms every day; some are irritating beyond measure, others delight and amuse us, some get into a sort of mental loop in our heads and we can't get rid of the image. It is this that the advertisers count on for a successful campaign. Once an image becomes compulsive, it becomes all powerful on the astral plane. The energy from human minds feeds the image, which grows stronger and demands more from the energy source. Then suddenly a new advertisement appears and takes the public fancy, the energy is diverted, and the old image shrivels and finally disappears back into the astral matter. Once you understand this, you can become immune to the subliminal messages often carried within the image.

A few years ago, England began to show a series of television commercials that were, in effect, miniature soap operas. One was for coffee and the other for a French liqueur. Each revolved around a couple and their relationship. The commercials ran for about three or four minutes on average, and portrayed the ups and downs of romance. The entire country was gripped by these mini-episodes, to the extent that friends recorded new ones for those who missed them because of work or holidays, and even, in one case, because a woman was on her honeymoon and wanted to know what had happened on screen.

It got to the point where annual awards for the best commercials were offered, and these "advertisement Oscars" are now highly sought after. My point is that all these are thought forms skillfully engineered to capture our attention and hold it until the character and the product become one in our minds. We admire the character . . . therefore, we buy the product.

The power of thought imagery is not fully understood by the ordinary public, but only too well understood by the advertising companies. The trained mind can use exactly the same techniques to build images on the inner levels that are so powerful they impinge on the primal creative matter and cause a ricochet effect down into the physical state.

All through this book you have been hearing and learning about the power of the mind to build forms with astral matter. Once you can do this with a fair degree of success, you can go further and create thought forms on the next level up: the mental level.

Here we come across a very different type of thought form. At this level we are dealing with emotions and desires one level up from those we have encountered on the astral. Magicians tend to think of emotions as being part of the astral, Yesodic level. But the mental level above that is where such emotions and desires originate. We only start to really get to grips with them and deal with them on the astral level.

All of us have a need for love. It is a driving force in every human being, and if we are deprived of it for any reason it can cause irreparable damage to the psyche. But just as devastating is to have known love and then lost it. Young widows and widowers, and older people who have enjoyed a loving relationship for years then suddenly lose their partner all suffer a serious deprivation. Contrary to the beliefs of younger people, sex does not cease on one's fiftieth birthday; if anything, desire increases at that time because one is freed from the fear of unwanted pregnancies. One has had more practical experience in the art of sexual stimulation. To be suddenly cut off from the closeness and companionship causes stress that borders on actual pain.

Most compensate by thought-forming an imaginary lover that may or may not resemble the lost loved one. These "demon" lovers can become extremely real. In medieval times they would have been known as incubi or succubi. Both men and women have described their erotic adventures with such thought forms over hundreds of years. In earlier times, of course, the church denounced these fantasies as being evil and sent by the devil. The fact is that they are, for the most part, harmless, and even beneficial in that they alleviate stress and loneliness. I said "for the most part" quite deliberately, because there are, as always, exceptions.

There are on every level natural life forms that are indigenous to that level. Those emanating from the astral and emotional levels can sense and are drawn to similar emotions on the physical level, often with disastrous results. They can be, from our point of view, both good and evil. From their point of view they are neither. However, they can have a very real effect on humankind.

Both incubi and succubi tend to exaggerate feelings that we would otherwise enjoy. Both begin by lying on top of their victim, who feel great pressure to the point of suffocation. Both ride their victim to exhaustion. In a normal sexual act, the weight of one's lover on top is a pleasant sensation of being enclosed and surrounded by love, and the exhaustion that follows orgasm is the sensuous tiredness of satiation. We have conflicting patterns here, one that we like and feels good, and one that, because it is nonhuman, overstimulates our senses and causes pain.

Because they exist and have their being on creative and emotional planes, these entities depend on human thought for their forms; in their natural state they are simply emotional ciphers that exist in a way we cannot begin to understand. But we do create imaginary lovers to feed our self-esteem and make us feel loved and wanted. If our dreams and desires get out of hand, they become not so much dreams as raw emotion. It is this that can draw the succubi down to our level and manifest in lucid dreams.

The virtual reality programs that are now entering the market are frighteningly close to an astral world where dreams can be materialized at will.[5] Within two years they will be as common as a video machine and in another five years will likely have taken over the film industry. Films as we know them will be gone forever. In their place will be the film version of karaoke. You will interact with your favorite film star, enter the film, and act it out to its conclusion. At least the films on long international flights won't be so boring!

---

5. I believe they actually *generate* astral worlds (J. H. B.).

Does all this thought-forming present any danger? Well, anything to do with magic has an element of danger, anything worthwhile doing has an element of danger. (Walking down the road can be dangerous!) But thought-forming can also be exciting and informative and mind-blowing. If you are going to stop and worry about how thought forming will affect you, close this book now and go back to science fiction. That's safe . . . almost.

Magic, above all else, needs common sense, application, and ethics. With these you will not go far wrong. Yes, you can give yourself nightmares. Yes, you can stir up your endocrine system and give yourself some bad times. But you can also touch spiritual ecstacy, and learn more about yourself and the universe around you than you thought possible. You can explore the inner universe, which is just as big and just as beautiful and just as exciting as the physical version. You can play safe all your life and miss out, or take chances and live it to the fullest.

Creating fantasies and worlds within worlds is possible. I have done it for years. But remember, you cannot stay there for too long. You have to return to this world and this level or be lost forever. You may have heard or read about men and women who have been "taken by the faery folk." Being lost on the astral is like that—your body is on earth, but your mind wanders, lost in the world of thought forms. You *must* have self-discipline to enter this world. It is not for the weak-minded or those wishing to escape reality. For them it can become a trap.

Never stay for long. Build an awareness of time into your scenarios. Remember this important fact: Everything you meet, good or bad, is literally a figment of your thought patterns.

20 HOMUNCULI (II)

Dolores on:
astral characters
as thought forms
on stage, screen,
and in literature;
invisible friends
in childhood;
ghosts and
poltergeists;
children of the
mind; astral
creations respond
to the
unconscious
needs of the
creator; what can
be created with
safety, and what
to avoid; the
animation of
Osiris.

THE UNSEEN WORLD OF the astral is filled with the thought forms of those who have gone before us. Some of them will persist for hundreds of years, some will disappear within a few weeks, months, or years. None will disappear entirely, for there will always be a faint echo, and all the form needs to return in full force is for two or more people to think actively and strongly about it. Strangely enough, we can find proof of this in the Bible (Matt. 20): "For where two or three people are gathered together, there also will I be."

When a small group of people come together, even if it is for no more than a drink and a quiet chat, they will form a Group Mind. That Group Mind is composed of a little of each person's consciousness, plus itself. That extra piece gives it the casting vote, so to speak. If the conversation gets intense and the subject is one about which they all feel strongly, it is a fair bet that an effect will be caused on the astral level.

If the object is the workplace and the boss, then an astral replica of the place and the person will materialize on the subtle levels for the duration of the meeting. If the talk gets hot and angry and opinions are strong,

185

then the object of the talk (the boss) may well feel uneasy, fearful, or apprehensive. If the subject is one where a strong astral form has already been built up at will, such as the Group Mind of a popular football team or a famous football player, it can cause an even stronger effect.

If the talk is complimentary, it will:

- strengthen the form;

- inject it with enthusiasm;

- feed it with the group's will to win.

If, however, the group is angry with the team or the player, it can:

- inhibit the will to win;

- cause a depressive aura to surround the team;

- cause them to lose because the Group Mind has been told it is a loser and follows what it perceives to be orders.

This is why one should *never* knowingly build a form based on someone real. The effect on a team of the good wishes of the crowd is known to be beneficial. This is why a football team usually does well when playing on its home ground. When they consistently lose or fail to play to the satisfaction of the crowd, it can make the dressing room a gloomy place indeed, and can affect future play.

Nowhere does this thought projection hit harder than in the creative arts. New shows, new films, new exhibitions, and new publications are all highly susceptible to the mind and thoughts of the public. Those who work in these areas are notoriously superstitious and sensitive to public opinion. A new show getting a bad review can flop within weeks even if all it needs is a tightening up of its content. Conversely, a film made for a small audience can sometimes catch the imagination of the filmgoers, sweep aside the multimillion-dollar epics with worldwide advertising, and dominate the awards shows—*The Full Monty* is a case in point. What you think, what you actually build in your mind in the form of images, is broadcast outward to the world. You don't have to be psychic or an extrovert—introverts are more intense about their thoughts and they usually have much more power behind them due to the build-up of emotion.

It matters what you think about and how you think of things and people. Thoughts are living, creative impulses that emanate from the physical brain in the form of vibrations. The three levels of thought are immensely powerful, even when they are unaware. When they are aware . . . they can create universes.

The physical brain is merely a tool, as much as a hammer or a screwdriver. The mind is what activates the physical brain and powers it up. What programs the mind, what tells it what to do, is *you,* and *you* are neither your mind nor your brain, you are something far and away beyond that. When you realize this fully, to the extent that it becomes real and understandable and acceptable, then things begin to happen because a knowing and purposeful intent is behind the thought process.

Film characters that have persisted and grown into archetypes might include Tarzan, Dr. Kildare, Flash Gordon, Zorro, Data, Yoda, Obi-Wan Kenobi, and a number of others. Many of these have been literary characters before being made into films. Sherlock Holmes, Captain Nemo, and James Bond have all caught and held the imagination and, therefore, the thoughts of us all. Children's minds are free of the hassle most adults have in their lives, so their thought forms can be immensely powerful. Today when many of them sit for hours before a screen, the commercials go straight into the deepest level. Anyone in advertising will tell you that if you can convince the children, the parents will follow.

The immensely popular puppet series of *Thunderbirds, Captain Scarlet,* and *Four Feather Falls* in the United Kingdom caught even the adults in their net. Until this time we have grossly underestimated the power of thought and its effect on us as intelligent beings, and through us on the world and the universe around us.

When a writer sits down to write a book, she has in mind a certain broad outline of the plot. It may even be a fairly detailed plot. However, as any writer will tell you, characters will almost certainly begin to take over at some point in the narrative.

Until they do, the book will not come alive. Katherine Kurtz is a longtime friend and a writer whom I (D. A. N.) admire greatly. In one of her intriguing *Deryni* novels, a character exploring a castle came upon a stairway leading to a tower. He climbed the steps, and as he did he began to get the feeling that something of great importance to him would be found at the top. Katherine had no idea what it was . . . she was as eager to find out as her character.

On reaching the top of the stairs he found a door that opened into a turret room. It was empty except for an old wooden chest. At this point Katherine had to stop writing for some days to attend a conference elsewhere in the United

States. All the time she was away, her mind kept wondering what was in the chest. She got back home and sat down to finish the chapter, breathless with excitement. Her character crossed the floor and pried open the lid . . . to find a set of richly embroidered religious robes. But until that moment Katherine had no idea what would be found. One's characters grow as the book grows, and often change and mature as would a living person. They are the writer's children in no uncertain terms, and can display temper, arrogance, annoyance, and stubbornness. They can force a change of pace, location, and temperament on to the perspiring author with a total disregard for her previous idea of the plot.

Authors use the same kind of thought-forming processes to build characters that you have been using to build astral forms, because that is exactly what a character in a book is—an astral form. Those who read the book later will either love or hate those "astral people," and if they like it, they will buy the book in millions. If the character touches a chord in us, we identify with it and want to go on reading about it. The phenomenal success of the Harry Potter books is an example. Harry Potter is alive and well on the astral plane . . . appropriate when you think he is a magician in the making.

At the time of writing, a new musical show is packing audiences into the Dominion Theater in London. *The Lion King* has translated very successfully from the screen to the stage. The costumes are almost surreal in that they are one-third costume, one-third puppet, and one-third the imagination of the audience. We see the actors *as* the animals because we *want* to see them like that and supply the missing pieces. These incredible costumes are fantasies made manifest. What can be done for a stage show can be done for anything, from a new car to a house to a diamond necklace.

Many children in their young days have invisible companions. These can be either animal or human. They are totally real to their "hosts," and can even be passed on to other and younger members of the family.

Ninety-nine percent of the time they are completely harmless and can even be of great comfort to a lonely child or one who spends long periods of time in a hospital. Abused children often invent companions who are like themselves. It comforts them to be able to comfort another. Sometimes they invent and build imaginary parents who will one day take them away from the hated foster home or orphanage.

When I was about seven or eight, I discovered what I took to be a gnome. He lived in a very old granite wall that I passed on my way to school every day. He was so real to me that I can still recall the feel of his leathery skin and the roughness of his beard. I called him Christopher. As an only child, I had had many unseen friends and never felt the need for human companionship; I was quite content with my dog, my books, and my "other" friends. One day I was caught by a teacher holding an animated conversation with . . . a granite wall! The result was a trip to a child psychologist, who happened to be Welsh and a psychic. He gave me the first advice I ever had on the subject of psychism: "Never let on that you can see things from other levels. Enjoy them and learn from them, but say nothing."

Some years ago, Hollywood made a film called *The Ghost and Mrs. Muir.* The story concerned a young widow with a small son who had to find a way to make a living. She came to live in a clifftop cottage that had once belonged to a sea captain. The captain's ghost took a liking to her and began to haunt her. He insisted on her writing a book that he dictated and which, when published, provided the money she needed.

This is a classic example of need and desire supplying what was needed. Often those who desperately need to see someone who has passed over will supply the emotion and the astral image needed to bring about an appearance of the dead. This doesn't happen in every case, but in a fair percentage.

If forms are "fed" recognition on a regular basis, they will certainly manifest at some point in a way that can be seen and even, on occasions, touched. Such forms will respond to the unconscious needs and desires of their creator.

But is this healthy and is it safe? Anything that helps a distraught human being to cope with loss, loneliness, or need cannot, in my personal opinion, be all bad. If it grows into an over-reliance on the form long after its usefulness has gone, that is a different matter. There are many cases where an astral companion has persisted for the lifetime of a human being and given meaning and comfort to what would otherwise have been a deprived and devastatingly lonely life. There are still prisons that use the practice of solitary confinement, and an astral companion in these circumstances could save the sanity of the person concerned.

The magician is not an ordinary human being. He stands outside of the throng of humanity. It has to be like that. In the main, a magician serves humanity, or should, and one can only serve if one is far enough away from it and gains a perspective.

Creating an astral form is only dangerous if you forget the simple rules of the game:

- never use it to excess;

- never copy the face and form of an actual human being;

- never use anyone's energy except your own to create a form;

- always dismiss a form by reabsorbing it and transmuting it back into energy;

- always bless the astral matter you have used;

- look up the word "ethics" in your dictionary and apply it.

What possible use can a created homunculi have? Created forms have been used from ancient times to act as messengers or protectors; to search out forgotten records and secret documents. The high-ranking lamas of Tibet have used such forms for centuries, often as simulacrums of themselves that were and are sent to other lamaseries to speak with their peers. And yes, I know I have told you not to copy the form of a living being, but these are top flight adepts of a different culture to ours, a culture used to a high level of discipline. Stick to what you have been told—it is highly unlikely that you are a high-level lama!

All astral forms are created in the same way by impressing a mental image onto a portion of proto matter. When separated from its matrix and programmed via a particle of your own energy, it can become a mobile energy unit suitable for small tasks. It will seldom become visible to other eyes unless you yourself have a substance in your physical makeup known as ectoplasm.

Homunculi have only a short span of existence. When the energy runs out, they return to the astral matrix in the same way that a drop of sea water returns to the ocean. This does *not* mean they can be abused.

Every time such a form is activated and imbued with human energy, the astral matter that provides its form is blessed by the close cooperation between humankind and the subtle level. *To abuse, torment, or otherwise demean that matter is to invite karmic retribution.* Remember that *you* are totally responsible for these forms. They cannot refuse you, they do not have the ability to distinguish good from bad, they are totally reliant upon you during their short period of existence.

You are not going to be able to create mobile forms on your first, second, third, or fortieth try. It can take years to perfect the task. It is not even the prime object of this book: that object is to teach you how to create forms and then manifest them in the physical world. The creation of homunculi is the highest level of such thought-forming. If you do try it, remember that if it goes wrong you must disintegrate it at once. Never try to recreate it exactly—the matrix holds a record and will simply set up the same sample complete with its original mistakes.

If, and it is an "if," you succeed, remember that to keep it going it will need to be recharged, but only for a maximum of three or four times, then it must be allowed to run down completely. If you attempt to keep it going and keep recharging it, it will slowly begin to exhibit a rudimentary intelligence of its own. If this happens it will begin to override your wishes and commands . . . frankly, you are in deep trouble at this point. You can find yourself "haunted," or your home filled with a presence that, while not evil of itself, can feel alien and disturbing.

One of the more disturbing aspects of this kind of work may occur at the moment of return. This takes the form of a momentary paralysis. You can find yourself unable to move, even unable to open your eyes at times. It will pass within a few minutes, but at the time it can cause panic in the inexperienced astral traveler.

Remember, I told you that an astral body is actually formed from proto matter as and when you need it, and that it does not actually "hang around" all the time. One of the things you have to learn when using an astral body is how to make it go where you want it to go and behave how you wish it to behave. It's not hard and you will find it easy to get the hang of it, but it can produce a few problems at the time.

I was a refugee from my island home during World War I, and one night at the height of the blitz on the Yorkshire city of Sheffield I decided to try and get back home. I built up an astral image of my old room, and outside of the room there was a walled garden. It had a window seat that was a part of the actual wall (the walls were some twenty-six-inches thick in this two-hundred-year-old cottage), and it was a favorite dreaming place of mine. Without any preliminaries, or indeed any warning at all, I found myself standing on the window seat with my face pressed tightly against the cold glass of the window. I was looking out onto the garden and could see quite clearly the full moon through the glass, but couldn't move. It was as if I was stuck to the window frame. I tried in vain to wrench myself free and began to panic, thinking I would not be able to get back and would find myself actually in Jersey and under Nazi rule. I heard movement behind me and realized for the first time that the cottage was occupied. There was a high-pitched scream and that shattered the frozen moment of time. I seemed to fall back into my bed in England with a thud. My heart was racing and I was drenched in sweat.

I related this to my parents in the morning, and they explained to me that this was something that happened when one was new to this form of bilocation. After the war I discovered the cottage had indeed been occupied at the time by a mother and her two young daughters.

I have always tried to take the advice of the Welsh psychologist from my childhood and keep what I have seen to myself. But every now and then there comes a time when the time seems right to share an insight.

When news of the D-day Normandy landings came, everyone went a little crazy—the end of the war was in sight. There was still a long way to go, but we felt that the tide had really turned. We listened to every bulletin as it came over the radio and it soon became clear that securing the beachheads would not be an easy task. Many young men did not even get off the beach on which they had landed with such hope.

By the beginning of the second day, things were still in the balance and every foot of sand was being fought for with dogged courage. That night, with the brashness of a teenager, I decided to go and see for myself. Born and brought up within sight of the Normandy coast, I knew it well enough to build its image as I had known it prewar. The image lasted for an instant, then I was in the thick of battle. There was no noise, though I could sense the vibration of it. There were landing crafts along the stretch of beach as far as I could see. Men were wading through knee-high water and hitting the sand with their guns already firing.

I seemed to be standing just below a sand dune about ten feet high and covered with rough coarse grass. Above me and set back from the actual beach was a concrete building of the type known as a bunker. Crouching below the dune were several soldiers, most of them sporting American flashes on their shoulders. I was intrigued by the fact that these flashes seemed to glow. As I watched, the group gathered itself for an attack. The first three men made it across the intervening space to a point beneath the bunker, the fourth stopped in midstride and spun round, his eyes wide with shock, and collapsed in a heap. For a moment it seemed as if he was only wounded, and he struggled to turn over to lie on his back. He looked right at me and saw me, smiled brilliantly, then his eyes went blank and I woke in my bed screaming my head off. I never tried looking in on a battlefield again, but I remember the battered and faint name on his helmet: "Larsen."

Did I have a vivid dream, or was it real? I have never tried to trace him. If it was a dream it did not matter. If it was real, then he passed with someone caring about him at the moment of death. It was as if I was there as a witness.

Note, however, that in order to get to my objective I first built an image on the astral of the place I wanted to get to. This was the way I was taught and it has always proved to be a good signpost.

Once you get into building forms out of the astral matter, you can sometimes be faced with somebody else's forms that have gone AWOL. Unless a form is absorbed when no longer needed, it can wrench itself free of the matrix and go wandering on its own. Because it has a portion of sentience, albeit a very low portion, it will seek out sources of energy to which it can attach itself like a limpet to a rock. In this, such AWOL forms are very much like a succubus, but they are easier to get rid of. Get into a shower and scrub yourself down with handfuls of coarse salt. Simple, yes, but it works, although *not* on succubi, I'm afraid. You can see the difference between such "shells" and other denizens of the astral. They are almost always hollow. Try to get behind them and you will see they are merely a facade. They will always try to face you and will never willingly turn their back on you.

We come now to a supposition on my part. I have long been interested in the half-human figures we come across in mythology, particularly in Greek mythology—Furies, fauns, centaurs, satyrs, or djinn, to say nothing of creatures such as mermaids, yeti, faeries, elves, and so on. I think it is more than possible that over long periods of time such creatures have been built up from astral matter and have achieved the status of archetypes. Having caught the imagination of human beings, they become caught up in the rich creative power of our life-wave and fed with curiosity, humor, lust, and dreams to such an extent that they have freed themselves from restraint and continue to exist on the astral level as separate entities. I also suspect that some of them—faeries, elves, and others—have managed to lift themselves to a higher level—the mental—and become fully self-empowering. They are then able to project themselves and their chosen forms into the mind and dreams of human beings.

One of the most fascinating and carefully researched books you can read on this and similar subjects is *Creatures from Inner Space,* by Stan Gooch. He is the author of many books on similar subjects (see references), and writes in an easy-to-read style and with a directness rare in this particular subject. He is also a man of letters and impeccable credentials. You will gain much information from this book, including the fact that if you are left-handed you are more likely to be psychic. Just don't read it late at night when you are alone in the house!

Astral forms can also be impinged upon your consciousness from a level higher up than that of the astral. Teachings and psychic experiences designed to awaken knowledge held deep within the higher self can be projected by beings from the mental and spiritual levels. This often, though not always, involves a disassociation from normal time. In appendix E, I (D. A. N.) have recounted an experience of my own that deals with this phenomenon, which remains, after some twenty-five years, as vivid in my mind as if it was yesterday.

Remember that all this information is subject to your own abilities and talents. Don't try to be clever, or fast. It can take a year of preparation and effort to create something useful, and even recognizable. There will be many mistakes, and they will require complete disintegration, plus the breaking-up of the intended program. You can absorb and transmute it, or turn it to ice and smash it, or cancel it by sending it into the unmanifest. Do not try to recreate the same program—always make it a little different.

Unlike an elemental created from a mixture of your own elements and proto matter, you must bring a homunculus to life by energizing it via solar energy passed through the solar plexus. This means it will run down after eight to ten hours and will need to be recharged. Because it bears the stamp of your personality, it will eventually begin to respond to situations as you would. The longer it exists, the closer it will get to becoming a "false" you. As soon as it shows this tendency, break it down and reabsorb it. If allowed to continue, it will begin to fill the house with a presence that can be extremely uncomfortable for all concerned.

There are precedents for this kind of half-life, and one can be found in the legend of the raising of Osiris. Having found her husband's body, Isis summoned the gods and demanded of them that they return his life to him. However, as Ptah, the god of life, reminded her, "Once life has departed its earthly shell, it cannot be called back."

However, the body, uncorrupted as it was, might receive a portion of life force donated by another. This would enliven it long enough to achieve the desire of

Isis to conceive a son. The next best thing to the actual seed of Osiris was that of his son Anubis, born to Osiris' full sister Nephthys. In offering a day and a night of his life force, Anubis would be returning a small portion of the life given to him by his father. Thus it would have been the seed of her foster son and nephew that impregnated the goddess and brought about the birth of Horus, the falcon-headed Avenger.

Although legend tells of the reanimation of Osiris, it is a tale that has grown in the telling over five thousand years. Anubis carried the same gene pool as his father and his aunt/foster-mother, so for her to conceive an "Osiris" child, the logical donor had to be his son. (Note that the modern techniques of genetic manipulation are very close to this kind of "magical" work.) The combination of a thought form of Osiris animated by the life energy of his son, and the enactment of the Great Rite of Hathor could have brought about the conception of a special child. We know little of the inner meanings of such rites, but the fact that the legend has been held in the racial memory for so long bears witness to its truth.

Controlling what you do or create is a vital part of all magical work. Self-control is at the top of the list. Controlling all three selves—physical, mental, and spiritual—must become a daily practice. To control anything, one must first know and understand the nature of what is to be controlled. Traditionally to do this one must name it; in other words, you must always know exactly what you are doing, its nature, and the projected outcome of the work. In the biblical story of Adam naming the animals created by God, we have an example: Adam was given rulership over the animal kingdom (a rulership we have consistently abused), and for this to be absolute, he needed to know and name each one.

Ask yourself here and now, *What do I know about myself at all levels?* When you can do this, you will know your *true* magical name. This will be far more than the often fanciful appellation you take at initiation. It will mean *you* at every level of your being, *you* as a potential divinity. By means of this you will come to know the world around you in the true sense of being *Adonai Ha Aretz*.

ASTRAL ELEMENTS

Because the astral level is a prototype, it contains the premanifested forms of all things, including the elements. Each level holds its own variation of them. The mental level variation on the elements is the concept of them, while the spiritual level holds them almost at their purest, but that is reserved for the level of the Primal Wave and contains the essence of them in the form of the Four Holy Creatures. But we may encounter the familiar elements on the astral level in many forms and variations.

Astral Water

Here we see the element of water as the Great Bitter Sea of Binah, the sea of dreams and desires. It may become the unseen River of Life that flows from birth to death and back again. It holds within it all the sea gods and goddesses, from Poseidon to Aphrodite.

It was from this inner sea that there emerged teachers such as Oannes, Ea, and Dagon, who taught the primitive tribes living on the coast of North Africa during the earliest times. It was from here that the disciples caught nets full of fish, the symbol of those they would teach in the future. It was the storm on such a hidden ocean that was calmed by Yehehsua, and upon which he walked to the consternation of the apostles.

It is the sea on which Odysseus sailed on his long voyage home after the fall of Troy, for that journey was surely not a physical one, but a cloak for the journey of initiation that he sought and was granted by Athena.

The fairy tales of nixies, undines, and mermaids all have their place here, as well as those tales of lunacy and werewolves when the moon is full. For we are creatures born of the physical sea and carry its traces in our salty blood. The great tides of the moon and the seasons sweep through us and affect us as surely as it affects the oceans of our world.

Such is the power of this inner ocean that we can use it to empower thought forms, especially in the religion of Wicca; witness its use in the ritual of "Drawing down the Moon." Moon power can add an extra infusion of energy if the thought form is built on a growing moon or during the night of a full moon.

Astral Fire

Fire has always been seen as a transmuting element, and the use of it as a means of offering a sacrifice to the gods has been in use since the beginning of recorded history. Its astral, unseen presence can take the form of solar winds and the radiation between the stars. It is also present as Light in the auric envelope of human beings and all living objects.

Physical fire has always been regarded with great awe, and the solar gods have been given rulership over prophesy, healing, and music, as well as light and heat.

What in occult terminology is called "the sun behind the sun" or "the sun at midnight" can also be seen as a part of the astral presence of the element of fire. Energy drawn from the solar winds, solar flares, or passed through the solar plexus nerve center can also be used to energize thought forms. A more advanced technique of building such forms could possibly be utilized using the creative essence of fire on the mental and spiritual levels. There is little to go on concerning this, but it would be an interesting project to try out at some point in the future.

Salamanders, the elementals of fire, are often used by adults and children alike to trace images in a coal or wood fire. The presence of fire has a stimulating effect on human beings, and its radiating heat and light often induce a flow of words giving rise to music or songs and stories told around a fire.

Astral Air

Air is a strange element, for even in a physical state it cannot be seen except if used to fill some form such as a balloon, a sail, a parachute, or a tire. Nevertheless, its astral power is manifested whenever we pray, invoke, evoke, or use breath to manifest words.

The ancient gods of air are always those who rule the other gods of that particular pantheon. They are the rulers of high mountains, thunder, and lightning, and the great winds are their servants. The astral power of air manifests as the words used to program thought forms, guardians, and homunculi. The power of the spoken word is second to none, and every magician worth her salt will develop the magical voice with which to summon or dismiss.

The sylphs of the element are often confused with the faery folk, but are not of that evolution at all. They are entirely separate and must be considered as such. Birds are another part of this, and their patterns of flight have often been used in the past to predict the future. Sound is another astral manifestation of air, since it cannot be seen but can be heard. The power of words is locked into the practice of the Magical Breath, and that, in turn, is the key to astral air magic.

Astral Earth

This area belongs to the practice of building the Inner Kingdom, an exercise that every aspiring magician should undertake. It takes the form of creating an inner world, which the magician gradually explores and makes his own. The creation of such a kingdom is a way of following in the footsteps of the Creator. In the same manner that a child will copy his parents, pretending to go to work or clean house, play at being a teacher or a truck driver, a nurse, or a fireman, so we human beings play at being God. By creating an inner universe and peopling it with carefully constructed thought forms of beings and animals of our own creation, we emulate the creation of our own universe.

The elementals of earth, the gnomes, are one small part of the faery race, and can often be found in houses and gardens where there is a happy and loving atmosphere. They often befriend children or take on the guardianship of homes for their own delight.

The inner aspect of earth encompasses the great Group Souls of the younger brethren of the animal, vegetable, and mineral world. It is one area in which we, the human race, have failed miserably. As guardians and initiators of this younger kingdom, we are a total failure.

21 DISMISSING A THOUGHT FORM

Herbie on: a European in Tibet; witness to marvels; Lung-gom-pa and tumo; the artist followed by the thought form of his God; Madame David-Neel creates "Friar Tuck"; the thought form exteriorizes; Dion Fortune's astral wolf; what to do when you lose control.

IN SEPTEMBER 1969, one of Europe's most remarkable women died peacefully at her home in France. She had attained the age of one hundred and two—something approaching a miracle, given the life she had led.

Madame Alexandra David-Neel read the science-fiction works of Jules Verne as a girl, and was inspired to a career of discovery and adventure. From an early age she began to travel. When she exhausted the potential of Europe, she set her sights farther afield and headed for Asia. There she became the first European woman ever to enter the mountain fastnesses of Tibet. She stayed—with one brief break—more than twenty years.

Alexandra David-Neel was no mundane tourist. She was fascinated by Tibetan culture, a medieval feudalism that had remained undisturbed for centuries. But most of all, she was fascinated by Tibetan religion and esoteric practice. In a land without roads, where the thin air and biting cold made even the shortest journey an ordeal, she traveled from monastery to monastery, from village to village, seeking out the hermits, mystics, and magicians who could teach her firsthand what she wanted to know.

So successful was she in her quest that she became the first European women ever to become a lama. But more importantly, she witnessed, investigated, and in some instances practiced the esoteric techniques that had made Tibet the magical capital of the planet.

On one occasion she watched the curiously loping figure of a *lung-gom-pa* runner, one of the country's mystic message-carriers, and later discovered the trance techniques that allowed these men to carry on without pause or exhaustion, mile after mile, until they reached their destination.

On another, she practiced *tumo*, the complex visualization of certain symbols, which, combined with an inner goddess contact, triggered the generation of great body heat. Madame David-Neel discovered that the real adepts of this technique were required to sit naked in the snow and dry out three blankets soaked in a freezing mountain stream using their body heat alone. When this ordeal was complete, they earned the title "Repa," after the thin cotton tunic that was their only garment thereafter.

But perhaps her most remarkable experience began one evening with the arrival in her camp of a well-known Tibetan artist she had met some years before.

The man had changed dramatically in the intervening time. He seemed distracted, almost feverish, and though he insisted he was not ill, he seemed constantly nervous and ill-at-ease. More peculiar still, Madame David-Neel was able to discern that he was perpetually followed by a monstrously large, shadowy presence, its shape no more solid than the last wisps of morning mist. From her studies of local Buddhism, she recognized the figure as one of the many fearsome gods in the Tibetan pantheon.

Intrigued, she began to question the man. Like most Tibetan artists, his paintings were of a religious nature, and since he had last met Madame David-Neel, he had formed a special devotion to a particular deity. Using old scriptures as a reference, he had painted the deity again and again. It had become the sole subject of his daily meditations. He had, he said, decided to devote his life to it. The deity he spoke of, Madame David-Neel quickly realized, was the same shadowy figure that now followed him.

As an initiate lama, Madame David-Neel was familiar with the Tibetan doctrine of the tulpa, a creature created by the power of thought, but this was the first time she had actually seen one. She was so fascinated she decided to find out if she could create a tulpa for herself. To this end, she began a daily regime of visualization. The creature she visualized was a plump little monk, modeled on Robin Hood's cheerful spiritual advisor, Friar Tuck.

At first she concentrated on seeing the monk in her mind's eye as vividly as possible, working hard to fill in the smallest details of his appearance. Once she had achieved this, she switched to visualizing him as if he were physically present, as Pema Tense did with his Yidam. It took some weeks to achieve, but she was finally able to see her creation as objectively real.

But while Madame David-Neel never lost sight of the fact that she had simply created a hallucination, as time went on strange things began to happen. The day came when she caught sight of her monk in the camp even though she had not visualized him. Two days later, he was back again, still without her input. The sightings became more and more frequent, and the monk himself underwent a sinister change, losing weight and taking on a shifty aspect. When others of her party began to ask about the mysterious visitor, she realized her creation had moved out of her control.

Something similar happened to the British occultist and psychic Violet Penry-Evans, better known by her pen name, Dion Fortune, when she discovered what she called an "astral wolf" lying on the bottom of her bed. Although she saw the creature as objectively real (it even had a degree of weight), her psychoanalytic training convinced her it was actually a projected thought form that had arisen in her own unconscious mind. Wolves and similar wild animals are often symbolic of repressed instincts, generally, though not invariably, sexual. When she tried to push the creature off the bed, it turned and growled at her—another thought form had shown itself to be out of its creator's control.

If it could happen to adepts like Alexandra David-Neel and Dion Fortune, it could happen to you. So what do you do if your conjured thought form decides to go its own way and cause mischief?

The first thing to remember is Pema Tense's basic insight: However real or powerful a thought form may appear, it is still a thought form. However thoroughly you have enshrouded it in astral proto matter, however powerful its source of energy, it is still essentially a creature of your imagination. And what a trained imagination can make, a trained imagination can unmake.

Thus, if you are faced with a rogue thought form created consciously or unconsciously, by yourself or someone else, your first line of attack should be imaginal. If the entity appears objective, "grip" it by internalizing its image and visualizing it as vividly and clearly as possible within your mind. Once you have done so, you can then visualize its destruction. You might, for example, imagine it catching fire and burning up or crumbling into dust, like a vampire staked by

Buffy, or exploding into fragments, or turning to water and sinking into the earth. Find the visualization that that suits you best and use it.

If you feel this sounds almost too easy to be true, you may be right. Some thought forms are resistant to this form of attack and need to be tackled differently. Broadly speaking, as you will have gathered from everything you've so far learned in this book, there are three basic types of thought form.

First, there is what I might call a pure thought form, which exists only as a mental construct. This type tends to become obsessive if you lose control and can sometimes communicate with others telepathically. The visualizations mentioned previously should be enough to deal with it.

Next, there is the thought form that has been injected, so to speak, with the elemental essence of proto matter—the type of magical thought form Dolores has been teaching you how to construct in this book. While you might possibly undermine one of these with an appropriate visualization, a banishing is likely to be more effective. Given our Qabalistic training, Dolores or I would tend to use the Lesser Banishing Ritual of the Pentagram. Qabalistically trained or not, you can use it, too—it's included as appendix C of this book, and you should use the astral techniques you've learned to potentize your visualizations.

Finally, there is the thought form that has absorbed something of its creator's essence. This was certainly the case with Dion Fortune's wolf, which emerged from her unconscious and represented an actual aspect of her psyche. It may also have been the case with Madame David-Neel's monk. In both instances, these two adepts decided on the third method of destroying their creations: absorption. In both instances, it proved an extraordinarily difficult process.

Absorption, or reabsorption, is a tricky, even potentially dangerous method that depends almost entirely on the skill and psycho-spiritual status of the user. If you have experience in the esoteric arts, decide for yourself whether you have reached a level where you can safely use it. If you are a beginner, or have no experience at all, you would be well advised to call in help, rather than attempt the operation yourself.

Should you decide to go ahead, this is what you have to do:

First, ensure you are in a state of total harmony and calm. This will require a period of meditation—sorry, tranquilizers won't hack it. It is an excellent idea to make a meditational contact with your spiritual ideal—the Christ, Buddha, Mohammed, or equivalent figure from your own tradition. Please don't skimp on this preparation. The operation is difficult, even for someone of experience, and you will need to lay down a firm foundation.

Once you are satisfied with your spiritual state, call up an astral image of the thought form you need to destroy, and try to divine its essential nature. This is a vital step and, like your initial preparation, can take some time. Use both intuition and observation for the job. The "feel" of the creature will give you clues, as will its attitudes and behavior. If you are attempting to destroy a malign entity—and it's difficult to see why you should be trying to destroy any other sort—you will probably find it is driven by anger, hatred, lust, or a desperation for self-preservation that leads to a type of vampirism. (By this latter category, I don't mean the mild absorption of energy so many thought forms indulge in, but rather an uncaring theft of energy that injures the victim.)

Once you have categorized the creature, you should begin to meditate on the opposite of the force that drives it—love for hate, sustenance for vampirism, detachment for lust, and so on. Continue your meditation until you are thoroughly suffused with the opposing quality.

Next—and this is the part that makes the entire operation so difficult—you must succeed in elevating yourself to a level of spiritual understanding from which you no longer feel anything toward the entity except perhaps pity for its state of ignorance. You must come to realize the essential emptiness of the thing you are about to absorb. Only when this is completely achieved can you safely proceed, and even then, you must proceed with compassion.

Once you have achieved the necessary state, open your aura and suck it in. (Vampiric thought forms will sometimes help you by forming an attachment through which they intend to draw off your energy. This will manifest on the astral as a cord connecting to your solar plexus. Use this cord to pull the creature toward you.) For your own sake, proceed slowly and gradually. A sudden interiorization of a malign thought form constitutes a considerable shock to your system, and you might not be able to maintain your spiritual equilibrium.

As you begin to absorb the thought form, you will feel your own nature resonate to its essence. If you are absorbing hatred, you could find your thoughts turning toward someone you dislike, if sexual lust, you may experience a turn-on, and so forth. Whatever the reaction, you must take immediate steps to neutralize it and regain your initial state of detached harmony.

Success in an operation of this type is marked by an unmistakable sensation of spiritual exhilaration and power. Enjoy it. It's the sign you've done a difficult job well.

Appendix A

THE STARBORN

THE FOLLOWING HTML CODE will allow readers with their own Web pages to experiment with the concept of cyberspace.

star1.html

```
<HTML><HEAD> <TITLE>star1</TITLE></HEAD><BODY
BGCOLOR="#ffffff"><H2 ALIGN=CENTER><FONT COLOR="#ED181E">THE
STARBORN</FONT></H2><P ALIGN=
CENTER><B>&copy; 1998 Dolores Ashcroft-Nowicki
</B></P><P> </P><P>  </P><P><B> Oh ye who stand within this Temple of the Mysteries listen unto to me. Place your heart within my heart and your hand within my hand and together we will set forth upon a journey to the realms of the spirit that dwell within each man and woman that liveth upon the earth.
</B></P><P><B> Relax your body and seek deep within yourselves for that seed of silence wherein lives the essential essence of the soul. </B></P><P><B> Stop up your earthly ears and listen only to the words that guide your inner and higher consciousness. </B></P><P><B> Leave behind the scents of earth and prepare your nostrils for the perfumes of Eden; fold your hands within your vestments and let my words touch and caress your souls. </B></P><P><B> I will pour you wine from grapes never seen upon the earth and feed you with bread that was never yet garnered from this planet's fields. Suspend your senses and live within their higher and finer selves, and so we will leave behind all that we know and hold dear. </B></P><P><B> From each heart there emerges a golden thread. It flows out to the Temple Chalice and pours itself into it. Thus we are linked and may begin our journey. </B></P><P
ALIGN=CENTER><A HREF="star2.html"> Begin
</A></P><P> </P><P>NOTES:</P><P> What is given here (and on subsequent pages) is the basic script for the pathworking, along with its relevant links. You should feel free to deal with each page creatively, adding such graphics, animations, or soundfiles as you feel would aid the visualization process. </P><P> There is a strong case for recording the entire script and inserting it, possibly without text, as a
```

series of sound files playable as streaming audio, assuming Web space and your technical expertise allow. </P><P> These notes are for your guidance only, and should be deleted from the finished page. </BODY></HTML>

star2.html

<HTML><HEAD> <TITLE>star2</TITLE></HEAD><BODY
BGCOLOR="#ffffff"><P><FONT
COLOR="#ED181E">STARBORN</FONT></P><P> </P><P> </P><P
><B> The Temple begins to move in a circle turning to the right, the sensation of
spinning grows stronger and stronger until we feel pinned to our seats and the whole
Temple spins out of this dimension and into another, higher one. </B></P><P
ALIGN=CENTER><A HREF="star3.html"> Continue
</A></P><P> </P><P>NOTES:</P><P> This would seem the perfect place for
an animated illustration. </P><P> These notes are for your guidance only, and should
be deleted from the finished page. </BODY></HTML>

star3.html

<HTML><HEAD> <TITLE>star3</TITLE></HEAD><BODY
BGCOLOR="#ffffff"><P><FONT
COLOR="#ED181E">STARBORN</FONT></P><P> </P><P> </P><P
><B> Still spinning, we feel that we are traveling through layer after layer of the
astral levels. Then gradually the movement begins to slow down, and finally it is a
gentle movement making a slow circle, then it stops. We open our inner eyes and discover that the Temple has subtly changed. </B></P><P> </P><P ALIGN=CEN-
TER><A REF="star4.html">Continue</A></P><P> </P><P>NOTES:</P><P>
Again, animation might be useful here, suggesting the changing nature of the Temple.
</P><P> These notes are for your guidance only, and should be deleted from the finished page. </BODY></HTML>

star4.html

<HTML><HEAD> <TITLE>star4</TITLE></HEAD><BODY
BGCOLOR="#ffffff"><P><FONT
COLOR="#ED181E">STARBORN</FONT></P><P> </P><P> </P><P
><B> Its pillars glow with light. Each one is a single block of crystal, through which
filters a diffused light. The altar is solid light. Beneath us the floor has gone and we

see only the star fields of the infinite cosmos. </B></P><P><B> We look up, and see the same thing; there are only the walls surrounding us, then gradually they, too, fade and disappear. </B></P><P><B> We sit in our chairs, the altar in the center, the pillars glowing either side of the east. </B></P><P><B> Then the altar blazes with light dazzling our inner sight, and fades from view; the same thing happens with the pillars, then with our chairs, so we are suspended in space. </B></P><P ALIGN=CENTER><A HREF="star5.html">Continue</A></P><P> </BODY></HTML>

star5.html

<HTML><HEAD> <TITLE>star5</TITLE></HEAD><BODY BGCOLOR="#ffffff"><P><FONT COLOR="#ED181E">STARBORN</FONT></P><P> </P><P> </P><P ><B> We come closer together and look at each familiar face, seeing it clearly, then the earthly forms fade away and instead of human shape, there are just glowing geometric shapes composed of millions of tiny points of light. </B></P><P><B> We come together and fuse into one beautiful star-shaped being. Be quiet now and allow yourselves to feel each others thoughts and patterns. We are one and yet we are separate. We can hide nothing from each other when fused like this. </B></P><P> </P><P ALIGN=CENTER><A HREF="star6.html"> Continue</A></BODY></HTML>

star6.html

<HTML><HEAD> <TITLE>star6</TITLE></HEAD><BODY BGCOLOR="#ffffff"><P><FONT COLOR="#ED181E">STARBORN</FONT></P><P> </P><P> </P><P ><B> Now the "Star" moves across Space, crossing the star lanes and the vast deeps where no stars shine. </B></P><P><B> We cross time and dimensions and come at last to the Great Central Sun, from which all Matter flows. </B></P><P><B> It is from this *sun* that all things have emerged and to which they will return. This is our true birthplace, for we are, as has been said, Starborn. </B></P><P><B> We are caught in the Sun's pull and begin to circle it, joining in the Great Dance of Becoming. </B></P><P><B> We are not the only ones; there are thousands of stars dancing together. Each one is sure of its place in the pattern drawn by the Great Sun. Each, in turn, swings close into the great Orb, and then out again, and so the light is woven into shapes that will become planets and galaxies in the far future. </B></P><P ALIGN=CENTER><A

HREF="star7.html">Continue</A></P><P
ALIGN=CENTER> </P><P>NOTES:</P><P> At this stage, music would be
an enormous enhancement of the experience. </P><P> These notes are for your guidance only, and should be deleted from the finished page. </BODY></HTML>

star7.html

<HTML><HEAD> <TITLE>star7</TITLE></HEAD><BODY
BGCOLOR="#ffffff"><P><FONT
COLOR="#ED181E">STARBORN</FONT></P><P> </P><P> </P><P
><B> Then we become aware of the voice of the Great Sun; it speaks to each one of
us as a person, telling us of our destiny and what has been created for us.
</B></P><P><B> We understand our Oneness with all things, and that even the Great
Sun is one part of an even greater *whole*; that there is another *Sun* behind this Sun to
which all others owe allegiance, and so it goes on. </B></P><P><B> We listen to the
voice within us, hearing and seeing our faults and our strengths and accepting the
teaching that is being offered to us, *if we so desire.* </B></P><P ALIGN=CEN-
TER><A HREF="star8.html">Continue</A></P><P
ALIGN=CENTER> </P><P>NOTES:</P><P> Resist the temptation to add an
audio message here in the voice of the Great Sun. If the experience of the working is
to have spiritual benefit, participants must listen to an inner voice at this stage.
</P><P> These notes are for your guidance only, and should be deleted from the fin-
ished page. </BODY></HTML>

star8.html

<HTML><HEAD> <TITLE>star8</TITLE></HEAD><BODY
BGCOLOR="#ffffff"><P><FONT
COLOR="#ED181E">STARBORN</FONT></P><P> </P><P> </P><P
><B> Then we are drawn out of the great dancing circle and once more traverse the
cosmos until we see the star forms we know and recognize. </B></P><P><B> Slowly
we withdraw from our union and become single entities again. In the quietness of
Time and Space we resume our human shapes and wait patiently. </B></P><P
ALIGN=CENTER><A HREF="star9.html">Continue</A></BODY></HTML>

star9.html

<HTML><HEAD> <TITLE>star9</TITLE></HEAD><BODY
BGCOLOR="#ffffff"><P><FONT
COLOR="#ED181E">STARBORN</FONT></P><P> </P><P> </P><P
><B> Around us form the walls of the Temple, then the pillars and the altar.
</B></P><P><B> The floor and ceiling return and we are once again within our own
Place of Worship. </B></P><P><B> It begins to spin faster and faster until we spin
out of this area of Time and into our own, gradually slowing down until we stop.
</B></P><P><B> There on the center of the altar is the chalice filled with our life
force. We withdraw the heart thread for it, and are fed with power, life, joy, and radi-
ance from the Grail. </B></P><P ALIGN=CENTER><A HREF="star10.html"> Continue </A></P><P> </P><P>NOTES:</P><P> A particularly good point for a
graphic, since participants are now at the stage of "earthing" their experience.
</P><P> These notes are for your guidance only, and should be deleted from the fin-
ished page. </BODY></HTML>

star10.html

<HTML><HEAD> <TITLE>star10</TITLE></HEAD><BODY
BGCOLOR="#ffffff"><P><FONT
COLOR="#ED181E">STARBORN</FONT></P><P> </P><P><B> Open
your earthly eyes my dear ones, open your earthly senses and your inner heart centers. </B></P><P><B> Open them and let what you have been given pour out into the
world on this Day of the Sun's Return. </B></P><P><B> Fill the earth with your
power and your joy; let it spill over, for this is the neverending flow of Light that fills
the cosmos. However, it must have a channel for its power to enter any planet. You
are such channels, now and forever. </B></P><P><B> Lift up your heads and rejoice,
for you are the vanguard of those that will come. Thus it shall be now and evermore.
The great traditions of the earth will unite and form a Gateway of Light, through
which shall come the Masters of the Hidden ways. </B></P><P><B> Look upon your
company and be glad, for *you are the starborn ones*. </B></P><P ALIGN=CEN-
TER><A HREF="star1.html">Home</A></BODY></HTML>

Appendix B

I, SQUARED

THEORIES ON WHETHER or not thought forms exist (and are usable) come to an interesting point when what you imagine is not physically possible. If what you imagine has nothing at all (or very little) to do with everyday reality, then how useful is the thought itself? I believe every thought is important, and even the oddest thoughts have many uses. The best example comes from complex algebra.

No groaning allowed for nonmathematicians: I'm not going to use more than a couple pieces of math, and none of these will be mind-blowing.

Complex math is a system of algebra that allows for roots of negative numbers. Remember that class in grade school in which the teacher taught that the square root of -4 was not -2, but that, in fact, it didn't exist? Maybe your teacher even stated cryptically that it became 2i, an imaginary number. In complex math, this little "i" is the heart and soul of every problem. The definition of "i" is: i2 = -1.

After being taught this form of math, I remembered that cryptic statement from the fourth grade: These numbers are imaginary. They don't exist in real life. Yet, thanks to my training in physics, I understand they produce answers experiment and observation dictate. How is this possible? If these numbers don't exist in 3-D reality, then how can they be used to predict correct answers?

My solution to that is that they do exist in reality, but not in a visible manner. They exist in your mind, that little corner of your consciousness (or unconsciousness) reserved for holding these numbers and performing calculations so you can write the answer down on the paper in front of you. But since that is the only place they exist, and they seem to be able to predict outcomes for real events, they have a direct impact on reality; therefore, your mind has a direct impact on reality.

I understand that psychologists have been stating this for a while now, and it's considered proper to think that your view of reality is completely fabricated by your unconscious mind based on input. But this implies that there is something that exists beyond the information that gives us the reality we perceive. Just as a computer will only show the end product on screen, and not the unbelievably long list of functions that were performed to get the product, your mind also leaves the useless details out. Unfortunately, these details include exactly where the information came from. But it's a fair assumption then, if we make any parallels between the mind and a computer, that, just like typing on a keyboard or clicking on a mouse, you can interject your thoughts and expectations into reality and expect to get feedback. I'm not implying that you can change reality completely just by thinking, any more than you can change the program you're in just by typing. But, just like the program, you can change the "program options" of reality to make your life easier. This is still only a subtle change, but a change nonetheless.

I've had a psychology professor tell me that if we were just heads on a lab shelf being fed computer-generated impressions of life, or just programs on a machine, we'd never notice. There's no way to tell if what we see is real. The notion of complex math, and my previous argument, suggests that there's more than what's being seen, and that we can affect it. But the idea that we can affect it at all is a good reason to believe that there is no such "program" that controls what we see. In the context of the computer example I used, some options that we can change should have "administrator passwords" on them to lock us out, but they don't seem to.

Now, I guess I had better offer some backing for my statements, before my argument dies of criticism. For the first point, I will ask a question: What makes up reality? I'll bet your answer can be rephrased to say, "Whatever I see, hear, taste, feel, and smell." Your answer might include feelings not attributed to these senses, but such feelings are always defined in terms of the five regular senses. You "feel" that slight gust of wind you intuitively know means you're not alone in the room. You "see" an event that you shouldn't be able to, but can. You "hear" things that other people can't. Anything that we receive as personal information comes from these five sources, whether the phenomenon is physical or not. The senses aren't just physical functions; they're concepts, axioms from which we define everything else. Even the idea that $1 + 1 = 2$ is validated because you can see the result.

I conclude that, since the only information we get about our external life is from these five senses, they, to all intents and purposes, define reality. Next, let's assume that you observe some event. It can be anything, but for this example let's say it's a mechanical event—a lever, or something moving past you at fast speed; something that has measurable quantities. Since you've seen this event, perhaps heard or felt it as well, it fits into the definition of reality.

Now let's reintroduce the complex math. There are methods of applying the math to the problem (quantum mechanics for the moving object, advanced engineering methods for the lever), so we'll gather the information in two ways. First, we'll take measurements from the event itself by use of whatever lab equipment necessary. This also fits into reality for the same reason.

Let me make a note here: I don't think its a valid point to say that complex numbers fit into reality the same way that the moving object does. In fact, everything we see and anything we learn points to the fact that the roots of negative numbers are not only a ridiculous notion, but also completely unnecessary. After all, since there is an infinite amount of observable numbers, why shouldn't they be able to solve all of our problems? Since a complex number can't be associated with something that is seen, heard, felt, tasted, or smelled, then it doesn't exist as far as your senses tell you.

Let's now predict the outcome of the experiment with our knowledge of math and physics. I'm sure that you don't want to see actual calculations performed, especially if you're not a physicist, but assume the answers match up. In the spirit of good scientists, let's repeat the measurements many times, and check the calculations for errors. Let's assume they still match. Since the math properly predicts the outcome of the experiment beyond coincidence, those imaginary numbers with no bearing on reality are now associated with something that is real. So, from that association, the numbers can, in a manner, be accessed by the senses, in the form of the event being predicted. The numbers have become a part of reality.

For mathematicians who live and die by their proofs, I'm not arguing that the mathematical proofs of complex numbers aren't sound. But I'm looking at it from an observational point of view. In mathematics, it's easy to get so caught up in the math itself, that the question the math was created to solve becomes less important. Mathematics is more than a tool; it's a powerful way of thinking. But it's only one way of thinking. And if a concept in math isn't describable in any way other than math, then that concept has a very limited usefulness.

Warning: physics philosophy ahead. I wrote this paper with the idea of showing that something so obviously imaginary as complex numbers could do something real. As I pointed out, complex numbers are involved whenever math becomes unthinkable any other way. My quantum mechanics professor tells me that we use complex notation in Lorentz transforms to "cheat the system," making the last component of a four-dimensional vector negative if you square it. It's used in crystallography because the structure of a crystal, when viewed by x-ray, is literally inside out and backward. These numbers are involved with practically everything that you cannot see. They can be used for things you can see, but so can real numbers. Generally speaking, complex numbers are used whenever you begin using more than three dimensions. In the context of four dimensions, it's the fourth dimension (that is, time) that is generally complex.

If we recognize more than three dimensions to the universe, then maybe complex numbers do exist physically in reality as a representation of what a higher dimension looks like in our 3-D perception. The existence of observable complex numbers doesn't go against my earlier argument that your thoughts affect reality. It actually fits very well into the concept of mental dimensions (that is, astral planes or inner planes). If you recognize multiple dimensions, and those dimensions are expressible by complex numbers, then those dimensions could quite possibly be imaginary in origin. This is not to say that you made them up on the fly; these dimensions might be where the individual mind draws its innate knowledge, where we send signals and receive information.

A current theory in physics espouses eleven dimensions, four of which we live in (the three spatial dimensions, and time), and seven other dimensions that are said to have "curled up" to a size that makes an atom look large. We're not going to notice anything that small, which means that the imaginary, even though it may actually have a place in the universe, must still be "imaginary" forever. You'll never know the process of your imagination, only the results. This idea also lends itself to Jung's idea of a Collective Unconscious. What he proposed in psychology might be explainable with modern physics.

The ideas in this paper are not really provable. But then neither is the idea of eleven dimensions, or most philosophical issues. The only things that can be proven are those that can be heard, felt, smelled, tasted, or, arguably, most importantly to humans, seen. And this is only true as long as you trust your senses. But the concepts seem to fit together very well, almost too well to attribute it to coincidence. I think that most, if not all, explanations of how the universe works will eventually converge into one idea, with pieces from all the other ideas it has replaced.

If we're lucky, it might even be the truth.

JAMES BECHRAKIS
JANUARY 4, 2000

Appendix C

LESSER BANISHING RITUAL
OF THE PENTAGRAM

1. Walk to the eastern quarter of the room and face east.

2. Perform the Qabalistic Cross as follows:

   a. Raise your right hand to a point about three inches above your head. Visualize a sphere of brilliant white light.

   b. Bring your hand down to touch your forehead.

   c. As you touch your forehead, vibrate the word "Ah-Teh."

   d. Bring the hand down to touch your breastbone.

   e. Vibrate "Mal-Kuth." Visualize a shaft of white light emanating from the sphere and penetrating your body to flower in a second sphere at your feet.

   f. Touch your right shoulder. Visualize a sphere of light there.

   g. Vibrate "Veh-Geb-Your-Ah."

   h. Bring the hand across to touch your left shoulder.

   i. Vibrate "Veh-Ged-You-Lah." Visualize a shaft of light emanating from the right shoulder sphere and penetrating your body to flower into a sphere at your left shoulder.

   j. Clasp your hands together in the form of a cup at a level with your chest. Visualize a flame burning within your cupped hands.

   k. Vibrate "Lay-Oh-Lah-Eem."

   l. Vibrate "Ah-Men."

3. Trace pentagram with your first two fingers, visualizing it in blue fire, like methylated spirit flame.

4. Stab pentagram.

5. Vibrate "Yod-Heh-Vav-Heh," imagining the sound rushing away.

6. Move clockwise to the south with your arm outstretched. Visualize a quarter-circle of blue flame traced by your first two fingers.

7. Trace second pentagram as before, stab it, and vibrate "Ah-Doh-Nay."

8. Move clockwise to the west, visualizing as before.

9. Trace third pentagram, stab it, and vibrate "Eh-Heh-Yeh."

10. Move clockwise to the north, visualizing as before.

11. Trace fourth pentagram, stab it, and vibrate "Aye-Geh-Lah."

12. Return to the east, continuing to visualize, and complete the circle by bringing your outstretched fingers to the center of the first pentagram.

13. Stretch your arms out sideways, standing in the form of a cross.

14. Vibrate "Before me Rah-Fi-El." Visualize telesmatic figure of the archangel in shimmering robes of silk shot with yellow and mauve. Cool breezes coming from this quarter.

15. Vibrate "Behind me Gah-Brah-El." Visualize archangel robed in blue offset by orange, holding a blue chalice and standing in a stream of swiftly flowing water that pours into the room.

16. Vibrate "At my right hand Me-Kah-El." Visualize archangel robed in flame red flecked with emerald, standing on scorched earth with small flickering flames at his feet and carrying a steel sword. Intense heat emanates from this quarter.

17. Vibrate "At my left hand Or-Eye-El." Visualize the robes as a mixture of olive, citron, russet, and black. He holds sheaves of corn in outstretched hands and stands within a very fertile landscape.

18. Vibrate "Around me flame the pentagrams. Above me shines the six-rayed star." The star is the Seal of Solomon or Megan David of the Israeli national flag. Visualize the ascending triangle (point upward) red in color, the descending triangle blue.

19. Repeat the Qabalistic Cross Ritual.

Appendix D

THOUGHT FORM PRACTICE

EXERCISE ONE

Look for a picture of a very simple Greek temple. A set of three concentric circles of marble forming a series of three steps, the topmost of which is the temple floor. Around this top circle is a ring of slender pillars, also of marble, that hold up a domed roof. There are no doors or walls; it is open to the elements. In the center stands a plain altar on which there is a sliver plate of fruit, barley cakes, and goat cheese. A jug of wine and a small silver cup complete the appurtenances of this temple. Set all this on a clifftop overlooking the Aegean Sea, with a winding path leading up to it.

Your task is to build this temple *with full attention to detail* over the space of a week. Having done this, build the thought form of the goddess Demeter and perform a rite in her honor.

EXERCISE TWO

Build a sandy beach under a night sky with a new moon above. Create the sight, sound, and scent of the scenery. Beyond the sea there is a small island; each night you will swim out to it and set about building a moon temple; your materials will be moonlight, shells, foam, and seaweed. You will continue until the night before the full moon. On that night you will create a thought form of Artemis, and on the full moon you will call the essence of the goddess into it and perform a rite of worship.

EXERCISE THREE

From the astral proto matter, create the inside of a small chapel of gray stone. Behind the altar is a stained glass window depicting three knights; the first is in silver armor bearing aloft a silver chalice; the second is in gold armor and carrying a black shield with a golden wheat sheaf on it; the third knight is in bronze armor and is bare-headed—he is older than the other two. The young knight is Galahad, the golden knight is Perseval, and the third is Bors. All three received sight of the Grail, but only Galahad actually touched it and was able to use it as a vessel during the Mass. Build his window slowly and carefully, and with attention to detail in armor and weaponry.

There are no chairs or seats in the chapel, only a small *prie-dieu* before the chancel steps. Man or woman will kneel here and offer whatever you feel able to offer, be it as small as one hour of your life exclusively to the Lords of Light, or the ultimate and Unreserved Dedication. (Do not make this last unless you really mean it; they *do* take up their options!) Remain here as long as you can, and keep your attention on the window. One of three things will happen:

- the Grail in the window will glow brightly and send a beam of light down and into your heart center;

- a priest will enter from the side and offer you communion from another chalice;

- Galahad, Perseval, and Bors will become real and three-dimensional. They will step down from the window and surround you. Together you will share bread and wine, after which you may leave the chapel and return.

This may either have a profound effect on you or leave you feeling flat, in which case, scrap the chapel and rebuild it until it has a positive effect. You are dealing with archetypes here, not belief systems, so you can go into the experience even if you are not a Christian or a practicing Christian.

EXERCISE FOUR

Create a glass bridge over a giant chasm. In the very center, raise up a castle of crystal. In the center of the castle you will find a treasure. What it is will depend on what *you* regard as a treasure. Also, it is disguised as something else, and you must seek it out, recognize its true form, and change it back. Then and only then can you cross over to the other side of the bridge.

If you have guessed wrongly, you may think you have crossed the bridge but you will in fact find yourself back on the other side where you began this exercise.

EXERCISE FIVE

Open up the astral matrix to find limitless space. Go forward as far as you feel able to do so. You will find your greatest fears will assail you during this time. You may have to attempt this several times before you come to a point beyond which you are unable to go. Wait until a point of light appears, and watch until it becomes solid. It will spin and vibrate and then begin to give out concentric circles of pure vibration, which you will feel as waves beating against your consciousness, or as the sound of voices and instruments chanting with awesome power. You may see it as light and color pouring into an as yet unmanifested space and creating forms of all kinds. You are here simply to look and experience, for this is the Point of Manifestation.

You may repeat these exercises as often as you like, but always do them in order, not as a random selection.

Appendix E

DOLORES' EXPERIENCE WITH TIME

SOME TWENTY-FIVE YEARS AGO, when our much loved bearded collie, Leah, was alive, I used to walk her down to the beach from my house every day in the summer months at about three o'clock in the afternoon. The route was always the same. Out of the house and turn left, down the road a bit and cross over and turn right down a narrow lane with a dog-leg turn at the end of it. At the end of this was a crossroads, not too busy but busy enough to warrant careful walking, especially with a dog on a lead. Over the crossroads and up another narrow street to another crossing, a very busy one leading directly to a park. This part of the walk would take, at the very most and including any waiting time for cars to pass, ten to twelve minutes.

On this particular day I began my walk and had reached the crossroads at the top of the dog leg. As I waited for a gap in the traffic, my sense of time and place shifted abruptly.

I found myself, minus the dog, standing under a railway arch in what I knew to be Waterloo Station in London. Facing me was a rough-looking individual, a vagrant. His eyes, however, were brilliantly blue and piercing in their intensity. He held out an envelope of thick handmade paper.

"Take this and read it, now. I will wait."

I opened it and found inside a letter written in a firm flowing hand, an airplane ticket, and some money—it looked to be about five hundred pounds.

The ticket was for Bombay, India, and onward to a town I had never heard of but one I felt was much farther north.

"You must go now, immediately," said the vagrant.

I protested that I couldn't leave on such short notice; there was my husband to consider, my job (I was working part-time), and the School of the SOL. He got very agitated and insisted that I leave now, this minute, and he would see to everything else. Somehow I found myself on a train with everything moving twice a fast as it should, then there was a period of darkness.

When I could see again I was in a busy airport facing a dark-skinned man in a Sikh turban.

"You must hurry," he said. "They have been waiting for a long time."

Then things got hazy; I remember looking down from a plane on mountains topped with snow and thinking to myself, "This is straight out of *Lost Horizon*. It is not real."

Then there was the "place" . . . set on a mountainside and made of red wood. A small boy in a black robe led me up a series of stairs to a room that looked out on to a mountain range of awesome proportions. The window had no glass, but was open to the elements. There was a narrow bed with a straw-filled mattress and pillow, on which lay a blanket and a cover of animal fur that stank to high heaven. There was a chair and a small table; a basin and jug stood on top of the table. On the bed was a dark red robe and a cord, along with a pair of felt boots. The boy indicated that I was to put these on, then he disappeared.

I waited for what seemed like hours, and finally the door opened and in came a man. He was of middle height and obviously Asian. The face was gentle and the eyes kindly, but I still felt apprehensive. Strangely, I had forgotten about my home and family at this point.

He sat down and told me that I had been brought here for a purpose, but that it was first necessary that my body be cleansed of all that it had brought with it. He opened the door and in came two young boys. One carried a wooden cup, along with a pitcher that contained dark liquid; the other carried two basins and some ragged lengths of cloth. Then they left. I was told to drink the liquid slowly, over a period of about an hour. I asked how I would know when an hour had passed, since everything, including my watch, had been taken away. My question went unanswered, and he left.

The liquid in the jug tasted foul, but I felt impelled to gradually get it down me. Then, having nothing else to do, I lay down and covered myself with the covers. I had never felt so cold. I thought I would never be warm again.

Just as I was about to fall asleep, my stomach revolted; I grabbed a basin and threw up, not once, but time after time. It was yellow and smelled terrible. Finally it stopped, and I fell back on the bed shivering, cold, and wretched. Then my bowels went the same way.

This brought the other basin into play, and the cloths. This smelled worse than the other, but I was beyond caring. Eventually I fell into a deep sleep. When I woke the basins had been removed, cleaned, and replaced, along with more cloths and another jug of the same liquid. The second day passed like the first, alternately vomiting and voiding my bowels until I thought I must be dying. A third day came, and by now I was too weak to reach for the basins and the bed was fouled with my waste. As I lay there unable to do anything, even move, my "jailer" entered and, with gentle hands, proceeded to wash me and clean up the room. Having done this, he poured more of the liquid down my throat.

I lost track of time. My whole existence was revolved around this violent purging, which, though it was happening less frequently, was nonetheless debilitating. Always he was there to clean me and clean the room. I was past embarrassment by now, and just let it happen.

Finally, after some time, it stopped. My body felt light and empty. The vomiting and voiding stopped and I was given no more of the drink, but instead, pure water and a thick porridge sweetened with honey. He fed me a small spoonful at a time. I was given slippers along with a robe of soft wool, and taken from the room to another, which was larger and had a small stove that gave a welcome heat. Now, at last, I was allowed to sleep for hours. It was a dreamless sleep, but one in which I was conscious of a voice speaking to me, feeding me information.

The bed was more of a platform with straw-filled cushions, and behind it a wall-sized tapestry of red and gold figures woven into it, most of which seemed to have either snake heads or snake bodies with human heads. I awoke feeling rested, but I knew there was more to be done. I felt very afraid. My companion came and sat with me. He did not speak but held my hand until I calmed down. Then he stood and removed his robe; I was not surprised to see that he was erect. He drew me to the platform and sat down, gently urging me to sit astride him. There was nothing erotic about it, simply a task that needed to be done, a rite to be accomplished.

The rigid flesh within me did not move, but the power and the force of the maleness was a flame that began at the coccyx and rose up until the whole spine was on fire. It rose slowly, and with every vertebrae another part of my consciousness opened up. Finally it reached the top of my head, and a tongue of flame flared up and was gone. I was lifted gently and urged to lie down and sleep. He left and I never saw him again.

The boys came with my clothes and took me to the gate. I looked back, but there was nothing to see. I passed through the gate and found myself crossing the road to the park, the dog's lead still in my hand. I "knew" I had been away for at least two weeks, but in fact it had taken place in the six or seven minutes, the time it took for my physical body to walk from the crossroads to the park. I never experienced anything remotely like it again. I know it had the appearance of a kundalini ritual, but why it was given to me I do not know. Herbie and my husband Michael are the only people with whom I have ever discussed it. The "forms" throughout were solid and touchable, but not of my making. I was in my forty-fifth year at the time, a number that adds to nine, the number of completion before a new phase begins. Shortly after, however, I received the inner plane "contact," which has been with me ever since.

Appendix F

CREATING A GOLEM WITH
THE SEFER YETZIRAH

IT IS MENTIONED IN THE Babylonian Talmud that rabbis who lived in the fourth century used the *Sefer Yetzirah* to create life:

> Raba said: If the righteous ones like to do so, they can create a world, for it is said: "For your sins separate [you from your God]." Raba created a man and sent him to Rabbi Sera; when he saw the man and spoke to him and he gave no answer, he said: "You seem to come from the companions (another possible translation would be: "from the magicians"); return to your loam! Raw Chanina und Raw Oshaaya studied the *Sefir Yetzirah* "Book of Formation" (or in another version, *Hilchoch Yetzirah*, "Rules of Formation") on the eve of every Sabbath (Friday evening), and created a small calf and ate it. (Sanhedrin 65 b)

The famous Qabalist Abraham Abulafia (1240–1296) mocks those who want to make calves with the *Sefer Yetzirah* and says, "Those who try to do so are calves themselves." An anonymous Spanish Qabalist writes that using the *Sefer Yetzirah* does not create a manifestation on earth but a "thougt form" (*Yetzirah machashawthith*). Moses Cordovero writes (1548) that the power that gives life to the Golem is *Chijuth,* "vitality," and belongs to the elemental forces. The idea that the letters have creative power was already known in ancient times:

> Betzalel (the builder of the Temple) knew how to "combine the letters with which heaven and earth were created." (Babylonian Talmud, Berachoth 55 a)

The living being created by the use of the *Sefer Yetzirah* is called a Golem. The Hebrew word "Golem" appears only once in the Bible (Ps. 139:16). The root G L M indicated something "not developed" or "not unfolded." In the medieval philosophical literature, the word "Golem" was used to describe the original formless matter, the *materia prima.* In other words, we are speaking about the matter of the Astral Plane. In later times, the figure of the Golem was often the subject of literature; for example, in Gustav Mayrink's famous novel *The Golem*.

The ritual of the creation of a Golem is based on an old description given by Rabbi Elieser ha-Rokeach of Worms (1160–1237) as a part of his comment to the *Sefer Yetzirah*. I have also taken the opening and closing of the rite from the *Sefer Yetzirah*. Many passages can be understood as descriptions of God's creation (for example: "He sealed the above . . . ") or as an instruction ("Seal the above . . . "). The author says that one should seal the directions with the letters of the NAME. There are many variations of these combinations. I have used those from the short version, which may be the oldest. Each of the seals is said to belong to one of the lower six Sefiroth.

It was always important for the old Qabalists to make sure this type of ritual did not result in arrogance or blasphemy of mankind. Therefore, it was pointed out that the Golem could not speak because it has no Ruach (that is, mental soul). Others considered it important that the Golem should be destroyed immediately after the creation. In writing this ritual, I have taken care to obey this rule.

The attributes of the archangels have been changed sometimes through the ages. For example, Michael and Gawriel (who is often called Gabriel by those who do not speak Hebrew) have changed the element they reigned over. The same is true for the directions some of the archangels belonged to. I have chosen to use the arrangement most Qabalistic students of today will be familiar with because I consider the Qabalah to be a living tradition, and not a rigid and dead thing.

PRONUNCIATION

I have tried to transliterate the Hebrew words in such a way that it is as easy as possible for an English-speaking person to pronounce them correctly. The letter *Cheth,* and sometimes the letter *Kaf,* are transliterated as "Ch." This is always pronounced as in the Scottish pronunciation of *loch*. I have transliterated the letter *Thaw* as "Th," in order to distinguish it from the letter *Teth*. However, both can be spoken like "T."

GLOSSARY

The word *belimah* describes the ten Sefiroth as the divine and unmanifest essence.

The *Nefesh* is the emotional or astral soul.

The *Ruach* is the mental soul.

The *Shechinah* is the female aspect of God. She is considered to be the divine presence in the world, especially in the temple.

INTRODUCTION

The ritual is written for three officers, but it can also be done with two officers, if the 2. officer takes also the lines of the 3. officer. (As the old descriptions say, it should be done with two or three people. I suggest the Magus should be a man and the 2. officer should be a woman.) However, I think it is possible to do this ritual with a bigger group. I like the idea of twenty-two upholders, each one of them representing one of the twenty-two Hebrew letters. Since the main part of the ritual is the chanting and pathworking, it is very easy to include some upholders.

Everybody should wear white robes. On the altar, some holy water will be needed —enough to purify everybody. In front of the altar should be a figure of the Golem made of loam or clay to help build up the thought form of the Golem later. "And he should take virgin earth from a place in the mountains, where no human has ever dug, and border the earth with water of life and make a Golem." The figure of the Golem should be purified with holy water.

THE OPENING

Magus: Looking upward, he draws in the air the invoking or opening hexagram, then points in the middle, and says:

> *By the seal of the six-pointed star and in the name of*
> *Yod Heh Waw*
> *I open the above.*

Then the magus looks downward, draws in the air the invoking hexagram, then points in the middle, and says:

> *By the seal of the six-pointed star and in the name of*
> *Yod Waw Heh*
> *I open the below.*

Then the magus goes to the east, draws in the air the invoking hexagram, points in the middle, and says:

> *By the seal of the six-pointed star and in the name of*
> *Heh Yod Waw*
> *I open the east.*

Then the magus goes to the west, draws in the air the invoking hexagram, points in the middle, and says:

By the seal of the six-pointed star and in the name of
Heh Waw Yod
I open the west

Then the magus goes to the south, draws in the air the invoking hexagram, points in the middle, and says:

By the seal of the six-pointed star and in the name of
Waw Yod Heh
I open the south.

Then the magus goes to the north, draws in the air the invoking hexagram, points in the middle, and says:

By the seal of the six-pointed star and in the name of
Waw Heh Yod
I open the north.

I have taken the order of the openings from the *Sefer Yetzirah* itself. This is why I have started with the opening of the above. This is indeed unusual, for normally I would have started in the east. I have decided to use the hexagram, because the whole opening is sixfold and there are six permutations of the divine name consisting of three letters.

INVOKING THE ARCHANGELS

2. **Officer:** Looks upward and says:

I invoke thee and I give thee welcome
Metatron,
Teacher of the mysteries.
Thou art called the prince of the face,
The most highest, and closest to God.
Let us understand and experience the mystery of creation.

Then he looks downward and says:

I invoke thee and I give thee welcome
Sandalfon,
Keeper of the secret knowledge.
Thou art the servant of the shechinah.
Let us become aware of
The divinity within.

Then he goes to the east and says:

> *I invoke thee and I give thee welcome*
> *Rafael,*
> *Thou art the master of the element of air.*
> *Make our words powerful.*
> *Give to our work the breath of life,*
> *For all life needs air to breathe.*

Then he goes to the west and says:

> *I invoke thee and I give thee welcome*
> *Gawriel,*
> *Thou art the master of the element of water.*
> *Give to our work the waters of life,*
> *For water is the element of life,*
> *And for out of the sea came all life on this planet.*

Then he goes to the south and says:

> *I invoke thee and I give thee welcome*
> *Michael,*
> *Thou art the master of the element of fire.*
> *Give to our work the power of life,*
> *For all life needs warmth and energy to exist.*

Then he goes to the north and says:

> *I invoke thee and I give thee welcome*
> *Uriel,*
> *Thou art the master of the element of earth.*
> *Give to our work the power of form,*
> *Because without form, there is no manifestation.*

Magus: Goes to the altar, stretches his arms out, and says:

> *Yah*
> *Yod heh vav heh*
> *Tzewaoth*
> *Elohej yisrael*
> *Elohim chajim*
> *U-melech olam*
> *El shaddai*
> *Rachum ve-chanun*

Ram ve-nisa
Shochen ad marom
Ve-qadosh shemcha
Fill this holy place with your divine presence.
Bless us, and inspire us,
So that our work will be successful.

All: Do the Qabalistic cross.

atah

malchuth

ve-gewurah

ve-gedulah

le-olam

amen

Magus:

In the name and under the protection of
the creator of the universe,
I declare this temple of the mysteries open.
The intention of the ritual is
to create a living creature from inanimate substance,
in order to understand the mystery of creation
and the creative power within us.

THE CREATION OF THE GOLEM

The fragment that this ritual is based on begins with a discussion of the question of why one may not do this ritual alone. Even though I do not believe this was a real part of the original ritual, I have included it in order to make everybody understand and remember the law of polarity, the divinity within, and the power of words.

Magus: *Bereshith bra elohim eth ha-shamaim ve-eth ha-aretz.* (Gen. 1)

2. Officer: *In the beginning, Elohim made the heaven and the earth.*

3. Officer: *Why does "bereshith" begin with the letter Beth?*

Magus: *Because the number of the letter Beth is two.*

2. Officer: *This is the law of polarity.*

3. Officer: *And because of this, it is written: two are better than one.* (Eccles. 4:9)

Magus: *Vayomer elohim nxasseh adam betzalmenu kid'mutheinu.* (Gen. 1:26)

2. Officer: *And Elohim said, "Let us make man in our image, like us."*

3. Officer. *Who are those, who speak?*

Magus: *They are: God . . .*

2. Officer: *. . . And the Shechinah.*

3. Officer: *The work of creation cannot be done alone.*

Magus: *Companions, will you assist me in the work that lies before us?*

2. Officer: *I will.*

3. Officer: *I will.*

Magus: *It was said that the righteous ones could create a world if they wished. And it is written: qedoshim tihju ki qadosh ani lhvh* (Adonai) *eloheichem.* (Lev. 19:2)

2. Officer: *You shall be holy, as I, Adonai your God, am holy.*

3. Officer: *But how can we be as holy as God?*

Magus: *We can be holy, because we were made in his image, like him.*

2. Officer: *We are the children of the creator and the creator is within us.*

3. Officer: *How did Elohim create life?*

Magus: *Elohim created life by the power of words. As it is written: vayomer elohim thotze ha-aretz nefesh chayah leminah behemah varemess, vechaytho-aretz lemineh vayehi-chen.* (Gen. 1:24)

2. Officer. *And Elohim said, "The earth bring forth living souls in their way, gregarious animals, and reptiles, and wild animals in their way"—and so it was.*

3. Officer: *Let us begin.*

Magus: *First we have to purify ourselves.*

2. Officer: *Ten sefiroth blimah, the number of ten fingers, five opposite five with a single covenant precisely in the middle, like the word of the tongue and the word of the genitals.*

3. **Officer:** *Ten sefiroth blimah, understand with wisdom, and be wise with understanding. Test with them, and probe with them, and make the thing stand in its purity.*

2. **Officer:** The 2. officer goes to everybody and purifies everybody's hands and forehead with holy water, saying to each one:

Ten sefiroth blimah
Five opposite five (touching the hands),
With a single covenant precisely in the middle
(touching the forehead).
You are purified.

Magus: (After the purification of everybody.) *Companions, now see with your inner vision the body of the Golem lying in front of you. See and feel the gray color and the hardness of the body made of cold loam. Look at the shape and expression of his face. Notice the position of his arms and legs. Look at his gray chest. Notice every detail of his body. Build up the astral form of his body with the power of your mind.*

(After some time to build up the thought form.)

Magus: *Twenty-two foundation letters, three mothers.*

2. **Officer:** *Seven doubles.*

3. **Officer:** *And twelve simple ones.*

Magus: *Command them, engrave them, change them, and combine them! And form with them the Nefesh of all that has been formed and the Nefesh of all that shall be formed!*

2. **Officer:** *They are set in a circle as 231 gates. And the circle rotates forward and backward.*

3. **Officer:** *How?*

Magus: *Weigh them and change them!*

2. **Officer:** *Alef with each one, and each one with Alef.*

3. **Officer:** *Beth with each one, and each one with Beth.*

Magus: *Form substance from the unmanifest, and make he that which is not!*

2. Officer: *Visualize and change, and make all that has been formed and all that has been spoken.*

3. Officer: *With the one name!*

(Text taken from *Sefer Yetzirah*, chapter 2.)

All: Everybody stands in a circle around the Golem. If possible, everyone is holding the hands of his neighbors. Then they chant the letters of the divine name combined with the alphabet. The 231 gates are combinations of two letters, Alef-Beth, Alef-Gimel, Alef Daleth . . . Alef-Thaw, Beth-Gimel, Beth-Daleth . . . Shin-Thaw. These 231 gates are combined with the letters of the tetragrammaton. To keep the idea of the original ritual, but simplify it, I have based it on the name Jod Heh Waw, which I identify with the three vowels I, A, and O, like the Greek transliteration. So in the simplest form possible, every gate will be spoken i-i; a-a; o-o. Please note that Alef and Ayin have no sound of their own. Among the seven "double-letters," Beth, Kaf, and Peh have a hard and a soft sound. They are spoken hard in the first syllable (B, K, P) and soft in the second syllable (W, Ch, F). So the first gate (Alef-Beth) would be chanted: i-wi, a-wa, o-wo. The second gate (Alef-Gimel) would be: i-gi, a-ga, o-go. The twenty-second gate (Beth-Gimel) is chanted: bi-gi, baga, bo-go. Chanting all the 231 gates will take about ten to fifteen minutes at the most. This will still be something like the original, which did in some descriptions include all possible combinations of five vowels, which means twenty-five instead of three combinations for each gate, and even for experts of the language this would take more than one hour, maybe two—and there are methods that are even more complicated. Since the whole thing needs to be done backward (as described later), this would have been a ritual of many hours. Yet, some say it is unlikely that it has been practiced like this. I do not know, but I think two times ten to fifteen minutes is a good choice. I am aware that the chanting is not really easy to do at the beginning, but I want to keep the original atmosphere. I do not think I can reduce this any more. However, since the original ritual was considered to be practiced only by master Qabalists, I expect that everyone taking part in this ritual knows the Hebrew alphabet and has practiced the chanting before, and maybe taken some time to meditate the meaning of the letters. It may also be helpful to draw the twenty-two letters around a circle and connect every letter with every other letter. Do this in the order of the chanting, and you will understand much better the meaning of the 231 gates. During the chanting, a dancelike step will be used, so that after each gate everyone moves one step in a clockwise direction. The tradition says that the whole thing has to be started again if a mistake happens. I think that it will be okay if at least one person will do the chanting correctly. This means that since it is unlikely for everybody to be wrong, such a problem is hopefully avoided. If it should happen, however, I suggest that it will be all right to repeat only the gate that went wrong. During the chanting of each gate, everybody visualizes a ray of light for each gate, which fills the astral form of the Golem with the creative power of the letters of this gate. It is very important to feel how the golem is filled up with this power, gate by gate.

Magus: After the last gate (Shin-Thaw), the magus goes to the Golem. Then the Magus writes on the Golem's forehead (or on a paper on the Golem's forehead) the word *emeth*, which means "truth," and says:

> *I write on your forehead*
> *the word "emeth,"*
> *the seal of the holy one, blessed be, the creator of the universe.*
> *By the power of the creator within all of us,*
> *I give life to you.*
> *May the power of life fill your body.*
> *May you live among us for a short while*
> *to the everlasting glory*
> *of the one creator.*

(Everybody goes to his seat.)

Companions, close your eyes now, and see with your inner vision. See the Golem lying in front of you. See and feel the gray color and the hardness of the body made of cold loam. Look at the shape and the expression on his face, still being emotionless and stiff. Notice the position of his arms and legs. Look at his gray chest. Notice every detail of his body, and now feel the energy of life that you have given to this cold body, radiating warmth from deep within it. The warmth fills up his body more and more. The hard surface slowly becomes more soft and the gray color turns into the color of human skin, shade by shade. Out of his hands and feet grow short fingernails and toe-nails, and his hair starts to grow to some inches of length. Feel and see how the power of life flows through his body. Almost imperceptibly you hear a small but regular sound. It sounds like a beat. It becomes louder, and you realize it is a heartbeat. You listen to the rhythm of his heartbeat and you look at his chest and you see how it seems to move. You notice the sound of wind or air from his nose. And you are witness to the very first breath of his life. His chest moves up and down while he continues to breathe. His fingers move slowly as if they had been stunned and are not yet used to moving. His arms and legs move a little bit, as if he was just in the process of awakening. Slowly he opens his eyes. Then he lifts up his upper body and stands up. He is alive—you have given life to this creature. You are his creators, his parents, and his masters. He turns around and looks in the eyes of everybody. He cannot speak, because he does not have a Ruach, but he does have a Nefesh and he does have emotions. In his eyes you can see the feeling of deep thankfulness for the short time that you have given to him the wonderful present of life. For even a small moment of life is an experience that will not be forgotten. He smiles as he looks into your eyes. And you feel that your heart is filled with the joy of life itself. No word can describe the feelings shared between you and him, a feeling almost like parentship of a different kind. (Small pause.) When he has completed facing everybody, he comes back to the center, and then he listens as I speak to him:

Creature made of earth,

formed by the power of the mind,

you have been given life, by the creative power of the holy name

And the twenty-two holy letters.

We bless you.

It is written: For everything there is a time and there is a right

moment, and for each thing under the heaven,

a time to be born and a time to die. (Ecclesiastes 3:1–2)

Your time among us is over, and you have to leave now.

You will take

with you the memory of the soul you once had.

And it will be absorbed into your own world for the benefit of your

kind of existence.

Lie down, back in your place!

Companions, the Golem is lying in his place;

let us say goodbye and farewell.

We know that what has been done could be done again!

The creator is always within us.

Creature made of earth,

I erase on your forehead

the letter "Alef," the letter with which begins the alphabet.

And where the word "emeth" was written,

now only "meth"—"he is dead"—remains.

In the name of the creator within all of us,

I take back the life that was given to you.

May the power of life go back to where it came from.

From earth you were made, and to the earth you will return,

but you will keep with you the memory of what you once were.

(The magus erases the "Alef.")

You watch the Golem closing his eyes. His arms and legs become stiff, and the breathing movement of his chest is irregular; after a while it stops completely. The heartbeat increasingly slows, until you cannot hear it anymore and it fades away. The expression of his face becomes stiff again. His hair, his fingernails, and his toenails become gray. The color of his skin, shade by shade, turns back to gray. The surface of his body changes to the hard and lifeless structure of dry loam. His body becomes cold again. Feel and see how the power of life withdraws into the center of the body of the Golem. The body of the Golem is lying in front of you, without any emotion or any sign of life. When you open your eyes, you still see the thought form of the Golem's body in front of you.

Magus: *Now the circle has to turn backward again. Take back what you have given, and absorb into yourself the power of life, which is now filled with the experience of the mystery of creation.*

All: Everybody stands in a circle around the Golem. If possible, everyone is holding the hands of his neighbors. Then they chant the letters of the divine name combined with the alphabet. This time the 231 gates are spoken backward. Also, the order of the vowels is reversed. They will be spoken -o -o; -a -a; -i -i. So the group starts with gate (Shin-Thaw), which would be chanted: SHo-THo, SHa-THa, SHi-THi. Then comes Resh-Thaw, then Resh-Shin . . . and the last one is Alef-Beth. The "double-letters" Beth, Kaf, and Peh are spoken hard in the first syllable (B, K, P) and soft in the second syllable (W, Ch, F), as before. Again, the dancelike step will be used, but this time in a counterclockwise direction. During the chanting of each gate, everybody visualizes a ray of light for each gate. Now he takes back from the astral form of the Golem what he has given to it. But the power of life he receives back brings with it the experience of the mystery of creation. So what everybody gets back is more than what he gave. Again, it is very important to feel how the power comes back, gate by gate.

(Small break.)

Magus: *The work has been done. Now let us give thanks to our friends, the archangels.*

THANKING AND SENDING BACK OF THE ARCHANGELS

2. Officer: Looks upward and says:

> *We thank thee and we bless thee,*
> *Metatron.*
> *Go back to thy place at the side of God.*

Then he looks downward and says:

> *We thank thee and we bless thee,*
> *Sandalfon.*
> *Go back to try place in the secret temple of the shechinah.*

Then he goes to the east and says:

> *We thank thee and we bless thee,*
> *Rafael.*
> *Go back to thy place in heaven.*

Then he goes to the west and says:

> *We thank thee and we bless thee,*
> *Gawriel.*
> *Go back to thy place in the waters of the upper world.*

Then he goes to the south and says:

> *We thank thee and we bless thee,*
> *Michael.*
> *Go back to thy place at the gate of paradise.*

Then he goes to the north and says:

> *We thank thee and we bless thee,*
> *Uriel.*
> *Go back to thy place in the garden of the lord.*

THE CLOSING

Magus: Looking upward, he draws in the air the closing hexagram, then points in the middle, and says:

> *By the seal of the six-pointed star and in the name of*
> *Yod Heh Waw*
> *I close the above.*

Then the magus looks downward, draws in the air the closing hexagram, points in the middle, and says:

> *By the seal of the six-pointed star and in the name of*
> Yod Waw Heh
> *I close the below.*

Then the magus goes to the east, draws in the air the closing hexagram, points in the middle, and says:

> *By the seal of the six-pointed star and in the name of*
> Heh Yod Waw
> *I close the east.*

Then the magus goes to the west, draws in the air the closing hexagram, points in the middle, and says:

> *By the seal of the six-pointed star and in the name of*
> Heh Waw Yod
> *I close the west.*

Then the magus goes to the south, draws in the air the closing hexagram, points in the middle, and says:

> *By the seal of the six-pointed star and in the name of*
> Waw Yod Heh
> *I close the south.*

Then the magus goes to the north, draws in the air the closing hexagram, points in the middle, and says:

> *By the seal of the six-pointed star and in the name of*
> Waw Heh Yod
> *I close the north.*

Magus: Goes back to his position and faces the altar:

> *In the name of the creator of the universe*
> *I declare this temple of the mysteries closed*
> *And the ritual ended.*

SALOMO BAAL-SHEM (STEFAN FIEBIG)

Appendix G

ASTRAL ENTRANCES EXERCISES

WHAT FOLLOW ARE THREE exercises promised elsewhere in the book to give you some ways into the astral that are not found when working in the usual format.

1. This way will take you into the "inner" astral and open up the astral memory area. This means you can call up and recreate images rather than building them. However, it will only work with images of objects that have existed at some time in the past.

2. This way will take you into the upper level of the astral, to a "gateway" leading to the mental level, and, if you can take the pressure, into the lower spiritual/angelic level.

3. The "Fourways" will take you into (respectively) the astral elemental kingdoms of earth, water, fire, and air.

EXERCISE ONE

Begin with a curtain of white mist that opens directly onto the all-white astral level. Remember that I described the feel underfoot as being similar to walking on a waterbed. Begin to walk forward and call the soft, slightly undulating feeling beneath you. These subtle levels are limitless, so you can keep walking as long as you need. As you do so, you begin to sink deeper into the astral matrix with each step. There is nothing to fear—just keep walking and you will sink deeper and deeper until it closes over your head (remember that you, too, are in an astral body at this moment), and you will meld into the matrix and become a part of it, but will still retain your human intelligence and abilities.

You can stop moving forward at this point, and rest in the proto matter around you. Summon what you want to see or hear or know about, and the images or sounds will manifest as thoughts or inner ear sounds. The imagery will not be crystal clear, but will appear dreamlike and often a little hazy, but if you persevere, you will soon be able to accept the images directly into the inner visual center. You can go with a clear-cut purpose, or simply browse.

EXERCISE TWO

Follow the same initial route into the astral, and pull up enough "matter" to create a curving stairway disappearing into the upper whiteness. Climb up, and as you follow the curve around, you will become aware of rainbow colors beginning to infiltrate the whiteness. Soon the colors will predominate and you will know you have entered the mental world. You will also notice small colored shapes and forms that change as they flutter past. These are human thoughts from the physical level. Most are simply stray thoughts, but those of almost solid color will be definite and purposeful. The shapes will also give you an idea of what the thought is about, but *not* who is thinking.

You can create another stairway and go on up to the beginning of the next level, or as far as you feel able to go. This will take you out into a level composed mainly of what look like stars, but which, in fact, are angelic beings. They are of all shapes, forms, sizes, and often colors, some of which you will not be able to see properly. If you begin to feel hazy or disoriented, return at once.

EXERCISE THREE

Use the same entry point, but stand still and face any direction. In fact, here all directions are the same, for there is no point of reference in space, inner or outer. Wait quietly and call upon the King of a particular element. Soon you will begin to see a change in the whiteness and a color will begin to appear. These colors will be those you associate with certain elements. For instance, pale gold may mean the gold of ripe corn and be your color for earth; or you might prefer a pale springlike green. Sea green or blue may be your choice for water, and a rich vibrant red for fire. A deeper blue or a rose might be your choice for air. Remember, this is *your* astral kingdom.

Herbie and I have enjoyed having you with us, and hope that you have enjoyed what we have shared with you. We will be glad to hear from you concerning any of these exercises or the information you have found in this book.

See you around on the astral!

REFERENCES

Adler, Alfred. *Practice and Theory of Individual Psychology.* London: Routledge, 1929.

Alexander, H. B., editor. *The Mythology of All Races* (12 volumes). New York: Cooper Square, 1964.

Barr, Murray L. *The Human Nervous System.* New York: Harper & Row, 1974.

Baskin, Wade. *Dictionary of Satanism.* London: Peter Owen, 1972.

Batcheldor, K. J. "Report on a Case of Table Levitation and Associated Phenomena." *Journal of the Society for Psychical Research.* Vol. 43, 1966.

Beck, Brenda E. F. "The Right-Left Division of South Indian Society."

Bentov, Itzhak. *Stalking the Wild Pendulum.* London: Wildwood House, 1978.

Bettley, F. R. Letter in *British Medical Journal.* Vol. 2, 1952.

Bowers, K. S. "Sex and Susceptibility as Moderator Variables in the Relationship of Creativity and Hypnotic Susceptibility." *Journal of Abnormal Psychology.* Vol. 78, 1971.

Breuil, Henri, and Raymond Lantier. *The Men of the Old Stone Age.* London: Harrap, 1965.

Broad, C. D. *Lectures on Psychical Research.* London: Routledge, 1962.

Brookes-Smith, C., and D. W. Hunt. "Some Experiments in Psychokinesis." *Journal of the Society for Psychical Research.* Vol. 45, 1970.

Burt, Cyril. *The Backward Child.* London: University of London Press, 1937.

Cade, C. Maxwell, and Nona Coxhead. *The Awakened Mind.* London: Wildwood House, 1979.

Chelhod, J. "A Contribution to the Problem of the Pre-eminence of the Right."

Clark, Margaret. *Teaching Left-Handed Children.* London: University of London Press, 1959.

Clarke, Arthur C. *Childhood's End.* London: Pan, 1954.

———. *Report on Planet Three and Other Speculations.* London: Corgi, 1975.

Clements, Michele. "What a Fetus Hears an Adult Remembers." *General Practitioner.* 13 April, 1979.

Cooper, S., M. Riklan, and R. S. Snider. "The Effect of Cerebellar Lesions on Emotional Behavior in the Rhesus Monkey." *The Cerebellum, Epilepsy, and Behavior.* New York: Plenum Press, 1972.

Cramer, Marc. *The Devil Within.* London: W. H. Allen, 1979.

Crick, Francis, and Graeme Mitchison. "The Function of Dream Sleep." *Nature.* Vol. 2. July, 1983.

Crowcroft, Andrew. *The Psychotic.* Harmondsworth: Penguin, 1975.

De Felitta, Frank. *The Entity.* London: Collins, 1979.

Dominian J. *Psychiatry and the Christian.* London: Burns & Oates, 1962.

Dow, R. S., and G. Moruzzi. *The Physiology and Pathology of the Cerebellum.* Minneapolis: University of Minnesota Press, 1958.

Durbin, Henry. "A Narrative of Some Extraordinary Things that Happened to Mr Richard Gile's Children." (Bristol 1800): quoted in A. R. G. Owen.

Ellman, Richard. *Yeats: the Man and the Masks.* Oxford: Oxford University Press, 1979.

Evans-Pritchard, E. E. *Nuer Religion.* Oxford: Oxford University Press, 1956.

Faron, Louis C. "Symbolic Values and the Integration of Society among the Mapuche of Chile." In Rodney Needham.

Fitzgerald, Randy. "Messages: the Case History of a Contactee." *Second Look.* October, 1979.

Fox, James J. "On Bad Death and the Left Hand." In Rodney Needham.

Frankel, F. H., and H. S. Zamansky, editors. *Hypnosis at Its Bicentennial.* New York: Plenum Press, 1978.

Freud, Sigmund. *Introductory Lectures on Psychoanalysis, Standard Works.* Vols. 15 and 16. London: Hogarth, 1963.

———. *The Interpretation of Dreams, Standard Works.* Vol. 4. London: Hogarth, 1958.

———. *The Psychopathology of Everyday Life, Standard Works.* Vol. 6. London: Hogarth, 1960.

Gardner, W. J., et al. "Residual Function Following Hemispherectomy for Tumour and Infantile Hemiplegia." *Brain*. Vol. 78, 1955.

Gazzaniga, M. S. *The Bisected Brain*. New York: Meredith Corporation, 1970.

Gibson, H. B. *Hypnosis*. London: Peter Owen, 1977.

Glaskin, G. M. *Windows of the Mind*. London: Wildwood House, 1975.

Goldsmith, L. E., and J. Moor-Jankowski. *Medical Primatology*. New York: Karger, 1971.

Gooch, Stan. "Left-handedness." *New Scientist*. 22 July, 1982.

———. *The Secret Life of Humans*. London: Dent, 1981.

———. *The Double Helix of the Mind*. London: Wildwood House, 1980.

———. "Right Brain, Left Brain." *New Scientist*. 11 September, 1980.

———. *Guardians of the Ancient Wisdom*. London: Wildwood House, 1979.

———. *The Paranormal*. London: Wildwood House, 1978.

———. *The Neanderthal Question*. London: Wildwood House, 1977.

———. *Personality and Evolution*. London: Wildwood House, 1973.

———. *Total Man*. London: Allen Lane, 1972.

Gooch, Stan, and Chris Evans. *Science Fiction as Religion*. Frome, Somerset: Brans Head Press, 1980.

Grad, Bernard. "Some Biological Effects of the Laying on of Hands." *Journal of the American Society for Psychical Research*. Vol. 59, 1965.

Grad, Bernard, et al. "The Influence of an Unorthodox Method of Treatment on Wound Healing in Mice." *International Journal of Parapsychology*. Vol. 3, no. 2.

Granet, Marcel. "Right and Left in China." In Rodney Needham.

Green, Celia, and Charles McCreery. *Apparitions*. London: Hamish Hamilton, 1975.

Guirdham, Arthur. *The Lake and the Castle*. Jersey: Spearman, 1976.

———. *We Are One Another*. Jersey: Spearman, 1974.

———. *The Cathars and Reincarnation*. Jersey: Spearman, 1970.

Gurney, E., F. W. H. Myers, and F. Podmore. *Phantasms of the Living* (2 volumes). London: 1886.

Harrison, Michael. *Fire From Heaven*. London: Sidgwick & Jackson, 1976.

Haynes, Renee. *The Hidden Springs*. London: Hollis & Carter, 1961.

Hertz, Robert. "The Pre-eminence of the Right Hand: a Study in Religious Polarity." in Rodney Needham.

Hilgard, Ernest R. *Divided Consciousness: Multiple Controls in Human Thought and Action.* New York: Wiley, 1977.

Hilgard, Ernest R. *Hypnotic Susceptibility.* New York: Harcourt Brace, 1968.

Hitching, Francis. *The World Atlas of Mysteries.* London: Collins, 1978.

Horney, Karen. *Our Inner Conflicts.* London: Routledge, 1946.

———. *The Neurotic Personality of Our Time.* London: Routledge, 1937.

Hull, C. L. *Hypnosis and Suggestibility.* New York: Appleton-Century, 1933.

"Human Brain." BBC TV. May/June, 1982.

Inglis, Brian. "In Light." Vol. 103, no. 1, 1983.

Iverson, Jeffrey. *More Lives than One?* London: Souvenir Press, 1976.

Iyengar, B. K. S. *Light on Pranayama.* London: Allen & Unwin, 1981.

Izumi, Tomoko. Personal communication to the author.

Jackson, S. M., editor. *The New Schaff-Herzog Encyclopaedia of Religious Knowledge.* New York: Funk & Wagnall, 1909.

Jacobson, Nils. *Life Without Death?* New York: Delacorte Press, 1973.

James, William. "Automatic Writing." *Proceedings, American Society for Psychical Research.* Vol. 1, 1889.

Jastrzembska, Z. S., editor. *The Effects of Blindness and Other Impairments on Early Development, American Foundation for the Blind.* New York: 1976.

Jenkins, Elizabeth. *The Shadow and the Light.* London: Hamilton, 1982.

Jung, C. G. *Aion.* Collected Works. Vol. 9. London: Routledge, 1959.

———. *Alchemical Studies.* Collected Works. Vol. 13. London: Routledge, 1959.

———. *Memories, Dreams, Reflections.* London: Routledge, 1963.

———. *Psychology and Alchemy.* Collected Works. Vol. 12. London: Routledge, 1959.

Kennedy, Margaret. *The Constant Nymph.* London: Heinemann, 1924.

Kolb, L. C. *Modern Clinical Psychiatry.* London: Saunders, 1977.

Krishna, Gopi. *Kundalini: The Evolutionary Energy in Man.* London: Stuart, 1970.

Kruyt, A. C. "Right and Left in Central Celebes." In Rodney Needham.

Krynauw, Rowland A. "Infantile Hemiplegia Treated by Removing One Cerebral Hemisphere." *Journal of Neurology, Neurosurgery and Psychiatry.* Vol. 13, 1950.

Lechler, Alfred. *Das Ratsel von Konnersreuth im Lichte eines Neuen Falles von Stigmatisation.* Elberfeld, 1933.

Lemkau, P., et al. "Mental-Hygiene Problems in an Urban District." *Mental Hygiene.* Vol. 26, 1942.

Lester, David. "Suicidal Behavior in Men and Women." *Mental Hygiene.* Vol. 53, 1969.

———. "Suicidal Behavior, Sex and Mental Disorder." *Psychological Reports.* Vol. 27, 1970.

L'Estrange Ewen, C. H. *Witchcraft and Demonaism.* London: Cranton, 1933.

Lindsay, Jack. *William Blake.* London: Constable, 1978.

Lloyd, Geoffrey. "Right and Left in Greek Philosophy." In Rodney Needham.

J. A. MacCulloch, editor. *The Mythology of All Races* (3 volumes). Boston: Marshall James, 1930.

Manning, Matthew. *In the Minds of Millions.* London: W. H. Allen, 1977.

———. *The Link.* London: Colin Smythe, 1974.

———. *The Strangers.* London: W. H. Allen, 1978.

Mason, A. A. "A Case of Congenital Ichthyosiform Erythrodermia Treated by Hypnosis." *British Medical Journal.* Vol. 2, 1952.

McFie, John. "The Effects of Hemispherectomy on Intellectual Functioning in Cases of Infantile Hemiplegia." *Journal of Neurology, Neurosurgery and Psychiatry.* Vol. 24.

Messerschmidt, R. "A Quantitive Investigation of the Alleged Independent Operation of Conscious and Subconscious Processes." *Journal of Abnormal and Social Psychology.* Vol. 22, 1927.

Mikhail, E. H., and W. B. Yeats. *Interviews and Recollections.* London: Macmillan, 1977.

Miller, Ron. "Do the Media Create UFO Sightings?" *Second Look.* November/December, 1979.

Moody, R. L. "Bodily Changes During Abreaction." *Lancet.* Vol. 251, no. 2, 1946; and Vol. 254, no. 2, 1948.

Morgan, C. T., and E. Stellar. *Physiological Psychology.* New York: McGraw Hill, 1950.

Milhl, Anita. *Automatic Writing.* New York: Helix Press, 1930.

"Multiple Personality." *Encyclopedia Britannica.* 15th edition, 1974.

Myers, F. W. H. "Automatic Writing III." *Proceedings, Society for Psychical Research.* Vol. 4, 1887.

Needham, Rodney. *Left and Right.* Chicago: University of Chicago Press, 1973.

"New Music from Old Masters." *Alpha.* July/August, 1979.

Nielsson, Haruldur. Congrës International tenu ‡ Varsovie (1923): quoted in A. R. G. Owen.

Ornstein, Robert. *The Psychology of Consciousness.* London: Cape, 1975.

Osty, Eugene. *Supernormal Faculties in Man.* London: Methuen, 1923.

Oswald, Ian. *Steep.* Harmondsworth: Penguin, 1966.

Owen, A. R. G. *Can We Explain the Poltergeist?* New York: Helix Press, 1964.

Oxford English Dictionary. Oxford: Clarendon Press, 1933.

Peterson, John M. "Left-Handedness: Differences Between Student Artists and Scientists." *Perceptual and Motor Skills.* Vol. 48, 1979.

"Philip the Man-made Phantom." *Alpha.* May/June, 1979.

Phylos the Tibetan. *A Dweller on Two Planets.* New York: Harper, 1974.

Pietsch, Paul. *Shuffiebrain.* Boston: Houghton Mifflin, ig8i.

Prescott, James. "Early Somatosensory Deprivation as an Ontogenetic Process in the Abnormal Development of the Brain and Behaviour." E. Goldsmith and J. Moor-Jankowski.

———. *Forebrain, Midbrain and Hindbrain Correlations.* (In press.)

———. "Phylogenetic and Ontogenetic Aspects of Human Affectual Development." R. Gernme and C. C. Wheeler, editors. *Progress in Sexology.* New York: Plenum Press, 1977.

Prince, Morton. *The Dissociation of Personality.* Oxford: Oxford University Press, 1978.

Pringle, M. L. K. *11,000 Seven-Year-Olds.* London: Longmans, 1976.

Puharich, Andrija. *Uri.* London: W. H. Allen, 1974.

Raine, Kathleen. *Blake and the New Age.* London: Allen & Unwin, 1979.

Rees, W. Demi. "The Hallucinations of Widowhood." *British Medical Journal.* Vol. 4, 1971.

Rhine, J. B., and Sara R. Feather. "The Study of Cases of Psi-Trailing in Animals." *Journal of Parapsychology.* Vol. 26, 1962.

Roberts, Jane. *Psychic Politics.* New Jersey: Prentice Hall, 1976.

Roll, William G. *The Poltergeist.* New Jersey: Scarecrow Press, 1976.

Rose, Ronald. *Living Magic.* New York: Rand McNally, 1956.

Roth, W. F., and F. H. Luton. "The Mental Health Program in Tennessee." *American Journal of Psychiatry.* Vol. 99, 1943.

Ruben, C. Gur. "Imagery, Absorption and the Tendency towards 'Mind Exploration' as Correlates of Hypnosis Susceptibility in Males and Females." In F. H. Frankel and H. S. Zamansky.

Ruben, C. Gur, and Raquel E. Gur. "Handedness, Sex and Eyedness as Moderating Variables in the Relation between Hypnotic Susceptibility and Functional Brain Asymmetry." *Journal of Abnormal Psychology.* Vol. 83, 1974.

Sackeim, H. A., et al. "Emotions Are Expressed More Intensely on the Left Side of the Face." *Science.* Vol. 202, 1978.

Schatzman, Morton. *The Story of Ruth Duckworth.* London, 1980.

"Schizophrenia: The Case for Viruses." *New Scientist.* 10 February, 1983.

Schopenhauer, Arthur. *Parerga and Paralipomena.* Oxford: Oxford University Press, 1974.

Schreiber, Flora Rheta. *Sybil.* Harmondsworth: Penguin, 1975.

Schurmacher, Emile, cited in Colin Wilson. *The Occult.* London: Hodder, 1971.

Selfe, Loma. *Nadia: A Case of Extraordinary Drawing Ability in an Autistic Child.* London: Academic Press, 1977.

Shackley, Myra. *Wild Men: Yeti, Sasquatch and the Neanderthal Enigma.* London: Thames & Hudson, 1983.

Shorter, Eric. "Raped by No One, But the Bruises Remain." *Daily Telegraph.* 1 October, 1982.

Shuttle, Penelope, and Peter Redgrove. *The Wise Wound.* London: Gollancz, 1978.

Sidgwick, Eleanor. "Phantasms of the Living." *Proceedings, Society for Psychical Research.* Vol. 33, 1922.

Sidis, Boris, and Simon Goodhart. *Multiple Personality.* New York: Greenwood Press, 1968.

Simon, Ted. "That Was No Lady, That's a Ghost." *The Times.* 3 January, 1983.

Singer, Isaac Bashevis. *The Seance.* London: Cape, 1970.

Sizemore, Chris, and Elen Pittillo. *Eve.* London: Gollancz, 1978.

Sklair, Freda. Personal communication to the author.

Smith, Aaron. "Speech and Other Functions after Left (Dominant) Hemispherectomy." *Journal of Neurology, Neurosurgery and Psychiatry.* Vol. 29, 1966.

Sperry, R. W. "The Great Cerebral Commissure." *Scientific American.* Vol. 210, 1964.

Spiegl, Anni. *The Life and Death of Therese Neumann of Konnersreuth.* Translated by Susan Johnson. Eichstatt, 1973.

"Spontaneous Hallucinations of the Sane." *Proceedings, Society for Psychical Research.* Vol. 10, 1894.

Stevenson, Ian. *Twenty Cases Suggestive of Reincarnation.* Virginia: University of Virginia Press, 1974.

Sulloway, Frank J. *Freud, Biologist of the Mind.* New York: Basic Books, 1979.

Summers, Montague. *The History of Witchcraft and Demonology.* London: Routledge, 1973.

———. *(Sinistrari de Ameno), Demonality or Incubi and Succubi.* London: Fortune Press, 1927.

Swedenborg, E. *Heaven and Hell.* London: Swedenborg Society, 1896.

Tarver, W. J. Letter. *New Scientist.* 24 October, 1968.

Taylor, Gordon Rattray. *The Natural History of the Mind.* London: Secker & Warburg, 1979.

Teng, E. L., et al. "Handedness in a Chinese Population." *Science.* Vol. 193, 1976.

Thigpen, Corbett H., and Hervey M. Cleckley. *The Three Faces of Eve.* New York: McGraw Hill, 1957.

Thurston, Gavin. "Preternatural Combustion of the Human Body." *Medico-Legal Journal.* Vol. 29.

Thurston, H. *Ghosts and Poltergeists.* London: Burns Oates, 1953.

Tomas, Andrew. *We Are Not the First.* London: Sphere, 1972.

Twigg, Ena, and R. H. Brod. *Ena Twigg, Medium.* London: W. H. Allen, 1973.

Underwood, Peter. *Dictionary of the Supernatural.* London: Harrap, 1978.

Usher, Shaun. "Can This Boy Be Ten Different People?" *Daily Mail.* 24 October, 1978.

Wallace, Marjorie. "The Day They Gave This Man His Memory Back." *Sunday Times.* 24 April, 1983.

Weitzenhoffer, A. M. *Hypnotism.* New York: Wiley, 1963.

Wheeler, W. M., et al. "The Internal Structure of the MMPF." *Journal of Consulting Psychology.* Vol. 15, 1951.

Wieschoff, Heinz A. "Concepts of Right and Left in African Cultures." Rodney Needham.

Williams, Mary. "The Poltergeist Man." *Journal of Analytical Psychology.* Vol. 8, 1963.

Willoughby-Meade, Gerald. *Chinese Ghouls and Goblins.* London: Constable, 1928.

Wilson, Ian. *Mind Out Of Time?* London: Gollancz, 1981.

Woolf, Leonard. *Beginning Again.* London: Harrap, 1964.

Wright, Pearce. "The No-Brain Genius May Be on its Way." *The Times.* 30 December, 1980.

Yeats, W. B. *Essays and Introductions.* London: Macmillan, ig6i.

Young, H. B., and R. Knapp. "Personality Characteristics of Converted Left-Handers." *Perceptual and Motor Skills.* Vol. 23, 1965.

INDEX